# The Many Sides of Jehovah God

By Philip North

ISBN 10: 1-58427-281-3

ISBN 13: 978-158427-281-6

Photo of author on the cover was taken by Jeri Pollett of Branson, Missouri.

**Philip North**
**P.O. Box 2271**
**Branson, Missouri 65615**

# Table of Contents

*This book is dedicated to my parents who tried to teach me right from wrong, along with all the great Bible class teachers and preachers at whose feet I had the pleasure of sitting to learn God's Word.*

# Foreword

Ever since a very young boy, I have been secretly fascinated with that Supreme Being known as Jehovah God. Like anyone else in one's youth, my imagination would run wild. Many were the times when this carried over into my religious training where the subject of this book is concerned. My parents were not what one would call religious fanatics, but they did try and teach me right from wrong, they were decent people, they held a reverential respect for God and his Bible, they faithfully attended church, and they took all four of us brothers there ever so regularly. I was the youngest of the four, and enjoyed church very much. My father was a deacon, and later served as an elder.

As us boys grew up, most of us became active in church work. Whether being instructed about God in Bible class or listening to the preacher expound on him from the pulpit, learning about this personality was quite interesting, amazing, and intriguing for me. I would often set my little head to concentrating on the extent of God's power and might. Boy, would it run fast and rampant! It was a combination of comforting and thrilling to know that someone actually existed whom nobody but nobody could overpower, elude, or outsmart! Such a thought would run through my young brain when experiencing a bully pick on me, or watching such a one pick on somebody else. I felt this same way when hearing proud, bragging, and arrogant words proceed from a person's lips, especially if these words were scornful, smart-alecky, belittling, and blasphemous. No matter who the individual, bully or otherwise, I was totally settled in my boyhood mind and thinking to myself, "You would not be able to stand up to *God* talking and acting like that! No!" The worse this person was, the more severe punishment I was sure God would bring that individual if change did not take place in his or her heart. Yes, feeling this way was a big comfort, along with a quiet sense of "victory" for me!

Too, like a good many children, some of my friends and I at various times would "play church." There would also be those occasions when I did so by myself. When doing so alone, I would always be the song leader, not the preacher—except on rare occasions.

I use the name "Jehovah" in this book's title so all who read will fully understand to specifically distinguish him from the other two persons in the God family, which are Jesus Christ and the Holy Spirit. All three make up the kindred known as the "Godhead." Jehovah is the Father, the head over all people, places, and things, both on earth and in Heaven. It is he whom I emphasize in this book. There are twenty-two chapters, each investigating a different characteristic of God, based only on what the Bible says, using the King James Version, known of course as the KJV.

Let not the reader get the mistaken idea that the other two members of the Godhead are being undermined or taken by this writer to not be very important. They most certainly are, due to the fact they work together for and with Jehovah to accomplish his purposes. Especially is this true of Jesus, Jehovah God's only begotten Son (John 1:14; 3:16).

Ever since being in my mid 40's, I have desired to write such a book as this, as my awe of God has greatly increased after studying the Bible all these years. I found myself wanting to do a lot of research on him. The word "God" itself is found well over 4,000 times in the KJV, and why should that not be? After all, it was the mind of God that caused this great book—the Bible—to be composed. The only book in the entire Bible where the name of God is never, ever mentioned is the Old Testament book of Esther. When reading that book, however, one cannot help but see God's Providence revealed. No matter how one looks at it, the Bible is God's book through and through. As old as it is, it can never be outdated, thus, "behind the times." God's Word keeps on replenishing itself, regardless of the passing of time, or how much this world of ours keeps changing. No other book can stay identically the same—unchanged—in its contents, while still remaining fresh and up to date generation after generation.

Upon reading this book of mine, one sees more and more with the completion of each chapter that God is like you and I in many ways. That is because we as humans were created with some of Jehovah's traits. Since God said in Genesis 1:26, "Let us make man in our image, after our likeness," we can look at humanity and notice how, in a number of areas, we are all like God. Indeed, he too possesses various feelings. The Bible records God as one who emotes anger, grief, shame, love, concern, satisfaction, and so on. That is you and I, is it not? Our Maker has a lot of sides to him, just as we ourselves do. It reminds me of some old sayings such as, "like father, like son," "the apple does not fall far from the tree," and, "a chip off the old block." Yes, this is all of us, for the beloved Apostle Paul said in the last part of Acts 17:28, as he was preaching on Mars Hill, when quoting from a poet, "For we are also his offspring."

When taking upon oneself the task of any project, the proper sources must be used. While working on a term paper in any grade level of school, those sources needing to be investigated will obviously depend on the subject. If that essay is to be on history, then sources on history must be utilized. If the subject is geography, then books on geography must be obtained. Should the assignment be on a particular person, books written about that person must be sought. Since this book is about the characteristics of Jehovah God, then the Bible is the source to read, and the Bible only, for it is the original source on God, having his approved words in its contents. No, I am not knocking any other writings published about our Creator, if those writings contain the truth; but this poignant subject known as truth can only come from the Bible, where the mind and commands of God are concerned. No subject can be regarded as pure truth if it does not come from its original source. Still another adage applies here: "Straight from the horse's mouth." The Bible is not a "second-hand book." It contains the original information on God—to the extent he wishes to reveal it, that is to say.

The reader will soon note after beginning this book, that many a verse of scripture is cited all throughout its pages, rather than just a few. This should not come as a surprise, given the theme. Of course, considering the amount of times God is mentioned in the Bible, it would be impossible to use every last verse containing his name. After all, this is supposed to be a book on the nature of Jehovah God, not a complete rewrite of the entire Bible, nor the composing of an encyclopedia! Some verses will naturally be used more than once, as they apply in more than one area. This writer, hopefully, did all possible to let the Word of God speak for its own self. Also, as demonstrated in the two previous paragraphs, a lot of old "down home sayings" and everyday adages were used, which turned out to be quite by accident.

In talking with a lot of people about God, I find that while the vast majority of those spoken to believe in his existence, many do not seem to know much about how God thinks and operates. This is said not as an insult to any human intelligence, but merely as an observation, for *none* of us knows all about everything or everything about all. Simple reasoning tells that if belief in God is there, why not learn all one can about him? Are we not everyone that way with our own friends and associates?

While researching for this book and composing it took many hours, as is the case with most any book written, this writer enjoyed the task very much. I ask you as the one reading to do so with an open mind, which I hope results in a receptive heart. As mentioned in the final chapter, when one reads the Bible, know for certain that is God and Jesus talking to us. The Bible is not just another "good book" to read. One should also meditate upon it. Ever so many of its verses are self-explanatory, so the Bible can, overall, be understood by anyone who has a mind to think and reason. It does not take a rocket scientist to understand a vast majority of the Bible's passages and teachings. Jehovah God would not have told those inspired writers to pen his words in some mysterious way so humanity could not understand them, and then turn right around and expect obedience. Such would make for an unfair God, thus, imperfect in his demeanor. How can one obey if there is no understanding? The Apostle Paul tells the church at Ephesus, "Wherefore be ye not unwise, but understanding what the will of the Lord is" (Ephesians 5:17). Paul also told them in chapter 1:18, "The eyes of your understanding being enlightened; that ye may know what is the hope of your calling, and what the riches of the glory of his inheritance in the saints." This writer pleads earnestly with you—do not listen to Satan! See for a fact that a greater portion of God's Bible *is* easily understood!

If the reader has yet to become really acquainted with this awesome, wonderful, majestic Creator, I believe most assuredly you will feel like you know him in many ways, or else know him better, by the time you finish reading all the pages that lie ahead. I say that not because I wrote this book, but again, it is due to the fact that the Bible is easy to comprehend in most of its pages. Great throngs of people seem to think God's Word is too hard, mysterious, and deep to basically grasp and understand, on the *sole* basis that it is the Bible. Such a concept could not be further from the truth! All with a mind capable of learning should know about God, as that is what he wishes and commands. What he desires us to know, he lets us know. What he does not want us to know, he remains silent on in his book. Read all of I Corinthians 2 in order to get an idea of how the mind of God was explored by the Holy Spirit, when it came to searching out God's commands.

Paul tells the young preacher Timothy the following: "All scripture is given by inspiration of God, and is profitable for doctrine, for reproof, for correction, for instruction in righteousness: That the man of God may be perfect, thoroughly furnished unto all good works" (II Timothy 3:16-17). The Apostle Peter wrote to a group of Christians and assured them, "Knowing this first, that no prophecy of the scripture is of any private interpretation. For the prophecy came not in old time by the will of man: but holy men of God spake as they were moved by the Holy Ghost" (II Peter 1:20-21). This is why, among other reasons, I am most thoroughly resolved that the Bible *is that book* which consists of the inspired and infallible words taken from the mind and mouth of God Almighty.

All efforts to destroy and abolish the Bible have failed, no matter how stoutly, staunchly, and strenuously they have been exerted. Such failure will forever continue, for God will see to that. Jesus said to his apostles in Matthew 24:35, "Heaven and earth shall pass away, but my words shall not pass away." The same exact words are recorded by him in the accounts of Mark 13:31 and Luke 21:33. The Bible perpetually remains the best seller year after year, in spite of what atheists, agnostics, and all others falling under the category of "skeptic" have said about it. This Divine Word lives today and always will! The fact that the Bible has lasted all of these centuries says so much in the way of total accuracy, in regard to its claims of origin.

I admit to having made many past mistakes and blunders, as I am only a man—nothing more. I will also be the first to confess the fact that there were those errors committed which were avoidable the first time around. No doubt, you as the reader will echo the same admission about yourself, whether your foul ups and wrongs have been few or many, as however the good Lord may judge us in comparison. Remembering and realizing my own faults and shortcomings have really humbled me when writing this book on that Being who is sinless and perfect in every way. When having investigated the scriptures for this book on everything pertaining to God, I am more convinced now than ever that not only am I not anywhere close to being flawless like him, I will also remain far, far so that way—all the way up to the time when I breathe my last.

Thank you for buying and reading my book. To those who have received it as a gift, thank you for accepting it and reading it. Every word of appreciation expressed here comes from the very bottom of this writer's heart.

While reading this book, think of it as my being your friend who is sitting right next to you, talking to you. To Jehovah God be all the credit and glory. He is commander over all. He is the one whom you and I should get to know as much as possible. He is the person of persons. He is GOD!

Philip North

Chapter 1

# God Is

God exists! Let us nail that fact down *now*! Such is not being overly opinionated. There is far too much proof, as opposed to thinking the contrary, if one's mind is logical. It has been argued so very long by those who do not believe there is a God, that if he can not be seen, he must not exist. This kind of people refer to the scientific phrase, "seeing is believing." Those of us who believe that Jehovah God *is* for real use the line, "we accept it by faith." Actually, it is more than by faith. This writer says it can be proven both ways—by faith *and* by sight. Though we cannot actually *see* that Supreme of beings with the naked eye, we can still prove the reality of his presence. The first part of Psalm 14:1 declares, "The fool hath said in his heart, There is no God..." The same words are found in the first part of chapter 53:1. Truly, one would have to be a fool in the final analysis when it comes to not believing in God, or the Bible would not say it. The evidence is very overwhelming. It is all right in front of our noses. It is usually much easier to *explain* something that it is to *explain away* something. Proving something *is* often constitutes a much easier task than proving something *is not*! After all, when something exists, it can be pointed out and seen. Not so with something not there.

Every product has its maker. Every invention has its inventor. This means that the maker is greater than the product, and the inventor is greater than the invention. The mechanic and those who work on the assembly line are greater than the automobile. The tailor is greater than the suit. The watchmaker is greater than the watch. The carpenters are greater than the building. This argument so goes with product after product. No product or invention can make itself. Something of a higher nature had to make it. Where God is concerned, that makes him greater than the Creation. Everything had to have its beginning, but that beginning had to have its *beginner*! This is what makes Evolution inconsistent. Those believing it have to come up with some kind of a beginning; but who, what, when, where, why, and how? There is the sensible argument to that. What is it?

Matter cannot make mind. Mind must make, and can only make, matter. The invention did not make the inventor, and the product did not manufacture the maker, anymore than the children gave birth to the parents. All three obviously came out vice-versa. No invention or product made itself. No son or daughter ever came into this world by one's own effort. Whatever the invention or product, some *mind* had to be behind the whole project, and no mind exists or has existed without some kind of body. Show me the mind, and you *have* to show me the body. Even a spirit has some kind of body. It is just not a body of flesh. Look around you at everything—big, little, or in-between. Notice every animal, human, fowl, and sea creature. Observe all the celestial bodies—the sun, moon, stars, planets, and all that make up outer space. Note how they hang upon nothing (as mentioned later in this book in detail). Study the revolving they do and how they operate. Eye all the terrestrial—the plants, flowers, bushes, trees, grass, and mountains. Take a look at the vast varieties of everything and how they function. See how *all* the celestial and terrestrial conduct themselves in the same constant cycle. How did they come about? It was not a *what* or an *it* that caused them to exist and function. It was a *who*! This *who* had to have a mind, and this mind was and is one far greater than yours or mine.

All individuals who do not believe in the existence of God must believe the earth came from no stimulation of any outside force. They must believe that something non-stimulating suddenly became stimulated. So what was that *power* responsible for that stimulation? Huh? These people must invent in their own minds some sort of theories; and theories are only theories until they are proven to be *fact*! That is why you have heard the title, "The Theory of Evolution." It will forever remain a theory, for it has never been proven a fact, nor indeed can be. It is interesting to note that all the fossils discovered in this world have never shown any kind of *metamorphosis* to back up Evolution or any other doctrine along its line. In simple words, there has been no *gradual change* discovered in these findings. Nothing was seen to be "in the process" of changing. If man evolved from monkey, where are the bones to indicate such? (I for one would be ashamed to tell my children and grandchildren that my ancestors hung from the trees by their tails, squealed, whined, fought constantly, scratched a lot, and had to survive mainly on bananas!) All that ever existed and exists now came from some being non-human. The Creation manifests itself as too great a phenomenon to believe that Jehovah God is a wild myth, or some fanatical, far-fetched, fearful, fraudulent fantasy that a child conjured up in his wildest imagination. Let us get real!

God is present! Every effect has it pre-existing cause. This is the first rule of science and the basis of all rational thought. Since the universe does exist, and since something cannot come from nothing where its origin is concerned, then something or someone had to always exist in order to cause to happen all that is now. Is the universe eternal, or is there a pre-existing force that created it? The truth is the universe both testifies and demonstrates by scientific law, common sense, and its very existence that it is not eternal. It has not always been around. In fact, many would argue that the universe is wearing out.

Here is another fact to consider: Matter can be, has been, and is now being, transformed into radiant energy such as light and heat. When each exchange takes place, the ratio of energy that is useless to energy that is useful declines. This is known as the second law of thermodynamics (a.k.a. law of entropy). Now, how could any human mind past, present, or future compose such a thing? How did mankind discover all this? You will reply, "By studying." That is correct! However, from where did all this *originate*? Was it from a man, animal, fowl, or sea creature? How about a fly, gnat, bee, or mosquito? Perhaps the wind was responsible? No! Some supreme mind far, far exceeding human intelligence had to be the cause of it all.

The greater the invention is, the greater the inventor. The greater the product is, the greater the maker. The greater the force is, the greater the one *behind* the force, which is actually the original force itself. Then there follows the mechanics and experts assembling and operating that product and invention. What about this amazing Creation? Why do the forces of nature behave the way they do? Why is it that most birds fly and humans do not? (Say! Why do the swallows fly to Capastrano the same identical day every year—March 19?) How come sea creatures must live in water to survive, but such is not possible for mankind? Why is man the highest being of intelligence? Why does he have only two legs, while the animal kingdom possesses four? Why cannot animal, fowl, and fish blood be transfused with human blood? We could ask "why" to so many questions about nature, and science can very well and truly *tell* us why on many of our inquiries, of which could go on ad infinitum. When the Apostle Paul gave his famous sermon on Mars Hill in Athens, Greece, he said the following about God in Acts 17:26-28: "And hath made of one blood all nations of men for to dwell on all the face of the earth, and hath determined the times before appointed, and the bounds of their habitation; That they should seek the Lord, if haply they might feel after him, and find him, though he be not far from every one of us: For in him we live, and move, and have our being; as certain also of your own poets have said, For we are also his offspring."

We need not ask if God exists, nor should we. Look all around you. God's works bare witness of his presence. God is in the trees. God is in the flowers. God brings about that harvest of crops. We use, see, and feel what has already been made. God is in the creating, revolving, and moving of everything. As goes the saying, "God's hand is in it all!" No human being could be ingenious enough to do any or all of this, and this writer declares that without any reservation. The question then arises: "How come God cannot be seen if he exists?" That issue will be dealt with in a later chapter.

Now back to the subject of skepticism. The unbeliever's attitude will be, "Show me God, and I will believe he exists!" Well, show me your brains, and I will believe you have them! Let us return to some earlier arguments here: Show me your mechanic, and I will believe that is an automobile you drive. Show me your watchmaker, and I will believe that is a watch you wear. Show me your tailor and fashion designer, and I will believe that is clothes you have on your body—suit or anything else. Show me your carpenters, and I will believe that is a building in which you live, along with its being a building where you work. How many of you can show me all those makers and inventors? Can you round them all up? If I demanded such, you would be frustrated—maybe angry—maybe disgusted. On this same note, you have that very identical argument to be made about proving the existence of Jehovah God. None of us would have to actually *see* those responsible for turning out any product or invention. *The proof of that inventor and maker is in the very existence of that product and invention*! So it is with God. The proof of his existence lies in his very works. They bear witness of God's being "alive and kicking!" They show ironclad and irrefutable proof of his unmatched ability. This writer is reminded about the bumper sticker that reads, "My God is alive. Sorry about yours." Doubtless, there is no way to sensibly argue that God is not real.

Since the universe cannot be proven to be eternal, it must have been caused by a force that already was; by one that was pre-existing. That force is called "God!" Psalm 19:1-6 declares, "The heavens declare the glory of God; and the firmament showeth his handiwork. Day unto day uttereth speech, and night unto night showeth knowledge. There is no speech nor language where their voice is not heard. Their line is gone out through all the world. In them hath he set a tabernacle for the sun, which is as a bridegroom coming out of his chamber, and rejoiceth as a strong man to run a race. His going forth is from the end of the heaven, and his circuit unto the ends of it: and there is nothing hid from the heat thereof." Psalm 27:1 says, "The earth is the Lord's, and the fullness thereof; the world, and they that dwell therein." There is much more proof that God is real; more than this writer or anyone else could possibly imagine or produce. Gentle reader, there is a God, and he is alive, even as you read this very book. God *is*!

Being the writer of this book, I will fully admit it was a somewhat difficult thing to separate the contents of this chapter on "God Is" from the next chapter entitled "God Is The Creator." So, the information in this chapter and the next one will be somewhat overlapped. That is to say, some of the things said in this chapter will be repeated in the next chapter, but using different examples, for the most part.

**Questions**

1. It is much easier to ____________ something than it is to ____________ ____________ something.
2. "The ________ hath said in his heart, "________________________ ____________________."
3. "The ___________ declare the glory of God, and the ______________ showeth his handiwork."
4. The existence of God can be proven both by ______________ and by _________________.
5. Pertaining to God, "we are also his ___________________."
6. Proving something _____________ often constitutes a much easier task than proving something ____________ ________ __________.
7. The celestial bodies hang upon ___________________.
8. _____________ cannot make ___________. Instead, __________ can only make ________________.

9. All the ____________ and _____________ conduct themselves in the same constant ____________.

10. In all fossils discovered, no _____________________ was ever found to have taken place.

11. The proof of that inventor and maker is in the ___________________ __________________________.

12. All individuals not believing in the existence of God must believe the earth came from ______________________________________ ____________________________.

13. "God's hand is ______________."

14. The universe both testifies and demonstrates by scientific law, common sense, and its very existence that it is not _________________.

15. When matter is transformed into radiant energy, it is known as the ___ ____________________________________________, a.k.a. ________ _________________________.

16. The greater the _____________, the greater the ________________.

17. "The earth is the ____________, and the ______________________."

18. Every product has its ______________, and every inventor has its _________________________.

19. The ________________ did not make the ______________, and the ________________ did not manufacture the _________________.

20. The unbeliever's attitude will be, "_____________________________ ___________________________________________."

Chapter 2

# God Is The Creator

Jehovah God is the Supreme Maker who is responsible for bringing all that is and has been in existence *into* existence. He was not part of a group who simultaneously put their heads together and unanimously decided, "Let us assemble the world." The very first verse of the Bible says, "In the beginning, God created the heaven and the earth" (Genesis 1:1). There was no shape nor substance to the earth, for verse 2 tells us, "And the earth was without form, and void; and darkness was upon the face of the deep. And the Spirit of God moved upon the face of the waters." All solid matter exists because God *commanded* it to do so, and not through the so-called billions of years, as Evolution claims. It shows a lot more feasibility to believe that everything had its beginning from God, than to try and explain away all of the Creation by claiming some form of *chance* took place without any power or stimulation behind it, or, as already stated, that man evolved from monkey. There is too much "proof in the pudding" to believe otherwise, and still keep the argument sane.

Let us start from the present time. How did you and I arrive in this life? We had a mother and father, did we not? From where did they come? They too had a mother and father responsible for bringing them into this world, who in turn had a mother and father responsible for doing so, who also had a mother and father likewise responsible, and well, how far back do we keep going? How far in the past do we trace it for one to establish that somebody was a monkey? Can such a thing be proven or documented? How much in the long ago can we trace the monkey heritage? As stated in the last chapter, there has never been any kind of *metamorphosis* existing when fossils of animals and people have been unearthed. There was no link found from man to monkey or from monkey to man. So, how far back do you trace the human race before you are forced to stop? To what extent does it go before one is backed into a corner and must finally reach a logical conclusion? This conclusion is that somewhere along the line of backtracking, you end up at the beginning, like the start of a book; like that first piece of concrete, asphalt, or dirt at the commencement of a road; like the connection of one pipe to another; like that spring of water coming from the ground and gradually connecting to another body of water; like the embryo of a human baby or some other form of fleshly life. Some area of original *birth* will--yes it will--be there! Some type of first *founding* is bound to be revealed! All of this draws one to an inevitable conclusion that whatever exists came from something else which also exists or existed, which came from something else that did too, and again, where is the *beginning*? There has to be one somewhere and in some way! What is it? Be careful, now! You will only be able to go back so far!

This same argument can be used in reference to any animal, whatever that animal be. The dog was once a puppy, but was that not also the same case in regards to its own mother and father? How many puppies and dogs do you trace back before you find yourself at the *beginning*? The *other* end of the investigation will appear, as well as the end where you began. Just where *is* the beginning? How about the cat? It was a kitten, as were its own mother and father at one time. How many kittens and cats do you backtrack on, before you find yourself at the *beginning*? Again, where *is* the beginning? The same thing applies to the lion, tiger, leopard, and so on. What about the bird? "Oh, it came from an egg," you will say! Where did the egg come from? It came from another bird, which came from another bird that laid the egg, which came from still another bird who did the same thing, and look here! You are once again forced to some kind of a *beginning*. (I will bet the reader is reminded of the age-old question, "Which came first, the chicken or the egg?") This writer asks again: Where is it? Who or what is responsible for it's initiation?

One even notices the same situation in regards to a tree. It came from a seed, which came from a tree, which came from a seed, and you know what? You end up going back and back and back until, well, when? How about the bushes, the grass, the flowers, and plants? How about anything that reproduces after it's own kind? How far back can you go, before you end up at the beginning somewhere in time? How about the formation of all hills, mountains, and valleys? Let us carry this issue still farther.

Suppose one could physically live forever, never to die, and had the power to actually *go* all the way back to the beginning of everything. How far back do you suppose you would get before you would truly *find* a beginning? (You would have to find one at some point!) When the whole matter was actually laid bare before your eyes, what would you see? What conclusion would you have to reach and accept, finally seeing the truth of it all? In what position would you find yourself? Whatever that position would be, you would have nothing to fall back on in the way of how you--and others--might have previously believed. The answer that would be right there in front of you would be unavoidable, whether accepted or not, for it would be staring square at you. After all, you will have gone as far back as you can possibly go in your search. There would be no more tracing or wondering to be conducted.

Remember we said before that matter is incapable of making mind. Instead, mind can only make matter. The whole universe is made up of molecules and atoms--matter! Matter is simply high, condensed energy. Matter is what forms solids. It is raw materials that make up everything and everyone. This matter could not have come about by some method of *self-stimulation*. (Remember we spoke on stimulation in the last chapter). Nothing cannot be stimulated by something, nor something stimulated by nothing, and thus, something cannot come from nothing, nor can nothing come from something. If nothing from nothing leaves nothing, then something from something must leave something. Therefore, something had to come from some force and source containing stimulation, or it could not and would not be present. Any term you want to use here--energy, power, force, drive, work, action, movement, or whatever, shows that some sort of *stimulation* was at hand that brought all into being which now exists or has existed. Is there some sort of pre-existing *casual* force that created the universe and all things contained therein, which just *happened* to be around with no movement? If so, how could no movement cause movement? How could no stimulation cause stimulation? How can something dead cause life? How can something non-existent cause existence? Remember again: We are going as far back as possible, and as deep as the mind can imagine. I ask still once again: Where is the beginning? Let us keep it all rational and in focus, and not start imagining what only *might* be the answer, or what you might *want* the answer to be. To do such would cross over into the ridiculous! Where was and is the start of everything?

The conclusion is evident. Some *eternal* force had to be behind it all. The universe testifies and demonstrates by scientific law that it is not eternal, as before argued. Each thing created reveals by its very size its design and purpose, along with the minimum level of power and intellect of its cause. This would show that the universe testifies for and about the force that caused it. The universe operates with great timing and exactness. The course of planets, stars, comets, and so forth, can be figured out years in advance by scientists. (Remember Halley's comet that appears for a short while about every 75 years?) From the largest star to the smallest living cell, one can discover the total cooperative relationship of all the creation as science learns and discovers more and more. Do we as humans think we are so independent? The very order of the universe is focused on the support and welfare of human life. If it changed its cycle and production, we would all die! For one example, I will ask you this: How would we breathe without the proper elements contained in the air?

That Jehovah God exists and is powerful, intelligent, and totally mindful of mankind and his needs, is an inescapable conclusion of the basic laws of science and reason. True scientific law and logic all agree with what the Bible says. The Apostle Paul told the Roman Christians, "For the invisible things of him from the creation of the world are clearly seen, being understood by the things that are made, even his eternal power and Godhead; so that they are without excuse" (Romans 1:20). How can something invisible be seen? Well, there are a number of invisible things: love, mind, conscience, joy, and other emotions, just to name a few. We cannot see these things with the human eye, for they are not matter, but we can testify to them in the sense of *feeling* them. We are *aware* of their presence. More on that is said in a later chapter.

Hebrews 11:3 says, "By faith we understand that the universe was formed at God's command, so that what is seen was not made out of what was visible." Just what is the writer telling us here? God *created* everything. The word "create" means, "Out of nothing, something comes." To easily phrase it, "create" means "to make something out of nothing." Since everything had to have it's beginning, then somewhere in tracing it all back, we simply find that the first of everything had to be created, and therefore, created completely grown. God did not start out with a seed or embryo. Such would not have been creating, except for the fact that he would still have needed to create that *first* seed or embryo, since every last thing, this writer avers again, had to have its *beginning*.

God started out with the finished product, which *produced* that first seed or embryo from each of those products. Otherwise, how could the product have been formed? How could it have come into existence? How could it have been created? How could the first seed and embryo exist? When something is *made*, it comes about as a form of *reproduction*, or, the composing of raw materials and matter already existing. However, when something is *created,* it has to be *originally* formed. Since it never existed before, so neither then could its seed and embryo. It could not possibly have existed previously *because it never was*! What never was cannot be *made*! It must first be *created* before it can be *reproduced*. Therefore, the Creation was the beginning of everything, as the book of Genesis explains. The very name of "genesis" comes from the scientific word "genes." Genes are what cause the forming of everything—the reproducing of its own kind. When someone talks about something being the "genesis" of it all, the explanation is in the first three words written in the book of the same name, which are also the very first three words of the Bible: "In the beginning." Genesis reveals the beginning of all that was involved in the Creation of the world.

So what about the origin of the human race? I say yet once again that nothing contained in the discovery of human fossils, regardless of how old their approximation was decided, revealed any type of metamorphosis taking place. Man did not come from monkey or any other type of origination pertaining to the so-named "Big Bang Theory." Here is one reason it makes more sense to believe what the Bible says concerning the initiation of everything and everyone: The Big Bang Theory tries to persuade us that all life came about due to some kind of a big *explosion* which came out of nowhere. If that were so, then who or what *caused* that big explosion? From where did it come? Remember that any formulation of energy can only be caused by *another* formulation of energy. Inaction cannot cause action. Chance cannot occur without chance already being there. Again, nothing cannot cause something, because nothing is just that--nothing! Life had to originate from some type of mind. I stress to the reader all the more again that matter cannot make mind. Matter must only be *formed by* mind. However, the Bible plainly states who *brought about* the heavens and the earth, along with what and who were brought about to *inhabit* the heavens and the earth.

After all of the Creation had been completed, we find the following words in Genesis 1:26-27: "And God said, let us make man in our image, after our likeness: and let them have dominion over the fish of the sea, and over the fowl of the air, and over the cattle, and over all the earth, and over every creeping thing that creepeth upon the earth. So God created man in his own image, in the image of God created he him; male and female created he them."

Thus began the human race. Mankind (a well known general term describing both men and women) has the highest intelligence of all animals, fowls, and sea creatures. None can equal this specie or rise above the intelligence level. No monkey, giraffe, or salamander can be educated. No fish, dog, or cat can so much as add one and one. No donkey, horse, or elephant can drive a car or motorcycle, fly a plane, maneuver a jet ski, or even ride a bicycle. There is no such thing as *marriage* when it comes to the animal kingdom, bird family, or underwater world. No chicken will ever be President, no rooster will succeed in becoming mayor, no hippopotamus can be elected governor, no rhinoceros will ever serve as senator, no lion will ever sit on the throne at Buckingham Palace, (even though he *is* recognized as "king of the beasts!") not one cow or bull can wait on people in restaurants or in any other business, no chipmunk can serve as a tourist guide, no zebra can cook, no skunk can act, no mouse can ever figure out an algebraic equation, no rat can deliver mail, no squirrel can write a speech or essay, almost no creature can talk (with the exception of myna birds, parrots, and a very limited number of other birds), and on and on and on this writer could rattle in illustrating the difference in brain level of the human race, compared to all the rest of the creatures of the flesh that God created! Even though some birds can talk, as said, the brain level is still far below that of the human race. The proponents of such areas as Evolution and the Big Bang Theory, however, still theorize that man evolved from monkey, and as he did so, his I.Q. increased in the process.

After all is averred, the Bible is specific in how man's existence came to be. Genesis 2:7 declares, "And the Lord God formed man of the dust of the ground, and breathed into his nostrils the breath of life; and man became a living soul." No member of the animal kingdom, fowls, or sea creatures "became a living soul." That is why the I.Q. is not the same as the rest of the creatures of the Creation, that is why mostly humans talk, and that is why humans were put in charge of this world's operations. It says, "*man* became a living soul." This fits in perfectly with what God said when he stated, "Let us make man in our image," then further said how man would be over all, or as God stated it, "have dominion over," all that was created.

If a creature is made "in the image" of someone, then various traits are going to be naturally inherited, as I stated in the "Foreword" section of this book. All through the Bible, we find where God talks, possesses absolutely everything in the way of knowledge and wisdom, and is in control of over all that he has created. Genesis 2:18 begins to tell how woman came into being: "And the Lord God said, It is not good that the man should be alone; I will make him a help meet for him." Look next at verses 21-23: "And the Lord God caused a deep sleep to fall upon Adam, and he slept: and he took one of his ribs, and closed up the flesh instead thereof; And the rib, which the Lord God had taken from man, made he a woman, and brought her unto the man. And Adam said, This is now bone of my bones, and flesh of my flesh: she shall be called Woman, because she was taken out of man."

Many body parts contained outside and inside a woman also compose the inside and outside of a man. How could that have happened if the woman did not come from the man? How could there be that many similarities and characteristics in common with these two creatures if one was not the offspring of the other? The forming of woman also had to do, like man, with being created "in the image of God."

It is an all too well known--and long proven--fact that man came from the ground, as we shall read. How is it proven? When a human body ceases to live, it eventually decomposes to dust. After the Bible records the disobedience of Adam and Eve in the Garden of Eden in Genesis 3, look at verse 19: "In the sweat of thy face shalt thou eat bread, till thou return unto the ground: for out of it wast thou taken: for dust thou art, and unto dust shalt thou return." Combine this verse with Genesis 2:7 already cited. They both tell the same thing: "And the Lord God formed man of the dust of the ground;" "till thou return unto the ground: for out of it wast thou taken: for dust thou art, and unto dust shalt thou return."

How can a body *return* to a certain something if it never *came* from that same something? To what does it *return*? It is the *dust*! That body, before it *was* a body, had to start out *being* dust, or else it could never *return* to dust. This same rule and cycle applies and occurs to all animals as well. Paul told the men of Athens, Greece in Acts 17:24, "God that made the world and all things therein, seeing that he is Lord of heaven and earth, dwelleth not in temples made with hands." It tells us here that God made the entire world, along with all the things contained in it.

No human mind could or can create, bring about invisible things, or plan with such great precision as the world we have around us and in which we live. Each invention and product that man produces must continually be revised and improved. God's work needs no improvement. What human could come up with so many different *kinds* of animals, species, and varieties? Look how many types of grass, flowers, plants, bushes, and trees are in the world. How could so many, many humans exist, and a vast majority of them not look alike, not develop alike, not talk alike, not think alike, have different colors of eyes, hair, and skin, along with varying personal tastes? A much *greater* mind had to do this, which means that greater mind, because it *is* greater, had to have a much bigger I.Q. In Isaiah 40:28 the prophet tells Israel, "Hast thou not known? hast thou not heard, that the everlasting God, the Lord, the Creator of the ends of the earth, fainteth not, neither is weary? there is no searching of his understanding." Only a mind with an unlimited amount of knowledge, wisdom, and forethought could have created all the wondrous beauties that encompass all around us.

Through this all, let us not overlook one important fact. Going back to Genesis 1:26 again, we note the first part of the verse which reads, "And God said, Let us make man in our image, after our likeness." The term "let *us*" would indicate there was more participation in the Creation of this world and mankind than solely by one Divine Being. That Being was Jesus Christ, the only begotten Son of Jehovah God. He was the one who actually *executed* the commands of God. John 1:1-3 says, "In the beginning was the Word, and the Word was with God, and the Word was God. The same was in the beginning with God. All things were made by him; and without him was not any thing made that was made." Some have called the book of John the "second Genesis," as it starts off identically the same as Genesis where they both say, "In the beginning." How can "the Word" be "*with* God," and at the same time *be* God? After all, that is what we just read. It says, "the Word *was* God." Such a sentence structure as this shows that the word "God" is sometimes used in the Bible in the *plural* sense. It is not always *singular*.

Three times in the Bible, the three personalities in Heaven are referred to, as stated before, as "the Godhead." There is God the Father, God the Son, and God the Holy Spirit. It is only human nature when we say the word "God" to refer to Jehovah, also known, as just said, as God the Father. We are referring to the highest Being, the Father, when we say "God." The whole point is that these three Beings of Deity are all in the God family, just as the wife and children all wear the same last name of the husband, if the children belong to the husband and wife biologically, of course. (Even then, some foster and stepparents will pay to change the children's last name). While these children are all different beings, they are everyone of the same family.

So it is with the Godhead. One can see how Jesus was the one who did the actual *work* of the Creation. Let us review verse 3 again: "All things were made by him; and without him was not any thing made that was made." How can we know for sure that it is Jesus whom John speaks of instead of Jehovah God? Dropping down to verse 14 it says, "And the Word became flesh, and dwelt among us, (and we beheld his glory, the glory as of the only begotten of the Father,) full of grace and truth." This explains clearly, connecting it with verses 1-3, that it was Jesus Christ who did the actual *work* of creating "the heaven and the earth." Hebrews 1:1-2 says about Jesus, "God, who at sundry times and in divers manners spake in time past unto the fathers by the prophets, Hath in these last days spoken unto us by his Son, whom he hath appointed heir of all things, by whom also he made the worlds." Jesus was simply obeying his Heavenly Father's command, as any obedient son would do. That fact that Jesus himself was also involved in the Creation makes it all the more awesome! (The Holy Spirit is known as the great *Lawgiver* of the Creation).

In speaking further about Christ's having a hand in the Creation, Paul said of him to the Colossian church, "For by him were all things created, that are in heaven, and that are in earth, visible and invisible, whether they be thrones, or dominions, or principalities, or powers: all things were created by him, and for him: And he is before all things, and by him all things consist" (Colossians 1:16-17). Indeed, Jesus *executed* Jehovah's commands at the Creation where all the who, what, when, where, and how were concerned. When his Father Jehovah said, "Let there be light," (Genesis 1:3), Jesus was the one who *caused* the light to happen. So it was as well with all the other things and beings that the Father wanted brought into existence.

All raw materials were created that mankind uses for production, survival, luxury, and business: oil, water, petroleum, silver, gold, copper, coal, and so on. Everything was created in tremendous quantities. Whatever the product made today, as in bygone days, it came from some type of raw materials that were created. A product can only be *made*, but the raw materials that make up the product had to be *created*. This all came from that wonderful Maker, Jehovah God, who in turn, had the *performing* of his commanded work done by his Son, Jesus.

This vast and powerful universe did not just happen! It came to be from the mind of somebody so far superior to any of us. It came from a supreme mind, so vehemently smarter than any fleshly creature who ever lived, lives now, or will live. The minds of Galileo, Copernicus, Einstein, and all other geniuses past and present *combined* are no match for this indescribable and unsearchable Mind of minds. The size, functions, and boundary lines of this enormous world are every last whit too great for even the very smartest and most gifted of scholars to succeed in pulling off, individually or collectively.

All of what you and I draw from to survive was not self-provided. They were all drawn up by God. We breathe *his* air, eat *his* food, drink *his* water, walk upon *his* earth, and all that we wear, buy, sell, trade, give away, and use are products and resources obtained from *his* raw materials. Mankind did not create one form thing! Psalm 102:25 tells of God, "Of old hast thou laid the foundation of the earth: and the heavens are the work of thine hands." These words are said again in Hebrews 1:10. This earth existed long, long before any of us were ever born or even thought of, to be sure. It will also continue to exist after each and everyone of us pass from this life, until God sees fit to bring time and all Creation to an end.

The very existence and sight of the heavens alone show the work, genius, expertise, and power of God Almighty. Psalm 19:1-6 tells us all the more of God's great work in the heavens and on the earth: "The heavens declare the glory of God; and the firmament showeth his handiwork. Day unto day uttereth speech, and night unto night showeth knowledge. There is no speech, nor language where their voice is not heard. Their line is gone out through all the earth, and their words to the end of the world. In them hath he set a tabernacle for the sun, which is as a bridegroom coming out of his chamber, and rejoiceth as a strong man to run a race. His going forth is from the end of the heaven, and his circuit unto the ends of it: and there is nothing hid from the heat thereof." The very works of God--in a personified way--actually *speak* for themselves to all who view it, as we just noted. The heavens talk of all its beauty and splendor, and the earth orates all its contents. The beauty of God's work is unspeakable in human terms, as are all his other traits. How often this writer has noticed the works of God, and then has felt so measly and insignificant!

For those who still insist on saying, "I want *proof* of God's existence by seeing him face to face," after their having read all this, I can only repeat my argument of tracing everything back to its origin. What maker or inventor do *you* know of who can *create*? What maker or inventor do *you* know of who caused all that you see around you to come into existence? What maker or inventor do *you* know of with the ability to trace the origin of every tree, flower, plant, bush, grass, star, planet, fowl, sea creature, animal family, animal, human family, and human being? What maker or inventor do *you* know of who can trace the very first appearance of the sun and the moon? What maker or inventor do *you* know of who has such an incredible ability and unmatchable know-how to calculate the functions and boundaries of all things big, little, or anywhere in the middle? Where under the beautiful name of Heaven would it all finally and at last have to stop? Yes, it *would* most assuredly stop, for there would (here come the words again!) have to be a *beginning*. Back to the first part of Psalm 14:1, also stated in Psalm 53:1: "The fool hath said in this heart, there is no God. . . ." I would be a fool not to believe in the existence of Jehovah God, after observing all the appearances and countless operations of this world.

There is a great Creator! He is up there in the heavens and has been since--and before--the beginning of time, all things, and all people. So much more could be shown in the way of evidence. Jehovah's mind and ways cannot be compared to mankind. In Isaiah 55:8-9, the wonderful prophet echoes the words of God to Israel: "For my thoughts are not your thoughts, neither are your ways my ways, saith the Lord. For as the heavens are higher than the earth, so are my ways higher than your ways, and my thoughts than your thoughts."

How little we are in stature and mind, when going up against God! How futile our ideas, achievements, and projects are when placed beside his Creation and its stupendous functions! Truly, how small we are in everything, when compared to that majestic and highest of all beings! Nothing created or made was done so by chance or man's device. It came from that one and only Creator—Jehovah God!

**Questions**

1. "In the beginning, _________ created the heaven and the earth."
2. Somewhere along the line of ________________, you end up at the ________________________.
3. It was ______________ who did the actual WORK of creating.
4. "Create" means, "__________________________________________ __________________________."

5. "By _______________ we understand that the universe was formed at _____________ command."
6. "Of old hast _____________ laid the foundation of the earth, and the heavens are the work of _____________ hands."
7. "And the earth was ___________________________________, and _________________ was upon the face of the deep."
8. The works of God show in a PERSONIFIED way. That means they actually ___________________________________.
9. Isaiah says that God is "the _____________ of the ends of the earth."
10. The Holy Spirit is known as the great ____________ of the Creation.
11. ___________, _______________, and the __________________ make up the God family.
12. God said, "Let us make ____________ in our____________, after our ____________________."
13. The word "God" is sometimes used in the ________________ sense, not always ________________.
14. As stated in the last chapter, there has never been any kind of _________________________ existing when fossils of animals and people have been unearthed.
15. _______________ cannot be stimulated by _______________, and vise versa.
16. Man was formed "from the ____________________________."
17. Woman was formed when God took a __________ from ________.
18. We exist, use, and consume everything due to __________ provisions.
19. Nothing was created or made was done so by ___________ or _______ device.
20. Man can only _____________, while only God can ____________.

Chapter 3

# God Is One

The identity of Jehovah God is like an individual's signature--the only one of its kind. God has no equal, superior, or replica. Exodus 6:2 says, "And God spake to Moses, and said unto him, I am the Lord."

Before this writer proceeds any farther, one crucial point needs to be made here. When reading the Bible, one should pay close attention to the *tense* in which a word is used, whether it be in the *singular* or *plural*, or whether it be in the *present* or *past* tense. Notice the three words in this verse showing that God is one: God uses the words "I," "the," and "Lord." All are singular, as the reader can see. That rules out any other god. That means Jehovah is the "one and only." No other god is to be considered or even thought of in one's mind and life. In Deuteronomy 6:4 Moses tells Israel, "Hear, O Israel: The Lord our God is one God." These same words were repeated by Jesus in Mark 12:29. In Deuteronomy 4:35 Moses says, "Unto thee it was showed, that thou mightest know that the Lord he is God; there is none beside him." Then look at verse 39: "Know therefore this day, and consider it in thine heart, that the Lord he is God in heaven above, and upon the earth beneath: there is none else."

So, no matter who, what, when, or where, (words used previously in this book) there is no other god but Jehovah. The song of Moses is recorded in Deuteronomy 32. In verse 39, Moses resounds God's words: "See now that I, even I, am he, and there is no other god with me: I kill, and I make alive; I wound and I heal: neither is there any that can deliver out of my hand." Job acknowledged those very last aforementioned words in the latter part of Job 10:7.

God has no partner or crony. No one can come anywhere near to his level or supersede him. He stands totally alone in his rank. When praying his famous prayer on unity in the Garden of Gethsemane, Jesus said to his Heavenly Father in John 17:3, "And this is life eternal, that they might know thee the only true God, and Jesus Christ, whom thou hast sent." "The only true God," Jesus declared. Our Maker is the only one of his caliber. He was not cut from any cloth or born from any womb. God stands alone and solely on his independence. He is his own original self. He is not the product of any creator or maker, for there is *no* other creator or maker, but Him.

Malachi the prophet makes an interesting illustration on this matter of there being only one God. He says, "Have we not all one father? hath not one God created us? why do we deal treacherously every man against his brother, by profaning the covenant of our fathers" (Malachi 2:10)? Along with stating the single existence of God in this verse, it cannot be argued in any form that all human beings do not have one biological father. All do. The same thing applies to the animal kingdom, the fowls, and all sea creatures. Here we just noted both a physical and spiritual parallel. The Apostle Paul stated in Ephesians 4:6, "One God and Father of all, who is above all, and through all, and in you all." Just like there is only one original father of every offspring, human or otherwise, so there is only one Father of all living things in the created world. That Father is Jehovah God. Paul also stated in Galatians 3:20, "Now a mediator is not a mediator of one, but God is one." Paul told the young preacher Timothy, "For there is one God, and one mediator between God and men, the man Christ Jesus" (II Timothy 2:5).

In I Kings 8:60, King Solomon says as he is speaking to Israel, " That all the people of the earth may know that the Lord is God, and that there is none else." In Isaiah 45:5, the prophet reiterates God's words: "I am the Lord, and there is none else, there is no God beside me: I girded thee, though thou hast not known me." Verse 18 says, "For thus saith the Lord that created the heavens; God himself that formed the earth and made it; he hath established it, he created it not in vain, he formed it to be inhabited: I am the Lord, and there is none else." Then look at verse 22: "Look unto me, and be ye saved, all the ends of the earth: for I am God, and there is none else." Chapter 46:9 says, " Remember the former things of old: for I am God, and there is none else; I am God, and there is none like me." I know that you as the reader noticed those same words this writer kept citing in regards to the singularity of God. God repeatedly said, "there is none else." This must mean, "there is none else!"

When King Hezekiah was praying to God that he would be delivered out of the hand of King Sennacherib of Assyria, he said in II Kings 19:19,

"Now therefore, O Lord our God, I beseech thee, save thou us out of his hand, that all the kingdoms of the earth may know that thou art the Lord God, even thee only." Notice again the *singular* forms used here. They were "God," "thee," "thou," "the," and "only." In speaking of one of the problems with false teachers, Jude said in his one chapter epistle in verse 4, "For there are certain men crept in unawares, who were before of old ordained of this condemnation, ungodly men, turning the grace of our God into lasciviousness, and denying the only Lord God, and our Lord Jesus Christ." God cannot be grouped into the same class with any being on earth or in Heaven. The very name of "Jehovah" thoroughly distinguishes him from any fleshly creature or other form of Deity.

There are so very many people on earth with the same name, but there is only one personality past, present, and future wearing the name "Jehovah." In Psalm 83:18 the writer declared, "That men may know that thou whose name alone is Jehovah, art the Most High over all the earth." Since his "name *alone* is Jehovah," then he has to be the only God with that name, plus, making him the only God, period! This leads us up to a most serious point in this part of the book.

Since God is one, there must be no other gods to come between him and mankind. He will not tolerate it. In fact, he stoutly *condemns* it! Just like no other man or woman should come between a married couple, so then no other god is to interfere with Jehovah and the human race. Looking at the very first of the Ten Commandments, we note Exodus 20:3-6: "Thou shalt have no other gods before me. Thou shalt not make unto thee any graven image, or any likeness of any thing that is in heaven above, or that is in the earth beneath, or that is in the water under the earth; thou shalt not bow down thyself to them, nor serve them; for I the Lord thy God am a jealous God, visiting the iniquity of the fathers upon the children unto the third and fourth generation of them that hate me; showing mercy unto thousands of them that love me, and keep my commandments."

We have a *direct command* here, do we not? "Thou shalt have no other gods before me," God declared! After the molten calf was destroyed, (mentioned later in this chapter in detail), Moses told Israel in Exodus 34:14, "For thou shalt worship no other god: for the Lord, whose name is Jealous, is a jealous God." Absolutely *no* graven images were to be worshipped, nor were they even to be purchased or constructed. This makes God, as the verse stated, jealous! Angry! Disgusted! Grieved! We find in Isaiah 42:8

where God says, "I am the Lord: that is my name: and my glory will I not give to another, neither my praise to graven images."

The Creator refuses all the way to be *shared* with those claiming to love and obey him. He will not even so much as, shall we say, "stomach" the presence of any other god. He wants to be rightfully recognized as the one God in service and praise, and not just in the form of a mere verbal *claim* by mankind. God's jealousy is discussed at length in a later chapter.

Let us now study the foolishness and vanity of idolatry. Why is it useless? Why does it amount to the sum total of nothing? Psalm 115:1-6 says this: "Not unto us, O Lord, not unto us, but unto thy name give glory, for thy mercy, and for thy truth's sake. Wherefore should the heathen say, Where is now their God? But our God is in the heavens: he hath done whatsoever he hath pleased. Their idols are silver and gold, the work of men's hands. They have mouths, but they speak not: eyes have they, but they see not: they have ears, but they hear not: noses have they, but they smell not: they have hands, but they handle not: feet have they, but they walk not: neither speak they through their throat. They that make them are like unto them; so is every one that trusteth in them." Almost the very same words are found in Psalm 135:15-18. In Deuteronomy 4:28 where Moses prophesies and warns Israel against idolatry, he says, "And there ye shall serve gods, the work of men's hands, wood and stone, which neither see, nor hear, nor eat, nor smell." Jeremiah 10:14 has the weeping prophet saying, "Every man is brutish in his knowledge: every founder is confounded by the graven image: for his molten image is falsehood, and there is no breath in them." Idol gods do not contain the five senses--smell, taste, touch, see, and hear. They cannot, therefore, communicate with any member of the human race, animal kingdom, or any sea creature.

Idols possess no ability to perform. They are nothing more than statues. Talking to them and worshipping them is equal to doing so with a telephone, automobile, furniture item, plaque, photo, or anything else incommunicable, because of their not containing those aforementioned five senses. One gets nowhere fast. Also, just because idols are made in the *likeness* of something or someone, does not rightfully make them an item of worship or an object of Deity. All are fashioned by *man's* device. Since man came from God (as said before in Genesis 2:7), and being as man has formed all graven images, it then follows that those images did not come from Heaven, nor did they create the earth and all things contained within it.

In writing to the Corinthian church, Paul tells these Gentile Christians who were formerly, among other things, idolatrous worshippers, along with some Jewish Christians who were offending the consciences of their Corinthian brethren, "As concerning therefore the eating of those things that are offered in sacrifice unto idols, we know that an idol is nothing in the world, and that there is none other God but one. For though there be that are called gods, whether in heaven or in earth, (as there be gods many, and lords many,) But to us there is but one God, the Father, of whom are all things, and we in him; and one Lord Jesus Christ, by whom are all things, and we by him" (I Corinthians 8:4-6).

"An idol is nothing," Paul stated. "There is none other God but one," he further declared. Paul then went on to say that while many lords and gods are recognized by some, according to the beliefs of those who pay homage to them, there is only one God who actually *exists* for us to worship! He is the only one truly *alive*!

It is rather amusing, and sad at the same time, when one thinks of why many people worship idols. One reason is that when one is praying to a graven image and asking permission to engage in a particular practice, that idol naturally is not going to respond (although there are those worshipping it who will claim otherwise). Since no answer is heard one way or the other, that individual feels it is okay to fulfill that particular desire. After awhile, that person feels they can live in any way they desire, because the idol is giving no feedback, thus, granting every request that is made. (This truly gives the term "wishful thinking" a whole new meaning!)

This writer will now refer to I Kings 18:15-40, and show the truly magnificent test of tests which took place involving the prophet Elijah, King Ahab of Israel, the idol god Baal, Baal's prophets, and Jehovah God. The following verses describing this great event should be self-explanatory. Here is what we read: "And Elijah said, As the Lord of hosts liveth, before whom I stand, I will surely show myself unto him today. So Obadiah went to meet Ahab, and told him: and Ahab went to meet Elijah. And it came to pass, when Ahab saw Elijah, that Ahab said unto him, Art thou he that troubleth Israel? And he answered, I have not troubled Israel; but thou, and thy father's house, in that ye have forsaken the commandments of the Lord, and thou hast followed Baalim. Now therefore send, and gather to me all Israel unto mount Carmel, and the prophets of Baal four hundred and fifty, and the prophets of the groves four hundred, which eat at Jezebel's table.

So Ahab sent unto all the children of Israel, and gathered all the prophets together unto mount Carmel. And Elijah came unto all the people, and said, How long halt ye between two opinions? if the Lord be God, follow him: but if Baal, then follow him. And the people answered him not a word. Then said Elijah unto the people, I, even I only, remain a prophet of the Lord; but Baal's prophets are four hundred and fifty men. Let them therefore give us two bullocks; and let them choose one bullock for themselves, and cut it in pieces, and lay it on wood, and put no fire under; and I will dress the other bullock, and lay it on wood, and put no fire under: And call ye on the name of your gods, and I will call on the name of the Lord: and the God that answereth by fire, let him be God. And all the people answered and said, It is well spoken. And Elijah said unto the prophets of Baal, Choose you one bullock for your yourselves, and dress it first; for ye are many; and call on the name of your gods, but put no fire under. And they took the bullock which was given them, and they dressed it, and called on the name of Baal from morning even until noon, saying, O Baal, hear us. But there was no voice, nor any that answered. And they leaped upon the altar which was made. And it came to pass at noon, that Elijah mocked them, and said, Cry aloud: for he is a god; either he is talking, or he is pursuing, or he is on a journey, or peradventure he sleepeth, and must be awaked. And they cried aloud, and cut themselves after their manner with knives and lancets, till the blood gushed out upon them. And it came to pass, when midday was past, and they prophesied until the time of the offering of the evening sacrifice, that there was neither voice, nor any to answer, nor any that regarded. And Elijah said unto all the people, Come near unto me. And all the people came near unto him. And he repaired the altar of the Lord that was broken down. And Elijah took twelve stones, according to the number of the tribes of the sons of Jacob, unto whom the word of the Lord came, saying, Israel shall be thy name: And with the stone he built an altar in the name of the Lord: and he made a trench about the altar, as great as would contain two measures of seed. And he put the wood in order, and cut the bullock in pieces, and laid him on the wood, and said, Fill four barrels with water, and pour it on the burnt sacrifice, and on the wood. And he said, Do it the second time. And they did it the second time. And he said, Do it the third time. And they did it the third time. And the water ran about the altar; and he filled the trench also with water. And it came to pass at the time of the offering of the evening sacrifice, that Elijah the prophet came near, and said, Lord God of Abraham, Isaac, and of Israel, let it be known this day that thou art God in Israel, and that I am thy servant, and that I have done all these things at thy word. Hear me, O Lord, hear me, that this people may know that thou art the Lord God, and that thou hast turned their heart back again. Then the fire of the Lord fell, and consumed the burnt sacrifice, and the wood, and the stones, and the dust, and licked up the water that was in the trench. And when all the people saw it, they fell on their faces: and they said, The Lord, he is the God; the Lord, he is the God. And Elijah said unto them, Take the prophets of Baal; let not one of them escape. And they took them: and Elijah brought them down to the brook Kishon, and slew them there."

This is one great story! Look at the way Israel made big *fools* of themselves by calling on the idolatrous god Baal all those hours! (All of them trying to pull one another's teeth would have made for a more *sensible* scenario!) We read how they injured their bodies by cutting themselves until their blood actually *gushed* out! Israel was crying out to a being that did not exist, that could not hear, answer, speak, or anything else having to do with receiving, acknowledging, and communicating! They could have yelled for a complete *century,* but it still would have been to no avail! To many, many of you reading this (and to this writer too), this was foolish. Yet, there are people who wholeheartedly worship and talk to these idols day after week after month after year, either because they were raised that way, or because they changed to that way of believing later on in life.

Show me the actual *work* of an idol god. What did they *create*? What did they so much as *make*? (Remember that we defined and illustrated the difference between "create" and "make" in the last chapter). What performance have they done which would merit any drawing of attention to them? What words ever came out of their mouths? What vocal chords do they have? Further yet, what words ever went into their ears? What thoughts ever entered into their heads? What type of brain do they possess? What movements have they ever made? What proof can they provide for their very own existence? What children did they ever have? (Such would prove them to not even be *human*, or of any fleshly nature, let alone, of *Deity*!) What credentials can they produce? How can they teach, guide, or counsel? How and what can they hear? How can they reason?

Sad is the case that so many idols are made, worshipped, maintained, and adamantly believed by countless numbers of people to be Divine. This is one grave danger in accepting some traditions. Remember, too, that, although these idols *represent* that accepted god, Jehovah still forbids it (Exod. 20:4).

Let me show even further still how idolatry contains no substance, weight, solidity, warmth, or life--period! The prophet Isaiah, in trying to persuade Israel to understand the folly of idolatry, says in chapter 44:9, "They that make a graven image are all of them vanity; and their delectable things shall not profit; and they are their own witnesses; they see not nor know, that they may be ashamed."

It is totally *vain* when one is into idolatry, as Isaiah said. It brings no actual profit to that individual spiritually, except for a false feeling of self-security. The fact that the idol is lifeless, and thus, produces no benefit, tells on its very self. "They are their own witnesses," we just read. This tells us that the proof of emptiness is in the actual *existence* of the idol.

Habakkuk the prophet tries to warn the Israelites about the judgment of the unrighteous, along with the total uselessness of idol worship: "What profiteth the graven image that the maker thereof hath graven it; the molten image, and a teacher of lies; that the make of his work trusteth therein, to make dumb idols: Woe unto him that saith to the wood, Awake; to the dumb stone, Arise, it shall teach! Behold, it is laid over with gold and silver, and there is no breath at all in the midst of it" (Habakkuk 2:18-19).

Just look how much of *nothing* comes from talking to an idol! It is the equivalent of attempting to converse or establish a relationship with one's clothes, books, house, towel, picture, tree, lamp, soap, shampoo, or anything else incapable of responding. We get into the absurd, yes we do! How and why is that? "There is no breath at all in the midst of it," the latter part of verse 19 says. Why talk to an idol? It does not, as previously noted, even have a *brain* to receive one's words! Therefore, what possible I.Q. could an idol have?

When Paul speaks of the heathen nations, take note of what he said to the Roman Christians: "Professing themselves to be wise, they became fools, And changed the glory of the uncorruptible God into an image made like to corruptible man, and to birds, and to four-footed beasts, and creeping things" (Romans 1:23). Claiming *wisdom*, this group of people were actually going in the other direction, and so, became *fools*! Jehovah God is not a man, a bird, a beast, or any creeping thing. As covered in a later chapter, and as the Bible *point blank* says by Jesus himself in the first part of John 4:24, "God is a *spirit*!" The people Paul mentioned just cited in Romans 1:23 were really *into* pagan worship. Verse 25 says, "Who changed the truth of God into a lie, and worshiped and served the creature more than the Creator, who is blessed forever. Amen." It is a most awful thing to have "changed the truth of God into a lie!" What does it profit someone--anyone--who serves "the creature more than the Creator?" What rewards and blessings can an idol give? Such devotion is a big throwaway of time and life. Idolatry profits and provides nothing, for such is utterly impossible! One may as well be attempting to walk from the earth to the moon!

Next, we will refer again to the weeping prophet, Jeremiah, and take note of the words that God wants him to relate to Israel on this matter of idolatry. In chapter 10:11 we read, "Thus shall ye say unto them, The gods that have not made the heavens and the earth, they shall perish from the earth, and from under these heavens."

This was one of my earlier arguments! What proof of *works* do these gods have as their credentials? Which of them created the heavens and the earth? I asked before, I ask again: Which of them can create *or* make? No idol can do either one. All idols shall perish, whatever and wherever they be found. Verses 14-15 says, "Every man is brutish in his knowledge: every founder is confounded by the graven image: for his molten is falsehood, and there is no breath in them. They are vanity, and the work of errors: in the time of their visitation they shall perish." "Brutish" means showing little intelligence or sensibility." Some of these same words were quoted a few paragraphs back. This verse illustrates that engaging in idolatry is a most foolish thing to do! It is forever wrong. It is tragic that many ignorantly engage in it. Others do so knowing better, as was the case with the Israelite nation.

There is no God, therefore, other than Jehovah God, and he will not stand for any idol impeding his presence. Chapter 5:7 declares by God, "How shall I pardon thee for this? thy children have forsaken me, and sworn by them that there are no gods: when I had fed them to the full, they then committed adultery, and assembled themselves by troops in the harlot's houses." We find in this text that God's punishment to Israel, which often consisted in allowing them to be led off into captivity by a heathen nation, could not be avoided, due to the fact that nothing else seemed to be effective in totally *cleansing* them from their love of pagan worship. Until or unless that time would come, God would *not* pardon them. Idolatry, as in other Bible verses, is compared to *adultery*, because in both evils, one spouse has been unfaithful to the person who is that *rightful* partner. This companion will make full use of the home shared by the other companion, then turn around and receive an outsider to whom there is no moral or legal obligation. The word "troops" in this verse simply denotes how Israel (Judah here, specifically) gathered in large numbers in the very temples of these false gods, and thus, took part repeatedly in their idolatrous worship. This leads us to an important question.

How badly will God punish the ones who worship these graven images? Ezekiel 14:4 has this prophet being told by God of his promise on the degrees of consequences: "Therefore speak unto them, and say unto them, Thus saith the Lord God; Every man of the house of Israel that setteth up his idols in his heart, and putteth the stumblingblock of his iniquity before his face, and cometh to the prophet, I the Lord will answer him that cometh according to the multitude of his idols." As the phrase so goes, "the punishment shall fit the crime." The deeper Israel would sink into idolatry, the more severe the punishment. So much of that same principle applies to civil law, both today and in the past.

We find God reminding the Israelite nation through Moses in Leviticus 26:1, "Ye shall make you no other idols or graven image, neither rear you up a standing image, neither shall ye set up any image of stone in your land, to bow down unto it: for I the Lord am your God." Verse 30 says, " And I will destroy your high places, and cut down your images, and cast your carcases upon the carcases of your idols, and my soul shall abhor you." This very clearly explains the tough hatred Jehovah God has for idolatry. He also reminded Israel again here, as he often had to do so throughout the Old Testament, "for I the Lord am your God." In Isaiah 2:18-22, the prophet tells Judah, "And the idols he shall utterly abolish. And they shall go into the holes of the rocks, and into the caves of the earth. In that day a man shall cast his idols of silver, and his idols of gold, which they made each one for himself to worship, to the moles and to the bats; To go into the clefts of the rocks, and in the tops of the ragged rocks, for fear of the Lord, and for the glory of his majesty, when he ariseth to shake terribly the earth. Cease ye from man, whose breath is in his nostrils: for wherein is he to be accounted of?"

Over and over again we read in the Bible how idolatry is vain and a serious sin, along with God's constant reminder to the people that *he* is the only God to be recognized and worshipped. Knowing God's A-1 loathe of idolatry, it should not surprise us that I Corinthians 6:9, Galatians 5:20, and Ephesians 5:5 all say in no uncertain terms that anybody who engages in this kind of life and worship will not go to Heaven. That is the *Bible* talking—not this writer! In 1 John 5:21, which is the very last verse in that book, the aged apostle says, “Little children, keep yourselves from idols.” Like John, I too plead with the reader to eschew idolatrous worship.

Let’s go back to some more of Paul’s sermon on Mars Hill in Athens, Greece. Athens was the very center of idolatry at this time in Biblical history. Paul tried to reason with a number of the Athenian men on the worship of idols. He did not speak in any intimidating way to them. Verses 24-30 say, “God that made the world and all things therein, seeing that he is Lord of heaven and earth, dwelleth not in temples made with hands; Neither is worshiped with men’s hands, as though he needed anything, seeing he giveth to all life, and breath, and all things: And hath made of one blood all nations of men for to dwell on all the face of the earth, and hath determined the times before appointed, and the bounds of their habitation; That they should seek the Lord, if haply they might feel after him, though he be not far from every one of us: For in him we live, and move, and have our being; as certain also of your own poets have said, For we are also his offspring. Forasmuch then as we are the offspring of God, we ought not to think that the Godhead is like unto gold, or silver, or stone, graven by art and man’s device. And the times of this ignorance God winked at; but now commandeth all men everywhere to repent.”

These verses just read teach that God does not *need* anything or anyone, no graven image can possibly be any likeness of him, and that “we are the offspring of God.” That is why we should pay homage to him, rather than to a graven image. That is why we should recognize him as the one to be adored and reverenced, instead of a lifeless idol. This is the God who “is Lord of heaven and earth.” This is the God that “dwelleth not in temples made with hands.” This all being so true, Paul says, “we ought not to think that the Godhead is like unto gold, or silver, or stone, graven by art and man’s device.”

The very fact that all idols were “graven by art and man’s device,” show they are worldly, earthly, and hence, did not originate from Heaven. Someone had to make them here on the planet earth, and thus, that takes away all Deity and spirituality from these idols, which never were theirs to start. May we all be like the Thessalonian Christians. Paul, in speaking of Macedonia and Achaia, said to them, “For they themselves show of us what manner of entering in we had unto you, and how ye turned to God from idols to serve the living and true God” (I Thessalonians 1:9). God commands all of mankind to do just that: "Serve the living and true God." Why serve something of which there is no possible reception or return of communication?

One particular episode cannot be left out here in reference to the severity of idolatry. This writer speaks of the incident involving the golden calf, known in the Bible as the "molten" calf. Like the aforementioned story of the prophet Elijah and King Ahab, so the following verses too should explain themselves. This happening is found in Exodus 32:1-9: "And when the people saw that Moses delayed to come down out of the mount, the people gathered themselves together unto Aaron, and said unto him, Up, make us gods, which shall go before us; for as for this Moses, the man that brought us up out of the land of Egypt, we wot not what is become of him. And Aaron said unto them, Break off the golden earrings, which are in the ears of your wives, of your sons, and of your daughters, and bring them unto me. And all the people brake off the golden earrings which were in their ears, and brought them unto Aaron. And he received them at their hand, and fashioned it with a graving tool, after he had made it a molten calf: and they said, These be thy gods, O Israel, which brought thee up out of the land of Egypt. And when Aaron saw it, he built an altar before it; and Aaron made proclamation, and said, Tomorrow is a feast to the Lord. And they rose up early on the morrow, and offered burnt offerings; and brought peace offerings; and the people sat down to eat and drink, and rose up to play. And the Lord said unto Moses, Go, get thee down; for thy people, which thou broughtest out of the land of Egypt, have corrupted themselves: They have turned aside quickly out of the way which I commanded them; they have made them a molten calf, and have worshiped it, and have sacrificed thereunto, and have said, These by thy gods, O Israel, which have brought thee up out of the land of Egypt. And the Lord said unto Moses, I have seen this people, and, behold, it is a stiff-necked people: Now therefore let me alone, that my wrath may wax hot against them, and that I may consume them: and I will make of thee a great nation."

How so bitterly angry and jealous God became at Israel! The people could not even be trusted to carry on properly while Moses was temporarily gone. They were like young children out of control. Too, how *absurd* it was for them to say, "These be thy gods, O Israel, which have brought thee up out of the land of Egypt." How disheartening, disgusting, and hurtful it must have felt to God upon hearing these words of idiocy and betrayal!

That is definitely taking leave of one's senses! The very thought of giving such credit to a molten calf, saying *it* was the god(s) which delivered the Israelite people from their Egyptian captivity! How could an "it" do such a thing? (Speaking sarcastically and nonsensically, try getting even a *live* calf to accomplish that for you! See how far you get!) Remember, once again, that even a *representation* of another god was wrong (Exod. 20:4). This is how idolatrous homage brainwashes people. Idolatry is damnable to one's very own moral and spiritual life alike, for God said in this text that the children of Israel "have corrupted themselves." Fortunately for these people, Moses was able to persuade God not to destroy them, as verses 11-14 explain. Jehovah lets his chosen people know again that *he* is the only God to worship and serve.

This writer would like to close out this chapter by quoting from the prophet Ezekiel again, where one cannot help but see the continued *resentment* that the one, true God has for those bowing down to idols. This is yet another story (a future event, actually) which is self-explanatory. In chapter 6:4-14, Ezekiel prophesies about the mass destruction God will bring upon the idolatrous mountains of Israel: "And your altars shall be desolate, and your images shall be broken: and I will cast down your slain men before your idols. And I will lay the dead carcases of the children of Israel before their idols; and I will scatter your bones round about your altars. In all your dwelling places the cities shall be laid waste and made desolate, and your idols may be broken down and cease, and your images may be cut down, and your works may be abolished. And the slain shall fall in the midst of you, and ye shall know that I am the Lord. Yet will I leave a remnant, that ye may have some that shall escape the sword among the nations, when ye shall be scattered through the countries. And they that escape of you shall remember me among the nations whither they shall be carried captives, because I am broken with their whorish heart, which hath departed from me, and with their eyes, which go a whoring after their idols: and they shall loathe themselves for the evils which they have committed in all their abominations. And they shall know that I am the Lord, and that I have not said in vain that I would do this evil unto them. Thus saith the Lord God; Smite with thine hand, and stamp with they foot, and say, Alas for all the evil abominations of the house of Israel! for they shall fall by the sword, by the famine, and by the pestilence. He that is far off shall die of the pestilence; and he that is near shall fall by the sword; and he that remaineth and is besieged shall die by the famine: thus will I accomplish my fury upon them. Then shall ye know that I am the Lord, when their slain men shall be among their idols round about their altars, upon every high hill, in all the tops of the mountains, and under every green tree, and under every thick oak, the place where they did offer sweet savor to all their idols. So will I stretch out my hand upon them, and make the land desolate, yea, more desolate than the wilderness toward Diblath, in all their habitations: and they shall know that I am the Lord."

That is what God says to all persons right now who are of the age and mind of accountability: "Know that I am the Lord!" Idolatry is spiritual adultery and will condemn one's soul. There is no sense, future, or benefit in practicing such a worship. Truly, God is *one*!

**Questions**

1. "Hear, O Israel: The Lord our God is _________ God."
2. "Their idols are ___________ and _________, the work of ________ hands."
3. "That all the people of the earth may know that the ________ is God, and that there is ______________."
4. "Thou shalt have ____________________________ before me."
5. All idol gods created _____________ and made _______________.
6. "Who changed the truth of God into a _________, and worshiped and served the ______________ more than the ______________."
7. "________ that made the world and _______ things therein, seeing that he is ________ of heaven and earth, dwelleth not in ____________ made with ___________; Neither is worshiped with ____________, as though he needed ______________, seeing he giveth to all _________, and ________________, and ______________________."
8. "I the _____________ will answer him that cometh according to the ______________________."
9. "And how ye turned to _________ from _____________ to serve the ____________ and ___________ God."
10. "And your _______________ shall be ______________, and your ________________ shall be ________________."

11. "How long halt ye between two __________? If the __________ be __________, follow him: but if __________, then follow him."

12. "The ______________, he is the God."

13. "Ye shall make you no other _________ or ______________________, neither rear you up a _____________________, neither shall ye set up any ____________ of ___________ in your land, to ___________ unto it: for I the ____________ am your __________."

14. "Professing themselves to be ________, they became __________, And changed the ___________ of the __________________ God into an ___________ made like to ___________ man, and to __________ and to _____________________________, and ____________________."

15. "Little children, keep yourselves from ____________."

16. "We ought not to _________ that the _______________ is like unto ___________, or ______________, or _________, graven by ________ and ________ device."

17. Idolatrous homage _________________ people.

18. "Then shall ye know that I am the ________, when their __________ men shall be among their _________ round about their _________, upon every ________________, in all the ________________________, and under every ________________, and under every ________________, the place where they did offer _________________ to all their ___________."

19. In 1 Kings 18, Israel was serving the idolatrous god __________.

20. "Wherefore should the _____________ say, Where is now their ______? But our _________ is in the _________________: he hath done whatsoever he hath ______________."

Chapter 4

# God Is A Spirit

There is absolutely nothing in the makeup of Jehovah God consisting of flesh, blood, bones, corpuscles, tendons, muscles, or any other human body parts, such as you and I have. He is totally a *spirit*! When Jesus was speaking to the Samaritan woman at Jacob's well, he said to her in John 4:24, "God is a Spirit: and they that worship him must worship him in spirit and truth." "God is a Spirit," the text reads. That excludes anything and everything pertaining to a physical body. Therefore, God never dies, ages, pains, tires out in the least, becomes sick, cuts himself, bleeds, loses any limbs, or has to deal with anything else pointing to existing as a creature of the flesh. For that matter, *no* spirit does. God should not be looked upon as "the man with the cigar" or "the man upstairs." Of course, it is understood that those who identify God as such are most likely, in their hearts, not intentionally showing any disrespect or irreverence to the Creator by labeling him in this manner. Rather, it is just their way of expressing themselves. However one examines it, God is not human.

After Jesus had resurrected and reappeared to his disciples, take note of Luke 24:36-43: "And as they thus spake, Jesus himself stood in the midst of them, and saith unto them, Peace be unto you. But they were terrified and affrighted, and supposed that they had seen a spirit. And he said unto them, Why are ye troubled? and why do thoughts arise in your hearts? Behold my hands and feet, that it is I myself: handle me, and see; for a spirit hath not flesh and bones, as ye see me have. And when he had thus spoken, he showed them his hands and his feet. And while they yet believed not for joy, and wondered, he said unto them, Have ye here any meat? And they gave him a piece of a broiled fish, and of a honeycomb. And he took it, and did eat before them." One key phrase to dispel all doubt about the difference between a spiritual body and a fleshly body is when Jesus said, "a spirit hath not flesh and bones."

No spirit has to deal with anything of the flesh, for it is not *of* that nature. However, Jesus was still in a body of flesh here, still human, still a man. He set out to prove it by asking for some food. When given a piece of fish and honeycomb, he ate it right in front of his disciples. No spirit eats and no spirit drinks, for no spirit hungers and thirsts.

So it is with God. He does not have to eat, drink, bathe, answer the calls of nature, sleep, or anything else that a physical body must do in order to survive. The whole summation is this: God flat out does not have to do *anything* to survive. He needs no maintenance, nor does he have to *perform* any maintenance on himself, so that means he does not *do* so. Jehovah needs no "survival kit." God is not a man. The Bible is very clear on this, and words it just exactly that way. In Numbers 23:19, Balaam says to Balak, "God is not a man, that he should lie; neither the son of man, that he should repent: hath he said, and shall he not do it? Or hath he spoken, and shall he not make it good?"

"God is not a man, " Balaam said. One can only take that in the most literal way in which it was said. If God is not a *man*, then he must be a *spirit*, as those are the only two *living* things in existence that talk (sensibly) and communicate.

When the prophet Samuel was rebuking King Saul for disobeying God, observe what is said in I Samuel 15:28-29: "And Samuel said unto him, the Lord hath rent the kingdom of Israel from thee this day, and hath given it to a neighbor of thine, that is better than thou. And also the Strength of Israel will not lie nor repent: for he is not a man, that he should repent."

Samuel, like Balaam, said ever so clearly of Jehovah God, "he is not a man," nor does he need to "repent." The word "repent," as it is used here, means that God will not change his mind about taking the kingship away from Saul.

God stays identically the same *all* the time in his appearance without any variation, shedding, rebirth, reform, or diminishing. God is not a *fickle* spirit in his character, either. He does not bounce around, in and out, up and down, or sideways in some kind of yo-yo fashion. God is not moody in his personality, or else that would make him a man; a mere mortal with weaknesses and shortcomings like you and I. In James 1:17, the apostle says, "Every good gift and every perfect gift is from above, and cometh down from the Father of lights, with whom is no variableness, neither shadow of turning." The fact that God is a being of "no variableness, neither shadow of turning," would do away with anything and everything connected to being human, for "neither shadow of turning" would indicate that God does not alter himself, nor is he altered by anybody or any thing in the least little way, not one iota, not any.

While this writer will discuss in another chapter the might and power of God, I wish to refer next to Jeremiah 23:24 as further proving my point on his being a spirit. There, the prophet sounds out some words of God: "Can any hide himself in secret places that I shall not see him? saith the Lord. Do not I fill heaven and earth? saith the Lord."

How in the world can any human being see everyone and everything all at once? It cannot be done! What did we just note? "Can any hide himself in secret places that I shall not see him?" How can any man, woman, boy, or girl "fill heaven and earth?" All reading this book know by the most *elementary* of logic that such is a total and utter impossibility! Only a *spirit* can do such a thing—an *extraordinary* spirit, at that! The very idea that one can "fill heaven and earth" displays an ability so much more superb to any form or level of human power. God, being a spirit, cannot be killed, annihilated, or so much as injured by any creature, any thing, any cause, any element, or any force. Such can only happen to a being possessing a body of flesh. Any spirit, though, never dies physically, for it is not a physical body. No *flesh* is there. Any physical body is limited in its intelligence, strength, durability, and capabilities. It is also limited in its length of life, be that a human or any other body of flesh, for the simple reason that all flesh ages and eventually dies, as does all *material* things, for that matter.

Our wonderful Maker is not of the flesh, so he is not human, which means he is not a man, even though he be of the masculine gender. Just think of this: No spirit can be harmed in any way by any body of flesh, for no spirit can be *touched* by such, regardless of how extensive the effort and attempt. God is an *untouchable*, which shows all the more that he is a *spirit*!

## Questions

1. "God is a ________________."
2. "For a _____________ hath not ____________ and ____________, as ye see me have."
3. "God is not a _________, that he should ________________; neither the

_________ of _________ that he should ___________."

4. God contains "no ________________, neither ______________ of ________________."

5. In speaking of God, it says that "the Strength of Israel will not ________ nor ___________: for he is not a ________, that he should __________________."

6. Since God is a ______________, he should not be looked upon as "the ____________ with the __________," or, "the _________ upstairs."

7. No spirit __________ and no spirit ____________, for no spirit _________ and __________________.

8. God has to do ________________ to survive.

9. "Do I not fill ______________ and ____________? saith the Lord."

10. A spirit never dies ____________, for it is not a ___________ body.

11. God, being a ____________, cannot be ___________, ___________, or so much as _______________ by any _____________, any _________, any ___________, any ________________, or any _____________.

12. To prove that Jesus was still in the flesh after his resurrection, he asked his disciples, "Have ye here any _____________? And they gave him a piece of a ____________________, and of a ________________. And he took it and did ______________ before them."

Chapter 5

# God Is Possessor of All Creation

In a previous chapter, it was shown how Jehovah God is the Creator of all beings and things. Genesis 1:1 says, "In the beginning God created the heaven and the earth." It would thus demonstrate by proper logic and reasoning that he completely *possesses* all of the Creation. Each item and living being making up the universe is his by sovereign right. Just like the baby born biologically belongs to the mother and father who collectively produced it, as is the case with any offspring in any category, (an example used previously) so then God rightfully and naturally has ownership of all that ever has been, and currently is, in existence. The Hebrew writer tells us, "And, Thou, Lord, in the beginning hast laid the foundation of the earth; and the heavens are the works of thine hands" (Hebrews 1:10). This was taken from Psalm 102:25.

Since the Creation came from *God's* hands, it belongs to *him*! That means without any ifs, ands, buts, or hum-hawing around that *all* we utilize came from God, which shows our being thoroughly *dependent* upon him for survival. This applies in both the spiritual and the physical areas. Nothing originated from the human race, because the human race itself originated from God. Not one object or live being is in this world which our hands can touch or ever will touch, or which any eye has fallen upon or will fall upon, because any man, woman, boy, or girl created it. *God* is the reason for it. Therefore, he can say without any reservation, "It is *mine*!" When Job was about to reach the end of his sufferings, God told him those very words: "Who hath prevented me, that I should repay him? Whatsoever is under the whole heaven is mine" (Job 41:11).

Every bit of credit, glory, and attribution traces itself all the way back to God. None of mankind need claim any of it. This means that the human race is not in ownership of anything or anybody, in regards to being the origin of it. Mankind can only be the maker of what God has already provided for him in the way of raw materials, as noted in another chapter.

"Does God really own *all* things," one may ask? Let us take note of what King David said in Psalm 24:1: "The earth is the Lord's, and the fullness thereof; the world and they that dwell therein." The Apostle Paul repeated the same words in I Corinthians 10:26 and 28. Verse 3 of Psalm 24 reads, "Who shall ascend into the hill of the Lord? Or who shall stand in his holy place?" David got specific in these verses when using the possessive pronoun "his." Not only is the earth itself God's, but so is every, last, single, solitary thing *in and on* the earth. All matter making up, residing inside, and touching the outside of this wonderful sphere known as earth, every magnificent planet stationed in the heavens, and all their objects, again I say, *in and on* those planets, belong to that bountiful Creator. The words "fullness thereof" would altogether spell it out. God not only created all things, he *owns* all things, because he *did* create all things. David declared somewhat the same words in Psalm 15:1: "Lord who shall abide in thy tabernacle? Who shall dwell in thy holy hill?" Along with the word "his," anytime one reads in the Bible words like "thy" and "thine," (archaic terms used in literary language) that too shows possession; ownership; belonging to oneself; and so, not to anybody else.

Moses exhorted Israel by saying in Deuteronomy 10:14, "Behold the heaven and the heaven of heavens is the Lord's thy God, the earth also, with all that therein is." Truly, God holds the complete "title" to every being and everything because *he is* that title to all. Exodus 9:29 has Moses also talking to the wicked and idolatrous King Pharaoh during the time God sent the plague of hail (the seventh out of ten different plagues) upon Egypt: "And Moses said unto him, As soon as I am gone out of the city, I will spread abroad my hands unto the Lord; and thunder shall cease, neither shall there be any more hail; that thou mayest know how that the earth is the Lord's."

There is yet another word which is used many times in the Bible referring to Jehovah God's being possessor of all things, and which word all of us have used in some form often in our lifetime: That word is "Lord." Just like a "landlord" and "landlady" are both recognized as owners of the land they bought and to which they have the title, whether residing on that land or not, so is God the "Lord" of everything and all flesh. When Paul was speaking to the men of Athens, Greece on Mars Hill in Acts 17, he says in verses 24-26, "God that made the world and all things therein, seeing that he is Lord of heaven and earth, dwelleth not in temples made with hands; Neither is worshiped with men's hands, as though he needed any thing, seeing he giveth to all life, and breath, and all things; And hath made of one blood all nation of men for to dwell on all the face of the earth, and hath determined the times before appointed, and the bounds of their habitation." God is the original "Landlord." He owns all of this entire globe and universe. He possesses and controls all functions. None of mankind has any "lien" on God's Creation.

Going back to the book of Job again, we see where Job is telling Bildad, "He stretcheth out the north over the empty place, and hangeth the earth upon nothing" (Job 26:7). That verse, in the mind of this writer, is one of the most startling and thought-provoking verses in the entire Old Testament! Our feet are touching some form of the earth so very much of the time. We lean upon objects that exist on the earth. However, what does the earth *itself* lean on? It is "nothing," as the eyes of the reader just plainly saw. There has to be some kind of control--regulation--some kind of special ability to keep something as big and weighty as the earth in the same identical place (orbit) second after minute after hour after day after week after month after year after century after millennium, hanging on "nothing!" Not to do so would make the earth constantly drift until it would sooner or later crash mightily with one of the other planets, or else one of those planets would eventually collide with the earth, which means *they too* hang upon "nothing," and yet, remain in the same exact spot all the time! It gives a new and higher respect to the words "possess" and "control."

That which God created, he controls. That which one controls, he truly possesses, hence, possesses all the way. You see, gentle reader, *real* power is what one *takes*, not what is *given*, for what is given can most always be taken away. Of course, God never had to take all the power contained in him, (which is indeed, *all* the power!) for it was never even given him. It was always his to *begin* with, oh yes! That is all the more reason for God's being complete Possessor over all the Creation.

It was once theorized that the earth is held up by a super, gigantic, muscular man known as "Atlas." Then came the question, "Who or what is holding up Atlas?" It was decided that a giant turtle was under him. The next question was, you guessed it, "Who or what is holding up that giant turtle?" On and on it went where one thing after another had to be "invented" as an attempt to explain how the earth was remaining in one spot in outer space, while it still continued to rotate on its axis, at that! To where does it all conclude, after becoming so imbecilic? The only possible answer is contained in what the book of Job said, written, like all the rest of the Bible, under the pen of Divine Inspiration: God "hangeth the earth upon nothing." See how silly and far out unbelief and speculation often extend? Speaking way out here, I have never heard any of those astronauts, while traveling in outer space inside their capsule, testifying to having seen a super, gigantic, muscular man holding up the earth with a giant turtle under him or anything or anyone stationed under that giant turtle; and neither have you nor anybody else, past or present! Nor will it ever be! For that matter, no photos taken of the earth, however far away or close, have ever revealed such a scene! This explains one reason why some theories will never be proven to be fact. *There is no proof!* That too, as commented elsewhere in this book, is why some theories will remain as just that--theories!

Jehovah is *God*! God is *Lord!* He is the Possessor—Owner—the one in control--over every area of this beautiful and gorgeous universe. As the saying goes again, "God's hand is in it all!" May we never take that saying lightly. No matter what or whom we have to claim as our own, technically speaking, we own nothing!

**Questions**

1. "Whatsoever is under the whole ____________ is ___________."
2. It was once theorized that the earth is held up by a super, gigantic, muscular man known as __________.
3. Underneath this muscular man, holding him up, was theorized to be a giant ______________.
4. "And the ______________ are the works of _________ hands."
5. Nothing originated from the human race, because the human race originated from __________.
6. "Who shall ascend into the hill of the __________? Or who shall stand in _________ holy place?"
7. "Lord who shall abide in _________ tabernacle? Who shall dwell in __________ holy hill?"
8. "That thou may knowest how that the earth is the ___________."
9. Paul said of God on Mars Hill that " he is _________ of ____________ and ___________."

10. REAL power is what one _____________, not what is ___________.
11. "He stretcheth out the north over the ____________ place, and hangeth the earth upon ________________."
12. God holds the complete _____________ to every ____________ and _________________________.
13. Concerning God, Paul also said, "and hath determined the __________ before ____________________, and the ____________________ of their _______________________."
14. That which one __________________, he truly possesses, hence, ____ ___________________________________."
15. "God's hand is _________________________."
16. No matter what we claim to have as our own, technically speaking, we own __________________.
17. Since the creation came from _________, then it belongs to ______.
18. Nothing ____________ from the human race, because the human race itself ____________ from ______________.
19. Since the creation came from ___________ hands, we are thoroughly ________________ upon him for ______________________.
20. "Behold the ______________ and the ____________ of ______________ is the __________ thy __________, the _____________ also, with ______ that therein is."

Chapter 6

# God Is Sinless

Jehovah God is absolutely *sinless*! He is completely without fault, flaw, weakness, or error. It can be safely said that he cannot *and* will not sin. God is perfect in every way. So perfect is God that he cannot be in the presence of sin without calling attention to it. This writer did not say, "*will* not be," but I said, "*cannot* be." His very nature never allows it. God cannot say, do, think, speak, or command anything wrong. His sinless character and never failing mind have no weak moments. How can plea after plea be made *by* God to mankind *not* to sin, while plea after plea is made *to* God by mankind to *forgive* sin, if God is not sinless? The Maker of all Creation is without discipline, guidance, or correction because his complete makeup is incapable of any wrong. Another way of saying it is that God is *infallible* to sin.

In Isaiah 59:1-2, the prophet tells a troubled Israel, "Behold, the Lord's hand is not shortened, that it cannot save; neither his ear heavy, that it cannot hear: But your iniquities have separated between you and your God, and your sins have hid his face from you, that he will not hear." God refused Israel's prayers because they did not repent of their sins. God further told Jeremiah, "I will scatter them as with an east wind before the enemy; I will show them the back, and not the face, in the day of calamity" (Jeremiah 18:17). In Ezekiel 7:22, God says to the prophet, "My face will I also turn from them, and they shall pollute my secret place: for the robbers shall enter into it, and defile it."

It is not like God is some kind of a "snob" or a "Mr. Goody Two-Shoes." The fact is that God simply cannot *be* where sin is. Just like none of us take kindly to any stinking odor or mistreatment, so then also does God feel the same way about sin. King Hezekiah tells Israel the following in II Chronicles 30:9: "For if ye turn again unto the Lord, your brethren and your children shall find compassion before them that lead them captive, so that they shall come again into this land: for the Lord your God is gracious and merciful, and will not turn away his face from you, if ye return unto him." King David declared in Psalm 11:7, " For the righteous Lord loveth righteousness; his countenance doth behold the upright."

Note the two very opposite comparisons here, gentle reader. First, we read where God cannot be in the presence of sin. Second, we saw where God will only be in the presence of righteousness. That is his nature. That is God. You name the sin, and God abhors it, for it is a complete "turn off" to him.

The same thing holds no less true in the avenue of *prayer*. I Peter 3:12 has the apostle telling the Christians to whom he wrote, "For the eyes of the Lord are over the righteous, and his ears are open unto their prayers: but the face of the Lord is against them that do evil." That is why many prayers are not answered, which is really the same as being answered with a "no." The individual not living as God commands need not be offended at a sinless God for not paying attention to their prayers. It will not work! Let us not deceive ourselves into thinking otherwise. We find these very words said from a blind man whose sight was restored by Jesus in John 9:31: "Now we know that God heareth not sinners: but if any man be a worshiper of God, and doeth his will, him he heareth." Indeed, Jehovah God is sinless. Therefore, he cannot be in sin's presence.

This also means that God can in no way *lie* to anybody about anything in any situation at anytime. The Apostle Paul said when writing to the young preacher Titus: "In hope of eternal life, which God, that cannot lie, promised before the world began" (Titus 1:2). In Hebrews 6:18 the writer says, "That by two immutable things, in which it was impossible for God to lie, we might have a strong consolation, who have fled for refuge to lay hold upon the hope set before us." The first verse quoted in this paragraph says, "God, that cannot lie." The second passage reads, "it was impossible for God to lie." Now if the two words "cannot" and "impossible" do not make it as crystal clear as a cloudless sky full of sunshine, pray tell, what does?

Since God is a sinless being, that means he cannot lie, for lying is a sin, as the Bible mentions a number of times, and for which some netted eternal death for doing so. The fact that God *cannot* tell a lie (as the legend goes about George Washington) is why he does not *ever* lie. Paul told the Roman church, "God forbid: yea, let God be true, but every man a liar; as it is written, That thou mightest be justified in thy sayings, and mightest overcome when thou art judged" (Romans 3:4).

God said to Job, "Wilt thou disannul my judgment? Wilt thou condemn me, that thou mightest be righteous?" (Job 40:8). God cannot be *condemned*, so it must follow that he cannot be *corrected*, either. Since God cannot lie, he, therefore, cannot even be guilty of *guile*, which means to tell only the *partial* truth, while omitting the rest, which should have been told. What was told was the truth, but the remainder of the story was intentionally left out. However, that is not God. He is altogether a *truthful* personality. There is nothing wrong with him. No fault, catch, or "glitch" can be found anywhere in his speech. Moses tells Israel of God in Deuteronomy 32:4, "He is the Rock, his work is perfect: for all his ways are judgment: a God of truth and without iniquity, just and right is he." The word "iniquity" means "lawlessness." Nothing can be *proven* false about God's speech, for nothing *is* false about it. God's sinless condition is sharpened to absolute and complete spiritual perfection!

2 Samuel 22:31 records King David's speaking to God in his song of deliverance, saying, "As for God, his way is perfect; the word of the Lord is tried: he is a buckler to all them that trust in him." Most nearly the same words are said by David in Psalm 18:30. (A "buckler" is a shield). David always trusted in God, and that is why he *won* the battles with his enemies as he did. He knew whatever God told him had to be the truth, for the simple reason it came from the mouth of Jehovah himself.

As Jesus was preaching his Sermon on the Mount, he said in Matthew 5:48, "Be ye therefore perfect, even as your Father which is in heaven is perfect." (Note: While the word "perfect," as it is used at times in the Bible, means, "Full grown; complete; mature," this writer is, of course, referring to that definition of the word commonly recognized by most all of us to mean, "Faultless; flawless; containing no wrong; without error"). No, we will never actually *reach* sinless perfection, but Jesus and His Heavenly Father expect us to work *towards* it. While one can never be sinless, one can *sin less* as one lives and follows God. The whole point of citing this verse is to further show the sinless state of God. There is nothing wrong with our Creator. Think about this: If God himself sinned, to whom would he repent and pray for forgiveness, seeing as he is the Supreme Being of them all? There is none higher. With him, "the buck stops here."

Since God is sinless, his very Bible must be too. Paul writes to another young preacher, Timothy, telling him, "All scripture is given by inspiration of God, and is profitable for doctrine, for reproof, for correction, for instruction in righteousness: That the man of God may be perfect, thoroughly furnished unto all good works" (2 Timothy 3:16-17). Only a sinless mind could write a sinless book. Go figure, right?

Peter wrote to a group of Christians, "Knowing this first, that no prophecy of the scripture is of any private interpretation. For the prophecy came not in old time by the will of man: but holy men of God spake as they were moved by the Holy Ghost" (2 Peter 1:20-21). The entire chapter of I Corinthians 2 shows by explanation and example how the Holy Spirit went down into the mind of God to see what things God wanted written, God told the Holy Spirit his commands, the Holy Spirit told the men what to write, (this makes up what is known as "Divine Inspiration") the men wrote down the words, and so, that is how we got the Bible. You see, that *is* the Bible, also known as the "Word of God," in which manner this writer has referred to from time to time in this book, as well as all of humanity who believe in it. James 1:25 teaches us by the apostle that God's Word is "the perfect law of liberty."

If you as the reader do not believe God is sinless, then you will not believe his Bible is either, for the words of that very book came from the mind of God. After all, if one does not believe (or like, either) certain characteristics said about the *author* of a book, then one is not likely to accept a single, minute *word* of what that author writes. (If one does accept anything said, it will be very little!) To believe the words is to believe the author, for the author is the one writing the words. They stand or fall together. The Bible is far too deep in its contents to have ever come from the mind of man, or even from the combined minds of any large *battery* of men.

Being as God is totally sinless, this brings us up to a very universal controversy about him. This writer affirms wholeheartedly that God is not to be blamed for any of the wrongdoing existing in this world--whether one speaks of crime, social injustice, or anything which brought sin into the world. Nor is the Almighty to be blamed for even *tempting* man to sin. God created a perfect world, hence, a perfect mankind, too. Can what I have stated in the second sentence of this paragraph be proven by the Bible? Yes, it can. In James 1:13-15, the apostle says, "Let no man say when he is tempted, I am tempted of God: for God cannot be tempted with evil, neither tempteth he any man: But every man is tempted, when he is drawn away of his own lust, and enticed. Then when lust hath conceived, it bringeth forth sin: and sin, when it is finished, bringeth forth death."

From time to time, someone is heard to lament how God (according to the way some people person believe) came and took their son, daughter, mother, father, grandchild, friend, or whomever, as a punishment to them. I say without any hesitation or reservation that *God did not do anything of the kind*! We just read in no uncertain terms where God does not tempt, nor can he be tempted to do evil from or to any person. That would not make him a sinless God. Rather, it is the one who is *being* tempted, thus, allowing oneself to yield "when he is drawn away of his own lust and enticed." When any sin is committed, it is the fault of that particular person, not God. God wants mankind to *obey* him, not *sin against* him. Why would God demand obedience to his commands, then turn around and "set up" some kind of temptation to lead man astray? God does not "throw a curve" at the human race. He does not operate like some of sinful man. He "shoots straight" every step of the way.

Regardless of how one quibbles over this matter or analyzes it, such just cannot apply to a sinless being, for the pure and simple reason no sin was or can possibly be committed, due to the very fact that this being is sinless. To be a tempter would make God imperfect, even if just by that one fault. That noticeable "wrinkle" and "crease" would be there.

In reading the first 11 verses of Matthew 4 that record the temptations of Jesus in the wilderness after his baptism, it states in no uncertain terms that the *Devil* is the tempter (verses 5, 8, and 11). Think about this too: Was God present in that wilderness tempting his own *Son* to commit sin? What kind of a loving and fair-minded parent would that be? Once more this writer says, let us get *real* here! It is not God who causes people to sin, but instead, it is their yielding to the devil by their own choice. What an awful thing to feel about a loving, caring, giving, and sinless God to say that *he* is responsible for any and all wrongs committed! Shame bemoans the individuals who persistently, consistently, and insistently blame God for the sinful condition of this world, or for what happens to them in the way of bad. Let us not ever accuse God, for it will prove by the Bible to be false every last time. Be it a person's own fault or not, God is not to be blamed here. He does not *cause* sin. He is not the perpetrator or instigator of tragedy or "freak accidents." He merely *allows* all these things to happen, because he does not exercise *favoritism*, the subject of which is dealt with in a later chapter.

To allow oneself to feel bitter like this is to permit Satan into one's heart.

Such is pure *rebellion* to that majestic being known as Jehovah God. Too, in the name of mercy and proper consideration to our own fellowman, it is understood that there are those who make such an exertion about God in a moment of weakness, but often retract it later. Howbeit, while there are things that happen to all of us as the result of someone else's wrongdoing, the only true blame falls on that person in the mirror when suffering the consequences of one's own mistakes. God does not tempt. He is without spot or blemish. He is *sinless*!

**Questions**

1. Jehovah God is absolutely _________________.
2. Since God is ______________, his very ___________ must be too.
3. After Paul tells Timothy that all scripture comes from God, he then ends the verse by saying, "That the man of God may be ____________, thoroughly _________________ unto all ______________."
4. God does not CAUSE _______. He merely _________ it to happen.
5. "As for God, his way is _________________; the word of the Lord is ____________; he is a buckler to all them that __________ in him."
6. A "buckler" is a ________________.
7. "For the ___________________ Lord loveth __________________; his countenance doth behold the ____________."
8. "In hope of eternal life, which God, that cannot ________, promised before the world began."
9. "Behold, the Lord's hand is not ______________, that it cannot _________; neither his ear ____________, that it cannot ________."
10. God's very own nature is so perfect, he cannot be in the presence of _________.
11. "That by two ____________________ things, in which it was impossible for God to _________, we might have a strong __________________, who have fled for _______________ to _______________ upon the _________ set before us."
12. The fact that God CANNOT tell a __________ is why he does not EVER ________________.
13. "Let God be _____________, but every man a ___________."
14. God's word, among other phrases, is referred as "the ___________ law of liberty."
15. "Let ______ man say when he is tempted, I am tempted of ________:

for _________ cannot be tempted with _________, neither tempteth he any _______: But ___________ man is tempted, when is is _________ of his own ___________ and _________________."

16. Since God is ___________, then he has the right to abhor _____ sin.
17. God is not the perpetrator or instigator of ________________.
18. "The face of the Lord is ___________ them that do ___________."
19. "Guile" means to tell only the ____________ truth, while ____________ the rest.
20. If you do not believe GOD is _________________, then you will not believe his _____________ is either, for the words of that very book came from the ____________ of God.

Chapter 7

# God Is The Original Source of All Intangible

That which is *intangible* is, of course, that which cannot be *touched* with human hands, but is still in existence. Only Jehovah God could be so wise and so unique as to have such a magnificent ability to create things that cannot be physically touched or physically seen, but nonetheless, can, on the other hand, in a sense, *actually be seen with the human eye, and its awareness recognized by the human mind.* That is right. Ironically, the intangible can be seen, in a way. It can be viewed in the sense of seeing it radiate from an individual. One witnesses various personalities, traits, and characteristics showing forth in people, along with other things not found in humankind. Just what are some intangible things that God created?

First and foremost is that of *love*. One cannot see it in the physical sense, but you can feel it from *within*, along with, as said, seeing it issue forth from an individual, as will apply to some other intangible things mentioned in this chapter. In I John 4:8, the apostle tells us, “He that loveth not knoweth not God; for God is love.” This verse does not say that love *came* from God, although that is ever so true. Instead, it says, “God *is* love!” This is all the more reason for recognizing him as “one of a kind.” The same thing is contained in verse 16, along with an example for you and I to consider: “And we have known and believed the love that God hath to us. God is love; and he that dwelleth in love dwelleth in God, and God in him.” The love of God is discussed in great detail in chapter 21 of this book, along with love itself, although one can never reach the bottom of it. The whole point here is that love is one of those intangible things created by God.

Next is the *soul*. Many believe it and the *spirit* are one and the same. While this writer would not try and be dogmatic about the two, it appears as though the spirit is that which is the *lively* part of the individual, while the soul is the very *reason* for having basic life *in* the body. There appears to be a fine line here, as both words will be used interchangeably in this part of the chapter describing the life of man. As the wise King Solomon was closing out Ecclesiastes, he said in chapter 12:7, "Then shall the dust return to the earth as it was: and the spirit shall return unto God who gave it." After Adam and Eve disobeyed God in the Garden of Eden, God tells them in Genesis 3:19, "in the sweat of thy face shalt thou eat bread, till thou return unto the ground; for out of it wast thou taken: for dust thou art, and unto dust shalt thou return."

While some people have claimed to see what a soul—or spirit—looks like, and while others have drawn their own ideas of one, the Bible does not say what the *appearance* of a soul is, although it does record the spirit of the prophet Samuel being brought up from the dead by the request of King Saul through witchcraft (I Samuel 28:7-20). However, all human beings who have lived had a soul in one's body. Those who exist now contain a soul, and all people who ever will live, yes, are going to be no different. That is what makes the body alive and moving. Genesis 2:7says, "And the Lord God formed man of the dust of the ground, and breathed into his nostrils the breath of life; and man became a living soul." It was only mankind that was given a "living soul." That soul will live on forever somewhere. That is illustrated in the aforementioned phrase, "and the spirit shall return unto God who gave it." Read the Parable Of The Rich Man And Lazarus in Luke 16:19-31as a prime example. Luke, who was a physician, writes, quoting Jesus, of definite proof of life continuing after death in that parable.

We read in the Bible—and know anyway—where the physical body dies sooner or later, then eventually returns to dust. We see further proof of that in Job 34:15 where young Elihu says to Job, "All flesh shall perish together, and man shall turn again unto dust." King David humbly declared of God in Psalm 103:14, "For he knoweth our frame; he remembereth that we are dust." No human body lives forever. Once the soul departs from it, the body, in time, goes back to the ground—the dust—where the good Lord originally formed it. When the Apostle James showed how faith and works are inseparable, he gave this comparison: "For as the body without the spirit is dead, so faith without works is dead also" (James 2:26). No body has any movement or is alive without the soul's *dwelling* in it.

We talk about how some music, poems, stories, and some choices of words "go all the way to one's soul." The soul is for sure the most precious thing to all those making up the human race. This is one thing that makes man so much more *above* the rest of God's Creation. The soul too is an intangible thing. It is in the body of every living human, and was so in all who have lived in the past, but cannot be physically touched or visibly seen.

Another of the intangible things from God is the *conscience*. Like love and the soul, it is also felt very deeply. This is the part of man that often draws certain limits as to what is said and done in life. Phrases like, "let your conscience be your guide," "my conscience bothers me," and "my conscience *would* bother me," hold ever so true in most people's lives. That brings up two important things to consider here: (1) The conscience will only guide a person up to the point where one has *trained* it, and (2) One should not *violate* one's conscience, for after continuous repetition of doing so, it most always leads to not caring about those individuals or situations around you anymore. Hence, training the conscience properly will maintain the practice of the Golden Rule, cause that individual to strive not to make the same mistakes repeatedly, hence, making for a happier life. We find the conscience mentioned a number of times in the Bible, along with how it works on a person. Like all other intangible things, it is truly amazing how this thing known as the conscience is, like the soul, in a manner of speaking, felt and touched, though never physically seen.

In John 8:1-11 where the scribes and Pharisees brought a woman to Jesus who was caught in the act of adultery, the apostle informs us they tempted him into trying to endorse her being stoned to death, as that was the penalty for such under the law of Moses. After he told them in the latter part of verse 7, "He that is without sin among you, let him first cast a stone at her," notice what "kicked in" as we read verse 9: "And they which heard it, being convicted by their own conscience, went out one by one, beginning at the eldest, even unto the last: and Jesus was left alone, and the woman standing in the midst." Jesus had "struck a chord" hard on these insincere people. It affected their consciences so badly, they could not go through with stoning that woman.

When the Apostle Paul stood before the Jewish Sanhedrin Council, we find Acts 23:1 saying, "And Paul, earnestly beholding the council, said, Men and brethren, I have lived in all good conscience before God until this day." Before Paul became a follower of Jesus, his conscience was good. After he became a follower, his conscience was also good. Paul indicated very clearly in the aforementioned verse that one's conscience is not always right, and therefore, this writer says again, it should be trained correctly.

In Romans 13:1-7, Paul tells the church there to be under subjection to the civil authorities, for they "are ordained by God" (verse 1). In verse 5 he says to them, "Wherefore ye must needs be subject not only for wrath, but also for conscience sake." Since God brought civil law into existence, and since the church there claimed to follow God's commandments, not to obey the law would mean for their consciences to bother them, for they would, in turn, not be obeying God. This is one example of *correctly* training one's conscience.

In all of Romans 14, and in all of I Corinthians 8, Paul instructs his Jewish brethren to respect the consciences of those Gentiles who were newly converted to Christianity by not eating meat in their presence, as those Gentiles were originally taught that any meat was only supposed to be used in sacrifice to an idol, their former religion. He also, in turn, tells in Romans 14 about the Gentile's need for respecting the consciences and rights of their Jewish brethren to eat that meat in their own privacy (verse 22). Thus, we find a good lesson in these passages of each person's respecting the consciences and rights of their fellowman, whoever that person is, and whatever that conviction be. It is a necessity.

The conscience is a tender thing, is it not? When writing to the young preacher Timothy, Paul tells him, "Now the Spirit speaketh expressly, that in the latter times some shall depart from the faith, giving heed to seducing spirits, and doctrines of devils; Speaking lies in hypocrisy; having their conscience seared with a hot iron" (I Timothy 4:1-2). Why were all these things being said and done? These people were acting in such an ungodly way over and over again, until finally, their consciences no longer bothered them. Notice the callous appearance on a guitarist's fingers after playing up and down those strings for a time. When that guitarist first started playing, those fingers hurt. (This writer, being somewhat of a guitarist himself, can testify to this!) After playing awhile, the pain stopped. This is on the same parallel with the conscience. This analogy also applies to any hardened criminal. The more murdering, raping, theft, etc. that is committed, the easier it is for that person to continue in such a way. Much of how one conducts oneself is dependent upon the conscience.

Paul earlier in his epistle to Timothy wrote, "Now the end of the commandment is charity out of a pure heart, and of a good conscience, and of faith unfeigned" (I Timothy 1:5). The word "unfeigned" means, "Not hypocritical; pure; sincere." One's conscience cannot be truly "good" unless one's very heart is "pure." Neither of the two will take place unless "charity" is first planted in the mind. In verse 19 Paul says, "Holding faith, and a good conscience; which some having put away concerning faith have made shipwreck." Holding to faith in God, along with following the Bible in its entirety, will keep one's conscience good. Therefore, the conscience cannot and will not mess up. This has caused many an individual to foolishly--and wrongfully--commit suicide. They have "made shipwreck" of their conscience so badly, they could no longer stand themselves. Even when no suicide has resulted, a hurt conscience often follows them the remaining days of their lives.

A violation of one's conscience has also caused many a person to lose sleep. From time to time we hear the remark, "I could not live with myself if I were to say that," or, "I could not live with myself if I were to do that." That is the conscience speaking, of course. It is telling the individual that such is a "no-no." Paul also said to Timothy in chapter 3:9, "Holding the mystery of the faith in a pure conscience." It seems as though the words "good" and "pure" cannot be separated, especially where the conscience is concerned, as stated in the last paragraph. When writing to the young preacher Titus, Paul told him, "Unto the pure all things are pure: but unto them that are defiled and unbelieving is nothing pure; but even their mind and conscience is defiled" (Titus 1:15).

Take away *purity*, and you cannot help but have a *defiled* conscience; one that is dirty; one that is corrupt; one that cannot think or say much, if anything, in the way of good; one that cannot do right; one that cannot be wholesome. (This writer, for one, does not like to be around someone who manages to make something off-colored out of everything said!) This is such a conscience that really *is not*! In Hebrews 13:18 the writer states, "Pray for us: for we trust we have a good conscience, in all things willing to live honestly."

Watch that conscience! Train it properly, and your troubles will be a lot fewer in life. Mend every fence possible. This is one of the very purposes for which the conscience was created. It is another intangible item from God. It can in no way, again, be visibly seen or physically touched.

Something else intangible is that of *light*. While light is most definitely *seen*, and we know it is impossible to live without some form of it, it is still intangible in the sense that light cannot be *touched*. This came from God, as well. In fact, the same thing is said in the Bible about God and light that is said about God and love. John says, "This then is the message which we have heard of him, and declare unto you, that God is light, and in him is no darkness at all" (I John 1:5). Just like "God is love," so also, "God is light." In speaking of heaven in his vision, this same John said in Revelation 21:23, "And the city had no need of the sun, neither of the moon, to shine in it: for the glory of God did lighten it, and the Lamb is the light thereof." Just like love, Jehovah God is not only the *source* of light, he *is* light. In James 1:17 the apostle says, "Every good gift and every perfect gift is from above, and cometh down from the Father of lights, with whom is no variableness, neither shadow of turning." This verse not only shows an unchangeable God, discussed earlier, but also refers to him as the "Father of lights." He is, as with all other things said about the Creation, the *origin* of light. Without God, there would be no light, whatsoever, for God *himself* is that first glow which caused the very *birth* of light, such as Genesis 1:3 tells us: "And God said, Let there be light: and there was light." Light is the very first thing God brought about at the commencement of this world. It was truly the origination of Creation.

Then there is that marvelous intangible possession known as faith. While it too cannot be physically seen or touched, it nonetheless manifests itself greatly in the human race in various ways every day. In Hebrews 11:1, we are told by the writer, "Now faith is the substance of things hoped for, the evidence of things not seen." Simply said, faith is, "believing and accepting without seeing." One cannot see or touch something, or find little, if any, in the way of proof, but belief of its existence is still there in that person's mind. When one has faith in another individual, this has often moved that person to try harder, make improvements, which in turn, makes for a better relationship and higher quality of life. Oh, what faith can do to both ourselves and others!

In John 20:24-29, we read an interesting story on the apostle who became known as "Doubting Thomas." John tells, "But Thomas, one of the twelve, called Didymus, was not with them when Jesus came. The other disciples therefore said unto him, We have seen the Lord. But he said unto them, Except I shall see in his hands the print of the nails, and put the finger into the print of the nails, and thrust my hand into his side, I will not believe. And after eight days again his disciples were within, and Thomas with them: then came Jesus, the doors being shut, and stood in the midst, and said, Peace be unto you. Then saith he to Thomas, Reach hither thy finger, and behold my hands; and reach hither thy hand, thrust it into my side: and be not faithless, but believing. And Thomas answered and said unto him, My Lord and my God. Jesus saith unto him, Thomas, because thou has see me, thou has believed: blessed are they that have not seen, and yet have believed."

Some have referred to what Jesus said to Thomas here as a mild rebuke. With Thomas, his seeing Jesus was his believing. He did not have faith at this particular moment, or else he would have totally believed and accepted what Jesus' disciples told him about their Saviour's being brought back to life. So it is with all of us from time to time. On some things and people, we do not believe and accept unless we see. (When it comes to some things and people, it is fully realized that we have *just cause* to feel this way!) At other times, we do believe and accept, even though we have not seen. What was it that Jesus said about this? He remarked to Thomas, "Blessed are they that have not seen, and yet have believed." Such is faith!

A lot of Bible scripture is listed on the subject of faith. In almost the entire chapter of Hebrews 11, the writer pens example after example of those in the Old Testament who conquered Satan, and hence, pleased God because of their great faith which had made them exert to the best of their ability: Moses, David, Abraham, just to name a few! Read the chapter! Is it not something how much of a high degree faith motivates people to do great things, which causes them to be respected so highly by God and others alike! Faith keeps one going when all else seems hopeless. It prevents a person from losing heart. It causes, and has caused, many an individual to "keep on keeping on." How unhappy life would be without this "substance," as afore worded in Hebrews 11:1!

In the second half of James 2, we are informed that works must accompany faith in order to prove faith's claim of real existence. Beginning in verse 17, it reads, "Even so faith, if it hath not works, is dead, being alone." Verse 20 tells us, "But wilt thou know, O vain man, that faith without works is dead?" The very last verse of the chapter, verse 26, used in a another chapter, summarizes the whole argument by saying, "For as the body without the spirit is dead, so faith without works is dead also." I challenge the reader to investigate all of James 2 and see the validity of this writer's argument. It is useless to claim any amount of faith within oneself and to God without willing to prove it by one's works. To profess such a thing is to have a *dead* faith, for this is indicative from the very start of not being *true* faith. Although it is an intangible thing, faith is still seen, in a manner of speaking.

*Hope* is another part of life from God that is intangible. The complete illustration of this subject is found in Romans 8:24-25 where Paul tells the church there, "For we are saved by hope: but hope that is seen is not hope: for what a man seeth, why doth he yet hope for? But if we hope for that we see not, then do we with patience wait for it." These verses contain what the country people call "pure, everyday, common, horse sense!" We do not hope for something we already have, for hope, like faith in II Corinthians 5:7, has then become "sight." No more faith is needed and no more hope is needed, for that which we now see and have, we no longer have to hope for, being as we have obtained--achieved--laid hold onto--what we were hoping. An individual may hope for an item, a reunion with a friend or relative, an event, help, relief, or whatever. Until what is hoped for comes to pass, it is still hope. However, when anything hoped for is realized, there is no longer a reason to hope. In fact, hope will then automatically melt into *reality*. Hope cannot be touched with the hand, nor is it physically optical, but it is still in existence, and constitutes another one of the intangible things created by Jehovah God.

None of the things mentioned in this chapter could possibly have been created or made by any member of the human race, for we are everyone *born* with many of those intangible traits inside us, which have been around from the very creation of Adam and Eve until now, along with those intangible things existing, as said earlier, which are not a part of man's physical makeup. What is unique about those traits mentioned in this chapter is that they come from *within* a person, and not from *without*, which glorifies God all the more. Of course, how things like the conscience, love, and faith are developed inside someone is determined many times by someone's surroundings, along with one's choices made in life. What also goes without saying is that what plays a big part is the kind of attitude that is present, which is often marked by whether one wishes to make or not make changes in life for the better. Before one can change one's way of *life*, one's way of thinking has to change first. This is because the offspring of all words, thoughts, and deeds stem from the mind.

Since mankind, as stated before, can only make things which have come from raw materials already created, God must then have been the one responsible for all that is intangible, for what mankind makes is all *material*. This in turn means they *can* be touched and seen. Things like all those discussed in this chapter, though, *cannot* be literally touched. What an amazing and heart-stopping ability Jehovah has! He is not only the Creator of the heavens and the earth, but is also the original source of all that is intangible!

**Questions**

1. God is the ______________ source of all intangible
2. "Intangible" means something cannot be ____________.
3. Name as many things as you can think of that are intangible: _______

_______________________________________________

_______________________________________________

4. Though not PHYSICALLY seen, some of the intangible, can yet BE seen, in the sense that it can ______________ from an individual. Explain this.
5. The human body, being tangible, along with all flesh, when death occurs, returns to the __________ from where it came.
6. "Man became a living __________."
7. "He that ____________ not knoweth not God; for God is ________."
8. "Then shall the ____________ return to the __________ as it was: and the ____________ shall return unto ________ who __________ it."
9. "All flesh shall ______________ together, and man shall turn again unto _________________."
10. A familiar phrase: "Let your _______________ be your _________."
11. "For he knoweth our _______; he remembereth that we are _____."
12. No body has any __________ or is alive without the __________ dwelling in it.
13. God said to Adam and Eve after they disobeyed him, "in the sweat of thy face shalt thou eat bread, till thou return unto the _________; for out of it wast thou ____________: for __________ thou art, and unto _________ shalt thou return."
14. "I have lived in all good ______________ before God until this day."
15. "God is ____________, and in him is no ________________ at all."
16. "Now _____________ is the ______________ of things __________ for, the _________________ of things __________________."
17. "Blessed are they that have not _________, and yet have ________."
18. God is called "the Father of ______________."
19. "For we are saved by ______: but __________ that is seen is not _________: for what a man have, why doth he yet ________ for? But if we _________ for that we have not, then do we with patience __________ for it."
20. Man cannot change his way of LIFE unless he FIRST changes his way of _________.

Chapter 8

# God Is Omniscient

The word "omniscient" is defined as, "Having infinite awareness, understanding, and insight; possessed of universal or complete knowledge." This means that Jehovah God knows *everything*! In speaking of God in a way that is not derogatory, we may say in its most literal sense that God is truly the one and only "know it all."

To all who are reading, think about the impact of this! Every last thing in the past and present that mankind has said, done, and invented--God *knows* all about it! Likewise is the case with every single thing that will be said, done, and invented in the future! God is able to describe each minute detail of it all without exception, and without omitting anything or anybody. He has it all perfectly straight and aligned in his mind, and can name it every bit as it happened—one, two, three, bam, bam, bam, and so on! This would as well tell us that God's mind not only possesses all *knowledge*, but also contains all *wisdom*. Since he is our Creator, it must then be every bit the truth to say that knowledge and wisdom *originated* with and from him.

God, being omniscient, can never think, say, or do anything wrong, as we studied in the chapter dealing with his being sinless. Therefore, all of his commands in the Bible are right and necessary for mankind to follow, which in turn means, again, that every word of his Bible is too. Like God's mind, so his commands too are *infallible*, which means they are incapable of containing any error. This would, in addition, make God's mind *infinite*; or, "without limits." It is like an abyss--no end to it.

The many scriptures to be cited in this chapter will show that very thing, along with all else that has been said in this paragraph. With God's being omniscient, that too means he knows and remembers every person who has lived, along with every animal, fowl, and sea creature—not to mention, all forms of vegetation. Such an all-knowing mind has to contain a perfect and unlimited memory.

We as human beings all have our limits. While there are those who have excelled mightily above others in physical strength, education, and intelligence, (and such feats are never to be taken lightly, but instead, should be given proper recognition), still, there is a *limit* to all capabilities within the human race. We only live so long. We can only do so much. We can only think of a limited number of things at one time. Our minds only go so far and so deep. Therefore, we can only *learn* so much and remember (retain) a limited amount, however much it might be. Any knowledge and wisdom we may possess only goes so far. The mind becomes tired after a period of time, so it must draw a line of limitation. Being as God knows all, however, shows that he is *limitless*! There is absolutely no end to his knowledge and wisdom. This fact makes God a perfect discerner in *all* of his judgments. They are without wrinkle, fault, or weakness.

Since God's knowing all is without exception, then mankind should not argue with him, doubt him, resent what he says in his Word, or disobey him. There is no such thing as the "erudite solution" with God. (The word "erudite" is the adjective form of "erudition," and means, "Extensive knowledge acquired chiefly from books: profound, recondite, or bookish learning.") God needs no books, teachers, professors, or classroom counseling. He is--and has always been--his own dictionary, encyclopedia, thesaurus, concordance, and textbook, for his knowledge and wisdom have forever dwelled in his mind--not only from "day one," but from everlasting to everlasting, since that is the way God himself is, as studied on in another chapter. There never was--and is not now--a moment in time or eternity that God has not been omniscient. Anything learned from the human race was already in the mind of Jehovah *eternally*! His mind is truly forever the zenith of minds. This is what makes God an all-knowing personality.

In Romans 11:33-36, the Apostle Paul tells the church there, "O the depth of the riches both of the wisdom and knowledge of God! how unsearchable are his judgments, and his ways past finding out! For who hath known the mind of the Lord? or who hath been his counsellor? Or who hath first given to him, and it shall be recompensed unto him again? For of him, and through him, and to him, are all things: to whom be glory forever. Amen." Who can teach God anything that he does not already know, since he existed before any human or any other part of the Creation? When Paul said that God is "past finding out," that very simply means he cannot be *found* out! You will never reach the *end* of God's mind--the bottom—the limit—for such does not exist. His mind is inexhaustible. In showing how so very far more superior God's mind is to man's mind, I cite again where he said through the prophet Isaiah to the Israelite nation: "For my thoughts are not your thoughts, neither are your ways my ways, saith the Lord. For as the heavens are higher than the earth, so are my ways higher than your ways, and my thoughts than your thoughts" (Isaiah 55:8-9).

Since God's mind is omniscient, he has to think so much exceedingly higher and superior to man, which would explain how and why he possesses all knowledge and wisdom. This is what makes everything about him so great, spellbinding, and marvelous! It indescribably surpasses human imagination! This is why God could bring into the picture such a great universe with so much versatility contained therein. The being that *knows* everything can *think of* everything, think it right and best, thus, always and forever be "on the mark!" Positively nothing will be left in the way of improvement, editing, assistance, criticism, correction, regret, error, weakness, or partiality. The all-knowing mind is able to create and make *perfectly!* A good many adjectives could be used in describing God's omniscience. Just like a video, CD, and DVD, God can replay anything in his mind in absolute accuracy every time, with nothing added, omitted, or forgotten.

In Exodus 31:3-6, God said the following to Moses about two men appointed by God concerning their assisting in the building of the tabernacle: "And I have filled him with the spirit of God, in wisdom, and in understanding, and in knowledge, and in all manner of workmanship, To devise cunning works, to work in gold, and in silver, and in brass, And in cutting stones, to set them, and in carving of timber, to work in all manner of workmanship. And I, behold I, have given with him Aholiab, the son of Ahisamach, of the tribe of Dan: and in the hearts of all that are wise hearted I have put wisdom, that they may make all that I have commanded thee." Virtually the same words are said in chapter 35:30-35.These verses tell us that *God* is the original container of knowledge and wisdom, hence, it is only *he* who can place it in man. Who else, pertaining to Bezaleel, can go so far as to have "filled him with the spirit of God, in wisdom, and in understanding, and in knowledge, and in all manner of workmanship?" The answer is in that very verse: It is God who can do it, for his mind, again, contains all knowledge and wisdom. Besides, whatever it be, one has to *have* before one can *give*.

In speaking of God's covenant with Israel, Moses tells his people in Deuteronomy 29:29, "The secret things belong unto the Lord our God: but those things which are revealed belong unto us and to our children for ever, that we may do all the words of this law." This warns us in no uncertain terms that what God wants us to know, he tells us. Those things he desires to keep a secret, he does so for reasons of his own, and we are not to complain or question such as to *why* he does not want to tell us everything. Besides, there are some things we could not handle even if we knew them. Too, many people have a hard time handling what God *has* chosen to reveal. It all tells us that we should not whittle on God's end of the stick. We should just leave some things alone! Let them be! Pay attention to only what God has *said,* and do not mess with his mind! To do so will cause the devil to mess with yours!

King Solomon played it smart, along with humble, when it came to asking God to provide him with what he really needed, showing all the more the unlimited knowledge and wisdom contained in God's mind. We find this in I Kings 3:5-12 as to why Solomon was the wisest man who ever walked this earth, save Jesus: "In Gibeon the Lord appeared to Solomon in a dream by night: and God said, Ask what I shall give thee. And Solomon said, Thou hast showed unto thy servant David my father great mercy, according as he walked before thee in truth, and in righteousness, and in uprightness of heart with thee; and thou hast kept for him this great kindness, that thou hast given him a son to sit on his throne, as it is this day. And now, O Lord my God, thou hast made thy servant king instead of David my father: and I am but a little child: I know not how to go out or come in. And thy servant is in the midst of thy people which thou hast chosen, a great people, that cannot be numbered or counted for multitude. Give therefore thy servant an understanding heart to judge thy people, that I may discern between good and bad: for who is able to judge this thy so great a people? And the speech pleased the Lord, that Solomon had asked this thing. And God said unto him, Because thou hast asked this thing, and hast not asked for thyself long life; neither hath asked riches for thyself, nor hast asked the life of thine enemies; but hast asked for thyself understanding to discern judgment; Behold, I have done according to thy words: lo, I have given thee a wise and an understanding heart; so that there was none like thee before thee, neither after thee shall any arise like unto thee."

When dealing with the other countries, the people were astonished at Solomon's wisdom. He asked God for the *right* thing, knowing his job as King of Israel was going to be great. I challenge the reader to read about his life and see for oneself. Solomon could not possibly have ruled as wisely as he did if God had not blessed him so bountifully as he did with wisdom. Solomon is a great example of illustrating how true knowledge and wisdom issue forth from God, who himself is the very *taproot* of it all, for he is omniscient. Of course, through all of his amazing wisdom, Solomon was still not perfect. He too made his mistakes and was guilty of sin at times, just like all of us.

The prophet Jeremiah said concerning God and his soon to be upcoming judgment on Babylon, "He hath made the earth by his power, he hath established the world by his wisdom, and hath stretched out the heaven by his understanding" (Jeremiah 51:15). Chapter 10:12 has the prophet saying the same identical words, except the verse ends using the word "discretion." Only God, being all-knowledgeable and having all wisdom, could have formed everything that make up the heavens and the world. Isaiah, in pronouncing God's woes upon the disobedient in Israel says, "Woe unto them that are wise in their own eyes, and prudent in their own sight" (Isaiah 5:21)!

Any real wisdom comes from God, not from the mind of any member of mankind. This is one of the fallacies contained in the minds of a lot of people who disbelieve God's existence and/or who doubt his omniscience. They are wise in their *own* sight, which means they possess *worldly* wisdom instead of *Godly* wisdom. What does God call such a person? Notice again Romans 1:22-25 where Paul says to the church there, "Professing themselves to be wise, they became fools, And changed the glory of the uncorruptible God into an image made like to corruptible man, and to birds, and four-footed beasts, and creeping things. Wherefore God also gave them up to uncleanness through the lusts of their own hearts, to dishonor their own bodies between themselves: Who changed the truth of God into a lie, and worshiped and served the creature more than the Creator, who is blessed for ever. Amen."

Only a *fool* would think that real knowledge and wisdom originates from the human mind! This is why some people conduct their lives in the manner that they do. Thinking that one can have wisdom in and of oneself just is not possible! "O Lord, I know that the way of man is not in himself: it is not in man that walketh to direct his steps" (Jeremiah 10:23). Mankind, being the sinful and unsettled creature that he is, cannot form in his own mind the means of saving his own soul or pleasing God, the elementary reason being that he does not think like God and God does not think like him. Since that is so, where is the compatibility, parallelism, or synchronicity? Such just is not there, period!

Looking once again at Job 26:7, where Job is talking to Bildad the Shuhite, he is saying of God, "He stretcheth out the north over the empty place, and hangeth the earth on nothing." This unimaginable ability not only takes real power, it also takes a special type of "know how" to do. By the very laws of gravity, weight has to *rest* on something. It cannot rest on air, for air is not a solid substance--not a material--not an object. However, what does this heavy world hang upon? We just noted where it hangs "upon nothing." No one on the topside of the good Lord's earth is able to hang any measure of weight, however light, "upon nothing." Only an all wise and all knowing God could cause such a thing to occur, for only God can change the *natural* into *unnatural*, since he brought about the natural from the very start.

Referring again to those who consider themselves wise because of their own ability, chapter 5:13 has Eliphaz the Temanite wrongfully accusing Job, while still remarking truthfully of God, "He taketh the wise in their own craftiness: and the counsel of the froward is carried headlong." There is nothing more foolish than attempting to mentally go up against God, for he will make pure *mincemeat* out of anybody's brain! When God is challenging Job, he says to him in chapter 39:26, "Doth the hawk fly by thy wisdom, and stretch her wings toward the south?" God was asking Job in so many words here, "Is it *your* wisdom which controls nature?" No, only God can do it because he *created* nature, due to the fact he had the almighty knowledge and wisdom to do so.

Just what does happen when one tries to figure out all of God's ways? Job 11:7-9 shows Zophar wrongfully reproving Job, but like Eliphaz, uttering this truth about God, nonetheless: "Canst thou by searching find out God? Canst thou find out the Almighty unto perfection? It is as high as heaven; what canst thou do? deeper than hell; what canst thou know? The measure thereof is longer than the earth, and broader than the sun." God may be *searched* out, but he can never, ever be totally *found* out. The search will be endless, resulting in so many more questions than answers. In Chapter 9:1-4 Job replies to Bildad by acknowledging God's justice: "Then Job answered and said, " I know it is so of a truth: but how should man be just with God? If he will contend with him, he cannot answer him one of a thousand. He is wise in heart, and mighty in strength: who hath hardened himself against him, and hath prospered?" We might as well keep our hearts soft and our tongues civil in life, especially where God's being omniscient is concerned. Such would be equivalent to a gnat battling an elephant!

I ask the reader to first read Job 38-41 for the purpose of seeing all the challenging and "bringing down" that God does to Job. Question after question is put to Job about God's ultimate knowledge and wisdom, versus man's knowledge and wisdom. Then, try and put yourself in Job's place and see how insignificant you would feel. After having all that "starch" taken out of him, Job could not have been more humble when he said these words in chapter 42:1-6: "Then Job answered the Lord and said, I know that thou canst do every thing, and that no thought can be withholden from thee. Who is he that hideth counsel without knowledge? Therefore have I uttered that I understood not; things too wonderful for me, which I knew not. Hear, I beseech thee, and I will speak: I will demand of thee, and declare thou unto me. I have heard of thee by the hearing of the ear; but now mine eye seeth thee: wherefore I abhor myself, and repent in dust and ashes."

It was time for *reality* to set in here, which it did. Job knew even more now that not he nor any other person could go up against God. *Job was talking directly with his Maker!* What would you as the reader say to God, face to face, if you had all those lines directly thrown at you? Do not answer too hastily, now! Remember: God's mind is limitless, while man's mind is limited.

Let us return to some of the Psalms now and note more on God's unmatchable knowledge and wisdom. King David declared in Psalm 19:7, "The law of the Lord is perfect, converting the soul: the testimony of the Lord is sure, making wise the simple." Why is God's law "perfect?" How can even the most "simple" people become "wise" by it? You probably guessed it! It is because God knows everything past, present, and future. So, his words have to be *right* all the way, every time, to the "nth degree." Chapter 104:24 says, "O Lord, how manifold are thy works! In wisdom hast thou made them all: the earth is full of thy riches."

We must mention that it was actually, and had to be, a *combination* of God's knowledge and wisdom that brought about all that has to do with the Creation. So, let us notice a very simple but vital point here: Knowledge in any form is read from a book and obtained from other people's minds, but it takes *experience* to get wisdom, for wisdom is the proper *application* of knowledge. As that is a fact, gaining all the knowledge in the world (if one could do such a thing!) would mean nothing unless that knowledge was put to use, and put to use properly. Such was no less true with the creating of all things and beings. With Jehovah God, however, that knowledge and wisdom *has always been*! He did not get either of them from any of mankind, so therefore, he did not learn either of them from any book or any other source. Again, it was all and always in his mind *eternally*!

There was no beginning or end with God, so there is no beginning or end to his knowledge and wisdom. In Psalm 94:10-11 the writer says of God, "He that chastiseth the heathen, shall not he correct? He that teacheth man knowledge, shall not he know? The Lord knoweth the thoughts of man, that they are vanity." One has to *know* before one can *teach*, and that is definitely one "cart" that you and I will not get before "the horse!" The rule applies likewise with knowledge and wisdom, respectively. Since God has all the knowledge and wisdom that can ever possibly exist, he is in the perfect condition to teach mankind right from wrong, wise from foolish, good from bad, etc. It is utter folly to reject any of God's words!

In the verses just quoted, it says that God has the ability to read minds. That is how high and deep his knowledge and wisdom excel. It says, "The Lord knoweth the thoughts of man." How are they compared to God? It reads, "they are vanity." How vain we can be about ourselves by letting our self-esteem and egos get too full! (Some people's egos are so big, if such were air, it would be a threat to national security! One burst with the pin, and the entire USA would blow clear off the map!) How well can God read you and I? I will let King David speak again. In Psalm 139:1-6 he remarks, "O Lord thou hast searched me, and known me. Thou knowest my downsitting and mine uprising; thou understandest my thought afar off. Thou compassest my path and my lying down, and art acquainted with all my ways. For there is not a word in my tongue, but, lo, O Lord, thou knowest it altogether. Thou has beset me behind and before, and laid thine hand upon me. Such knowledge is too wonderful for me; it is high, I cannot attain unto it." David appears *flabbergasted* here! May his humility be in all of us.

Since God knows all things, that means he can read our minds. If he could not, that would prove his knowing of all things and all people to be limited, as would be his absolute and complete control. He knows what is going on in your mind and all minds this very minute and second. He knows whether it is "G" or "X" rated. He reads us all like a book (and just like you are reading this very book now, so too he reads you loud and clear!) When it comes to God, we have no *privacy*!

As "way out" as it may seem to some of you readers, (while others will not be shocked) there are those who either think they know *more* than God and/or know *better* than God. Of course, when it comes to human behavior, we cannot help but observe all kinds in the world. It arranges from the most humble to the most haughty. Read what the prophet Ezekiel says when God tells him to repeat the following words to the prince of Tyrus: "The word of the Lord came unto me saying, son of man, say unto the prince of Tyrus, Thus saith the Lord God; Because thine heart is lifted up, and thou hast said, I am a God, I sit in the seat of God, in the midst of the seas; yet thou art a man, and not God, though thou set thine heart as the heart of God: Behold, thou art wiser than Daniel; there is no secret that they can hide from thee: With thy wisdom and with thine understanding thou hast gotten thee riches, and thine heart is lifted up because of thy riches: Therefore thus saith the Lord God; Because thou hast set thine heart as the heart of God; Behold, therefore I will bring strangers upon thee, the terrible of the nations: and they shall draw their swords against the beauty of thy wisdom, and they shall defile thy brightness. They shall bring thee down to the pit, and thou shalt die the deaths of them that are slain in the midst of the seas. Wilt thou yet say before him that slayeth thee, I am God? but thou shalt be a man, and no God, in the hand of him that slayeth thee. Thou shalt die the deaths of the uncircumcised by the hand of strangers: for I have spoken it, saith the Lord God" (Ezekiel 28:1-10).

No doubt, a vast many of you reading those verses quoted above would exclaim, "How arrogant!" This writer could not agree more! However, it is all too evident that many a person has allowed knowledge to get to the ego. In fact, somebody once said that mankind is a tender specie: Pat him on the back, and he gets a swelled head! Jehovah God is the very *origin* of knowledge and wisdom, so no member of the human race has any right whatsoever to be *stuck* on oneself at anytime. While there is everything right and necessary in gaining all the knowledge and wisdom possible, still, each of us must remember who is the very *source* of it all. This writer is just a man--nothing more. You who read this book are merely human--nothing more. We are all finite creatures of the flesh—nothing more. No matter how long we live or how much we learn, we will never learn and know everything, nor will we ever be able to figure out the "why" or the "wherefore" to all things, or solve all mysteries. We are not *omniscient*, in other words. No individual but Jehovah God can make such a claim.

Daniel, like King Solomon, was another individual who realized God was a personality composed of all knowledge and all wisdom. Daniel 1:19-20 shows how King Nebuchadnezzar respected and admired Daniel, along with three other men, for the great wisdom Daniel and those men possessed, because Daniel and them received it from God: "And the king communed with them; and among them all was found none like Daniel, Hananiah, Mishael, and Azariah: therefore stood they before the king. And in all matters of wisdom and understanding, that the king inquired of them, he found them ten times better than all the magicians and astrologers that were in all his realm." Daniel and these three others had more wisdom than all those working for the king who excelled in magic and astrology. Why? Because they were *godly* men! Let us all learn from that, please!

Daniel 2:20-23 records Daniel's praising God and giving him the proper glory for the wisdom he (Daniel) possessed: "Daniel answered and said, Blessed be the name of God for ever and ever: for wisdom and might are his: and he changeth the times and the seasons: he removeth kings, and setteth up kings: he giveth wisdom unto the wise, and knowledge to them that know understanding: he revealeth the deep and secret things: he knoweth what is in the darkness, and the light dwelleth with him. I thank thee, and praise thee, O thou God of my fathers, who hast given me wisdom and might, and hast made known unto me now what we desired of thee: for thou hast now made known unto us the king's matter."

Any *genuine* wisdom we have springs forth from God, so by unavoidable logic, we must also admit the same thing about Biblical knowledge, for again, we should all constantly be aware that the Bible came from the mind of God. You and I must be like Daniel and thank the Lord on this matter. God knows it all—not you nor I—*not ever you nor I!* Remember that Daniel said of God, "who hath given me wisdom and might."

Of course, when talking about God's omniscience, the book of Proverbs cannot be overlooked, one of the books written by King Solomon for the most part. Chapter 3:19-20 states, "The Lord by wisdom hath founded the earth; by understanding hath he established the heavens. By his knowledge the depths are broken up, and the clouds drop down the dew." We are warned in verse 7, "Be not wise in thine own eyes, fear the Lord and depart from evil." If one is not careful, one will allow one's mind to channel the areas of acquired knowledge in the direction of evil, thinking one has become invincible. Many is the egotist who has fallen, either by loss of power, business, family member(s), friendship, or life because that individual became "wise in thine own eyes." Chapter 21:30 tells us, "There is no wisdom nor understanding nor counsel against the Lord." This writer asks again: What can any of us teach God? What teaching can ever, ever, be given to God, who is the one being already containing full knowledge and full wisdom in every area? No one can be taught something they already know. Yes, one can be *told*, but one cannot be *taught*!

Proverbs 23:4 says, "Labor not to be rich: cease from thy own wisdom." The word "labor" would carry with it the idea of striving towards something, hence, making it our prime goal--in this case, to be rich. There is nothing wrong in being rich, but if that is one's greatest aim in life, then it is not truly *wise*! The things that are *intangible*, as we spoke on elsewhere in this book, are the things that are the most *valuable*. The term "thine own wisdom" teaches us that any wisdom of our own is, ironically speaking, not really wisdom; that is to say, not wisdom that is beneficial to us. May we take heed from a man named Agur in Proverbs 30: 5-6: "Every word of God is pure: he is a shield unto them that put their trust in him. Add thou not unto his words, lest he reprove thee, and thou be found a liar." The same idea is in Romans 3:4, where agian, Paul tells the church there, "God forbid: yea, let God be true, but every man a liar; as it is written, That thou mightest be justified in thy sayings, and mightest overcome what thou art judged."

Since it is God who truly knows all, we should listen to *his* words, and not to the worldly wisdom of *man*, for the simple reason man's wisdom is not from God. We are warned of such by Paul in Colossians 2:8. There, he tells the church, "Beware lest any man spoil you through philosphy and vain deceit, after the traditon of men, after the rudiments of the world, and not after Christ." Wherever one reads in the Bible, the words are plainly stated that it is *God* who should be heeded, for only *he* has all the knowledge and wisdom there is to be had. The main "why" of this goes back to what the reader noted in a previous chapter—God is *sinless*!

The same type of warning also comes from Paul in Romans 12:16: "Be of the same mind one toward another. Mind not high things, but condescend to men of low estate. Be not wise in your own conceits." *Worldly* wisdom too often, along with drawing the individual away from God, makes that same one possessing it conceited. This is due to worldly wisdom's centering largely on *self*. "Condescend" means, "To ascend to a less formal or dignified level." Even when one has developed a lot of Biblical knowledge, (of which there is nothing wrong in and of itself) that person is not to act *superior* to others who are less knowledgeable, for that is thinking too highly of oneself. Verse 3 teaches us not to behave that way: "For I say, through the grace given unto me, to every man that is among you, not to think of himself more highly than he ought to think; but to think soberly, according as God hath dealt to every man the measure of faith." It is no wonder that with some people, the phrase applies: "A little knowledge is a dangerous thing." None of us should ever act a "cut above" everybody else. This writer for one does not care for the company of such a one! It is also a crying shame, a disgrace, and most insulting to others when someone will use one's high I.Q. to make fools out of people, talk down to them, commit crimes, along with tricking and manipulating one's fellowman. Then there are those who are quite "full of themselves." (Is the reader familiar with the "Narcissus complex?") Look at the very character of God himself. Even *he* is still merciful, gracious, and compassionate, though he knows all things. That is something to think about!

1 Corinthians 2:16 says by Paul, "For who hath known the mind of the Lord, that he may instruct him? But we have the mind of Christ." First of all, as was already said, God cannot be taught anything because he is *omniscient*. Second, to truly "have the mind of Christ" means to be obedient to every command of God, which is always right, for that is the way Jesus conducted himself before his Heavenly Father, the very God I write of in this book. Verse 13 says of the truthfulness of the apostle's preaching, "Which things also we speak, not in the words which man's wisdom teacheth, but which the Holy Ghost teacheth; comparing spiritual things with spiritual." God's words are not man's words, neither is God's wisdom man's wisdom. This writer cites yet again Isaiah 55:8-9: "For my thoughts are not your thoughts, neither are your ways my ways, saith the Lord. For as the heavens are higher than the earth, so are my ways higher than your ways, and my thoughts than your thoughts." This is the very reason that we should all *listen* to the Lord! We are not sinless, while God is. We do not know everything, but God does. We do not possess all wisdom, while God does. We have not always existed, as God has. Our judgments are not infallible, unlike God's most definitely are.

1 Corinthians 3:18-20 says, "Let no man deceive himself. If any man among you seemeth to be wise in this world, let him become a fool, that he may be wise. For the wisdom of this world is foolishness with God. For it is written, He taketh the wise in their own craftiness. And again, The Lord knoweth the thoughts of the wise, that they are vain." Paul was quoting

from Psalm 94:11. We just read where one is a fool to be wise in a *worldly* sense, for that brand of wisdom does not issue from God. In speaking of his mission to the Gentiles, Paul said in Ephesians 3:10, "To the intent that now unto the principalities and powers in heavenly places might be known by the church the manifold wisdom of God." "Manifold" means, "Much varied." God's wisdom is made up of so much versatility and complexity, mankind cannot, by any possible attempt, *comprehend* it all, which also means, again, that the knowledge of God would have to be sharpened to *absolute perfection* for his wisdom to be "manifold." The more we read of God's being *omniscient*, the more we realize how much we do not know, or will ever be able to figure out. How truly limited our minds are! Even the most gifted genius is nothing, compared to God's omniscience!

When Paul wrote to Timothy, he said, "Now unto the King eternal, immortal, invisible, the only wise God, be honor and glory for ever and ever. Amen" (I Timothy 1:17). The same basic thought is expressed in Jude 25: "To the only wise God our Saviour, be glory and majesty, dominion and power, both now and ever. Amen." Jehovah God is "the only wise God." With this verse in mind, I now refer to II Timothy 3:15, where Paul reminds Timothy of his upbringing: "And that from a child thou hast known the holy scriptures, which are able to make thee wise unto salvation through faith which is in Christ Jesus." What are the "holy scriptures" able to do? They "are able to make thee wise," Paul said. This is all the more proof that actual wisdom comes from our Maker, "the only wise God," which can be gotten exclusively from the obtaining, containing, retaining, maintaining, and sustaining of Biblical knowledge, which in turn, can only derive from the mind of the all-knowing God. What a superb cycle, reader friend!

The writer James challenges all who read his book to find out what true wisdom is and its source. He says in James 3:13-17, "Who is a wise man and endued with knowledge among you? let him show out of a good conversation his works with meekness of wisdom. But if ye have bitter envying and strife in your hearts, glory not, and lie not against the truth. This wisdom descendeth not from above, but is earthly, sensual, devilish. For where envying and strife is, there is confusion and every evil work. But the wisdom that is from above is first pure, then peaceable, gentle, and easy to be entreated, full of mercy and good fruits, without partiality, and without hypocrisy." The word "conversation" in the Bible means, "Manner of living." These verses say quite a bit as to what *real* wisdom does and does not contain, hence, how it will and will not behave. *Godly* wisdom is *real* wisdom, because it is not warring, divisive, or arrogant. Notice the last verse again: "But the wisdom that is from above is first pure, then peaceable, gentle, and easy to be entreated, full of mercy and good fruits, without partiality, and without hypocrisy." Only a being with the knowledge of *everything* can contain *perfect* wisdom, along with having the ability to distribute it to any member of the human race desiring it. This is God!

It is one thing to have the wisdom to *make* something, (and some truly have fantastic abilities along this line) but how about having the wisdom to *create* something? Remember yet again that anything *made* comes from, and can *only* come from, something that has been *created*. Therefore, it had to take a "mind" to make the "matter." (Perhaps the phrase "mind over matter" just came into your head!) No mind of any man, woman, boy, or girl could accomplish such a feat as *creating*, because, as afore said, "create" means, "Out of nothing, something comes." Only such a mind as God has containing total knowledge and complete wisdom could *create*, while nearly any mind with some degree of normalcy can *make*. Only such a mind as God's can *read* minds. Only such a mind could be *totally original*. Only such a mind could be impossible for anyone to *teach* and *correct*. So, only such a mind could be right every time, *without exception*! This is what makes up the omniscient mind of God. Compared to the things stored in the mind of the Almighty, you and I really know ever so very little. We all make mistakes. God does not. God never has to "proofread." Our memories fail us from time to time. Not so with the Creator.

I will close this chapter by citing I Corinthians 1:18-29, which I believe says it all in comparing God's knowledge and wisdom to man's knowledge and wisdom. The following verses should, again, for the greater part, be self-explanatory. God is truly *omniscient*! He is completely furnished in knowledge and wisdom. May we everyone profit from the following words where godly knowledge and godly wisdom are concerned: "For the preaching of the cross is to them that perish foolishness; but unto us which are saved it is the power of God. For it is written, I will destroy the wisdom of the wise, and will bring to nothing the understanding of the prudent. (This last verse--19--was taken from Isaiah 29:14—PN) Where is the wise? where is the scribe? where is the disputer of this world? hath not God made foolish the wisdom of this world? For after that in the wisdom of God the world by wisdom knew not God, it pleased God by the foolishness of preaching to save them that believe. For the Jews require a sign, and the Greeks seek after wisdom: But we preach Christ crucified, unto the Jews a stumbling block, and unto the Greeks foolishness; But unto them which are called, both Jews and Greeks, Christ the power of God, and the wisdom of God. Because the foolishness of God is wiser than men; and the weakness of God is stronger than men. For ye see your calling brethren, how that not many wise men after the flesh, not many mighty, not many noble, are called: But God hath chosen the foolish things of the world to confound the wise; and God hath chosen the weak things of the world to confound the things which are mighty; And base things of the world, and things which are despised, hath God chosen, yea and things which are not, be bring to nought things that are: That no flesh should glory in his presence."

**Questions**

1. To be "omniscient" means "______________________________ ______________________________ ______________________________."
2. "O the __________ of the __________ both of the __________ and __________ of God! How __________ are his judgments, and his ways __________! For who hath known the __________ of the Lord? Or who hath been his __________? Or who hath first __________ to him, and it shall be __________ unto him again? For _____ him, and _______ him, and _____ him are all things: to whom be __________ forever."
3. "Erudition" means, "______________________________ ______________________________."
4. God gave Solomon "a __________ and __________ heart."
5. "He hath made the earth by his __________, he hath established the world by his __________, and hath stretched out the heaven by his __________."
6. "O Lord, I know that the way of man is not in __________: It is not in __________ that walketh to __________ his steps."
7. "The __________ things belong unto the ________ our _______."
8. "I have given thee a __________ and __________ heart; so that there was none like thee __________ thee, neither after thee shall any arise like __________ thee."
9. There is __________ that God does not know.
10. The word "infinite" means, "______________________________."

11. Since God's mind is "infinite," that makes OUR minds "_________."
12. Anything learned by and from the human race was already in the mind of God _________________."
13. To know everything means to possess _______ knowledge and _______ wisdom.
14. God's mind is mentioned in this chapter in comparison to an "abyss." This means that there is no _________ to it.
15. "And I have filled him with the ___________ of _________, in ____________, and in _________________, and in _______________, and in ________ manner of _______________________."
16. "For _____ thoughts are not ________ thoughts, neither are _____ ways _______ ways, saith the Lord. For as the heavens are _____________ than the earth, so are _______ ways _____________ than _______ ways, and _______ thoughts than _______________ thoughts."
17. The mind of God is truly forever the ______________ of minds.
18. God is an _____________________ personality.
19. When it comes to the silence of God, we should not "____________ on ____________ end of the stick."
20. "Woe unto them that are ____________ in _________ own eyes, and ________________ in ____________ own _______________."

Chapter 9

# God Is Omnipotent

Jehovah God is "omnipotent." That means he is "all powerful." Both the definition and illustration are spelled out with the prefix "omni" meaning "all," and the word "potent" meaning "powerful." We often hear it how some chemicals and drugs are "potent." One might very well think the word "omnipotent" should be pronounced "omni-PO-tent," but it is actually pronounced "om-NI-potent."

There is without exception no being or force anywhere more powerful than our Creator. Such has never existed in the past, it does not now, nor will there ever be any type of force, occurring in the future. God possesses *all* power! That earns him the rightful name of the "Almighty God." As argued in a previous chapter, the inventor is greater than the invention. Therefore, since God is the one who "created the heaven and the earth," (Genesis 1:1) this makes him the Supreme Being of all power, thus giving him complete authority as well. His power cannot be beaten, matched, or even closely competed. This Power of powers is not only mighty in his strength and ability, but also in his very *appearance*, especially where his countenance is concerned. With God, the power comes no greater. As stated about his omniscience, it has reached its *zenith*!

Concerning those in prison soon to experience the death penalty and the Psalmist pleading for their rescue, Psalm 79:11 records Asaph telling us, "Let the sighing of the prisoner come before thee; according to the greatness of thy power preserved thou those that are appointed to die." The term "the greatness of thy power" just cannot be stressed to the point of exaggeration. May the mind of the reader meditate on that term for awhile, in order to realize why God commands the respect that he does. This term is also used elsewhere in the Psalms. Psalm 66, in speaking of the great works of God, says in verse 3, "Say unto God, How terrible art thou in thy works! through the greatness of thy power shall thine enemies submit themselves unto thee."

We always think of the word "terrible" to mean something extremely bad; awful; and at times, catastrophic. In much of the Bible, "terrible" comes from the same Hebrew word meaning "reverend." It contains various shades and degrees of meaning, including those of "respect" and "dread." In the latter part of the aforementioned verse, it shows "dread." Commanding this "respect" and "dread," it is easy how God makes and brings all enemies to "submit themselves" to him. No one stands any chance of defeating him. God controls all people. God controls all things. Nothing or nobody was created by God but what he *does not* or *cannot* control!

In view of this, it should not surprise us that God has control over nature. After all, he created it too. It stands to reason. Read all about the great Flood that took place in Noah's time in the entire chapter of Genesis 7. Notice verses 17-24: "And the flood was forty days upon the earth; and the waters increased, and bare up the ark, and it was lifted up above the earth. And the waters prevailed, and were increased greatly upon the earth; and the ark went upon the face of the waters. And the waters prevailed exceedingly upon the earth; and all the high hills, that were under the whole heaven, were covered. And all flesh died that moved upon the earth, both of fowl, and of cattle, and of beast, and of every creeping thing that creepeth upon the earth, and every man: All in whose nostrils was the breath of life, of all that was in the dry land, died. And every living substance was destroyed which was upon the face of the ground, both man, and cattle, and the creeping things, and the fowl of the heaven; and they were destroyed from the earth: and Noah only remained alive, and they that were with him in the ark. And the waters prevailed upon the earth a hundred and fifty days."

God controlled *all* actions in this Flood. He controlled when it rained, (and rain had not ever fallen upon the earth up to this time), how long it rained, and how much power was *behind* the rain. He controlled who and what died and lived during this great period. To actually control nature shows a different mode of power. Remember earlier in this book it was said that *real* power is *taken*, not *given*. If nowhere else in the Bible shows how God is powerful over all things and beings, what occurred in this great Flood does.

Read about how God made the sun stand still for Joshua, so the Israelite nation could defeat the Amorites in Joshua 10:12-14: "Then spake Joshua to the Lord in the day when the Lord delivered up the Amorites before the children of Israel, and he said in the sight of Israel, Sun, stand thou still upon Gibeon; and thou, Moon, in the valley of Ajalon. And the sun stood still and the moon stayed, until the people had avenged themselves upon their enemies. Is not this written in the book of Jasher? So the sun stood still in the midst of heaven, and hasted not to go down about a whole day." This shows another example of Jehovah God's control of Nature itself. The sun, sometimes called the "ball of fire," was set by God to do its job constantly without change, as likewise with the moon. To be able to control these two phenomenal pieces of the creation takes indescribable power. No one else could succeed in such a feat but God—the one who *created* them.

Then there is the parting of the waters of the Red Sea when the Israelites were fleeing from their bondage in Egypt while King Pharaoh's army was in hot pursuit of them. Exodus 14:21-31 says, "And Moses stretched out his hand over the sea; and the Lord caused the sea to go back by a strong east wind all that night, and made the sea dry land, and the waters were divided. And the children of Israel went into the midst of the sea upon dry ground: and the waters were a wall unto them on their right hand, and on their left. And the Egyptians pursued, and went in after them to the midst of the sea, even all Pharaoh's horses, his chariots, and his horsemen. And it came to pass, that in the morning watch the Lord looked unto the host of the Egyptians through the pillar of fire and of the cloud, and troubled the host of the Egyptians. And the Lord said unto Moses, Stretch out thine hand over the sea, that the waters may come again upon the Egyptians, upon their chariots, and upon their horsemen. And Moses stretched forth his hand over the sea, and the sea returned to his strength when the morning appeared; and the Egyptians fled against it; and the Lord overthrew the Egyptians in the midst of the sea. And the waters returned, and covered the chariots, and the horsemen, and all the host of Pharaoh that came into the sea after them; there remained not so much as one of them. But the children of Israel walked upon dry land in the midst of the sea; and the waters were a wall unto them on their right hand, and on their left. Thus the Lord saved Israel that day out of the hand of the Egyptians; and Israel saw the Egyptians dead upon the seashore. And Israel saw that great work which the Lord did upon the Egyptians: and the people feared the Lord, and believed the Lord, and his servant Moses."

What great power God displayed here! It was yet another act of controlling the very course of Nature. Look at all the weight water has behind it, and yet, it remained a stationary wall for hours. This defies the very laws of *gravity*! The *wind* also came into the picture here, and it too was controlled by God. The ground whereupon the people walked was made *dry* by God. Who else could control and/or change the gravitational laws? The question is self-answering.

God also showed his power over nature when sending the ten plagues upon Egypt, each in mass numbers, as a means of punishing King Pharaoh in his refusal to release the Israelite nation from their captivity. Exodus 8-12 records the plagues occurring in the following order: Blood, frogs, lice, flies, murrain (an infectious disease) of cattle, boils, hails, locusts, darkness, and the killing of the first-born. However, none of these plagues affected the Israelite people. Only the Egyptians suffered from them. Even when it comes to pestilence, God is still in control because he is omnipotent—all-powerful, and so, all controlling. His regulation is always present. Job declared of God in the latter part of Job 10:7, "...there is none that can deliver out of thine hand."

Example after example is given throughout the Bible, especially in the Old Testament, about God's omnipotence. Nobody need try to out run, out think, out wit, or out argue Jehovah. Compared to his power, we are too weak for words to possibly describe. The very next time we watch the rain fall, hear that clap of thunder, view that flash of lightning, see and hear the blowing of the wind, notice any natural disaster, witness the tide rise and fall on an ocean, sea or gulf, let us remember that such is the result of God's limitless power. Since he *created* all, it would lead to the simple and sensible conclusion that he has *power* over all!

Whether one interprets it exactly as it is worded in the following verse, or in a figurative way, the power of God is also displayed at the writing of the Ten Commandments. Exodus 31:18 tells us of God, "And he gave unto Moses, when he had made an end of communing with him upon mount Sinai, two tables of testimony, tables of stone, written with the finger of God." Even in its most literal interpretation, one can only ask another question that provides its own answer: Who else could write on stone—engrave—with their finger, and hence, not use a tool? No human or animal can. It is only God who is able to do so. How great and marvelous his power truly is!

The word "omnipotent" itself is only found once in the Word of God, but it is certainly manifested in many other Bible verses, nonetheless. The Apostle John says in Revelation 19:6, "And I heard as it were the voice of a great multitude, and as the voice of many waters, and as the voice of mighty thunderings, saying, Alleluia: for the Lord God omnipotent reigneth." Anytime in the Bible that a word ends with "eth," that shows continuity; that of always being around; constant. Hence, God *always* reigns because God is always *omnipotent*! His power never wanes or gives out. It continues to be the same today as it was yesterday, and will continue so, never, ever to cease. God never weakens, tires out, or has to rest. Therefore, God never *dies!*

Let us return to the book of Job to read some more on God's omnipotence. We find Eliphaz once again wrongly rebuking Job in Chapter 5:17, saying that his sufferings were brought about by sinning, when it was not: "Behold happy is the man whom God correcteth: therefore despise not thou the chastening of the Almighty." Still, as before, Eliphaz was right when he said that God punishes all wrongdoing. There is a consequence, be it minor or major, for every sin committed. As goes the saying, "Every *action* has its *reaction*." The same thing applies to each right and good thing that has its reward, as discussed elsewhere in this book on God's being a *rewarder*. The fact that Jehovah God is omnipotent would imply—and show—that he catches every thing said and done wrong and punishes such, as does he with rewarding everything said and done right. Paul tells this to the churches at Galatia: "Be not deceived; God is not mocked: for whatsoever a man soweth, that shall he also reap. For he that soweth to his flesh shall of the flesh reap corruption; but he that soweth to the Spirit shall of the Spirit reap life everlasting" (Galatians 6:7-8). This permanent "rule of thumb" applies to everyday life, as well as in the spiritual realm. *When seeds are sown, some kind of a harvest is reaped*! No one escapes paying for wrongs done, be it soon, or later on in life.

Hence, God's omnipotent power controls all "results," shall we say, of what is said and done, right or wrong. I refer to Job 26:7-14 where Job says, "He stretcheth out the north over the empty place, and hangeth the earth upon nothing. He bindeth up the waters in his thick clouds; and the cloud is not rent under them. He holdeth back the face of this throne, and spreadeth his cloud upon it. He hath compassed the waters with bounds, until the day and night come to an end. The pillars of heaven tremble, and are astonished at his reproof. He divideth the sea with his power, and by his understanding he smiteth through the proud. By his Spirit he hath garnished the heavens; his hand hath formed the crooked serpent. Lo, these are parts of his ways; but how little a portion is heard of him? But the thunder of his power who can understand?"

Truly, these verses, some of which have been already cited a number of times previously in this book, demonstrate so much more than one trait of God. Too, how so puny and helpless we as humans are in power and strength, compared to the omnipotent God!

All people are limited as to what and whom they can control, but God has *no* limits. (And those known as "control freaks" usually take full advantage in this area!) God has control of all places, things, and beings, for he *brought* them into existence. Job 33:4 finds Elihu saying to Job, "The Spirit of God hath made me, and the breath of the Almighty hath given me life." As in many other places in the Bible, God is once again referred to as the "Almighty." Why are you alive and kicking right at this very moment? (This was a question asked in the chapter dealing with the soul, one of God's *intangible* things created). It is because God's power and ability made you, along with the very breath that was breathed into you! God has the power to *give* life, and he has the power to *take* it. Hence, none of us can control God in the "giving" and the "taking." In chapter 1:21, after Job's children had died due to all four corners of his house caving in on them, it records some humble and admitting words of good old Job: "And said, "Naked came I out of my mother's womb, and naked shall I return thither: the Lord gave, and the Lord hath taken away; blessed be the name of the Lord."

Elihu speaks again in Job 36:5 where he says, "Behold, God is mighty, and despiseth not any: he is mighty in strength and wisdom." How very true the words are--much more than you and I could imagine! When rebuking Job, God said in Chapter 40:2, "Shall he that contendeth with the Almighty instruct him? He that reproveth God, let him answer it." Verse 9 records God telling Job, "Has thou an arm like God? Or canst thou thunder with a voice like him?" Verses like these make this writer want to shake his head in disgust at those who are conceited; those who will not let anybody tell them anything; those who think they know it all; those who act like they themselves are God! The inescapable truth is that God controls even *them*! People who are fools such as this are just too wrapped up in *themselves* to see it! God's dominance over them happens without it ever *registering* in their own foolish minds. Such individuals think they are so smart, so wise, so powerful, and so controlling of everything and everybody, and yet, it is the omnipotent God who is really in charge, not them! Arrogance knows no limits, sad to say. The individual who "plays God" will somewhere along the line find his "role" taken away from him.

One would do well to read the entire 148th Psalm anytime Satan tempts that individual to behave haughty and high in mind: "Praise ye the Lord: Praise ye the Lord from the heavens: praise him in the heights. Praise ye him, all his angels: praise ye him, all his hosts. Praise ye him, sun and moon: praise him, all ye stars of light. Praise him, ye heaven of heavens, and ye waters that be above the heavens. Let them praise the name of the Lord: for he commanded, and they were created. He hath also stablished them for ever and ever: he hath made a decree which shall not pass. Praise the Lord from the earth, ye dragons, and all deeps: fire, and hail; snow, and vapor; stormy wind fulfilling his word: mountains, and all hills; fruitful trees, and all cedars: beasts, and all cattle; creeping things, and flying fowl: kings of the earth, and all people; princes, and all judges of the earth: both young men, and maidens; old men, and children: let them praise the name of the Lord: for his name alone is excellent; his glory is above the earth and heaven. He also exalteth the horn of his people, the praise of all his saints; even of the children of Israel, a people near unto him. Praise ye the Lord." We find some forms of *personification* in this psalm. (Personification means, "Giving human qualifications to something non-human.") All forms of the Creation praise God, for their very existence points right back to him as their origin. If those things not part of the human race must—and do—praise God, how much more commanded by God are you and I as human beings, those creatures possessing the highest form of intelligence, to do so? This Psalm does not omit any gender, age, race, or social standing. We all need to praise the Almighty God! Amen and amen!

Like most all other traits of God, the Psalms speak of his omnipotence. King David has the following to say in all of Psalm 29: " Give unto the Lord, O ye mighty, give unto the Lord glory and strength. Give unto the Lord the glory due unto his name; worship the Lord in the beauty of holiness. The voice of the Lord is upon the waters: the God of Glory thundereth: the Lord is upon many waters. The voice of the Lord is powerful; the voice of the Lord is full of majesty. The voice of the Lord breaketh the cedars; yea, the Lord breaketh the cedars of Lebanon. He maketh them also to skip like a calf; Lebanon and Sirion like a young unicorn. The voice of the Lord divideth the flames of fire. The voice of the Lord shaketh the wilderness; the Lord shaketh the wilderness of Kadesh. The voice of the Lord maketh the hinds to calve, and discovereth the forests: and in his temple doth every one speak of his glory. The Lord sitteth upon the flood; yea, the Lord sitteth

King for ever. The Lord will give strength unto his people; the Lord will bless his people with peace."

David is relaying here to us that God deserves all the glory and praise one can render him, for he is behind the existence of all power. That is because God *himself* is all power! Even if one never, ever was allowed to see God in the next life, or even if the angels and all the host of Heaven were forever prohibited to see God's form, his very *voice* would be enough to make everything react, along with everyone sitting up and taking notice, as we just read.

It did not take much persuasion for the Israelite nation to understand the strength in God's voice. Talk about an "attention getter!" Exodus 20:18-21 tells us, "And all the people saw the thunderings, and the lightnings, and the noise of the trumpet, and the mountain smoking: and when the people saw it, they removed, and stood afar off. And they said unto Moses, Speak thou with us, and we will hear: but let not God speak with us, lest we die. And Moses said unto the people, Fear not: for God is come to prove you, and that his fear may be before your faces, that ye sin not. And the people stood afar off, and Moses drew near unto the thick darkness where God was."

The thought of one's very *vocal chords* being so powerful that it shakes the earth, brings about thunderings, lightnings, noise like a trumpet greatly magnified, along with causing a mountain to smoke, should cause us to *respect* our Maker with all humility and willingness! To be so afraid of such a voice that one fears *death* if that voice keeps speaking is too awesome for words to define in any language. In Ezekiel 1:24 the prophet says about his vision of some living creatures, "And when they went, I heard the noise of their wings, like the noise of great waters, as the voice of the Almighty, the voice of speech, as the noise of a host: when they stood, they let down their wings."

No matter how many measured *decibels* any one individual or any size crowd of people can possibly achieve, God's voice is still so much, much stronger. It is like no other sound that man has ever heard or has ever been able to produce, this writer cares not how many P.A. systems mankind has the ability to hook up to any number of circuits. Such is but a small bit of God's being omnipotent. It most definitely gives a whole new and different concept to "the voice of authority!"

We now go to Romans 1:20 where Paul tells this of God: "For the invisible things of him from the creation of the world are clearly seen, being understood by the things that are made, even his eternal power and Godhead; so that they are without excuse." One aspect of God's omnipotence is that his is an *eternal* power, which is discussed in a later chapter. It never ceases or subsides, for, like Jehovah himself, as already noted in the chapter on his being everlasting, *it always was*! One cannot ever seize any of this ever-dominating power from God because he has always possessed it.

In Hebrews 12:29, the writer says, "For our God is a consuming fire." Since fire is a very powerful agent, try and multiply it in your mind how much *more* powerful God is than any fire! How *hot* can you imagine? How *consuming* can you figure it to be? No such an exuberant power can be comprehended! We find the same thing taught in Deuteronomy 9:3 where Moses says to Israel about their future conquering of the land of Canaan, "Understand therefore this day, that the Lord thy God is he which goeth over before thee; as a consuming fire he shall destroy them, and he shall bring them down before thy face: so shalt thou drive them out, and destroy them quickly, as the Lord hath said unto thee."

Imagine the great Chicago fire in 1871 that burned up a large number of blocks. Imagine the amount of fire and lava spewing forth from a volcano, especially the one that buried Pompeii in A.D. 79. Imagine a fire so hot, you could not come within 100 miles of it! That, gentle reader, is God! That is but another "drop in the bucket" of his being omnipotent, as the prophet Isaiah said *just* that of God: "Behold, the nations are as a drop of a bucket, and are counted as the small dust of the balance: behold, he taketh up the isles as a very little thing" (Isaiah 40:15). What seems so very enormous to us is ever so small to God and oh so easily regulated by him. Since God is *omniscient*, as we spoke of in the last chapter, we should also then understand him to be *omnipotent*. That leads us to the next point.

With God's being every bit potent, we should realize how his Word, the Bible, would be no different. We have, after all, compared the Bible to some of God's other traits in previous chapters of this book. Hebrews 4:12 says, "For the word of God is quick, and powerful, and sharper than any two-edged sword, piercing even to the dividing asunder of soul and spirit, and of the joints and marrow, and is a discerner of the thoughts and intents of the heart." We said before that anyone who contains all power has the ability to seek out what is in the hearts of all people every moment. This verse shows the Bible to be the most powerful book ever to exist! There is not any department of the mind in which it does not search out, reveal, and touch. To be "quick, and powerful, and sharper than any two-edged sword" means to contain the maximum power. It explains that the Bible could not possibly be any stronger or any deeper in its penetration. This is why no other book or gifted style of writing can match it.

The omnipotence of God, as said, does not even exclude his very *appearance*. He is so mighty and powerful, that none can possibly look upon him and live! Does that sound too farfetched? Well, I will show you as the reader something else. I care not what any person past or present may testify or claim, the Bible says that no human being (except for Jesus) has ever seen Jehovah God. John the Apostle says, "No man hath seen God at any time. If we love one another, God dwelleth in us, and his love is perfected in us" (I John 4:12). Now being as the Bible is the inspired Word of God, completely coming from the mind of God, John must mean just what he said--"No man hath seen God at any time!" "No man" means, "no man!" That means no exceptions. This means that no creature of the *flesh* has laid eyes upon the face of Jehovah God, *period*! The same words are found in John 1:18: "No man hath seen God at any time; the only begotten Son, which is in the bosom of the Father, he hath declared him." This also tells us that any testimony from anyone claiming otherwise, no matter what is averred or how strongly, is *false* testimony! Jesus *himself* said that no man ever saw the face of God (John 6:46). God's countenance is so mighty and bright, absolutely and positively *none* of mankind could survive gazing upon his face! You know, the fact that the sun itself is too bright to view without either going blind or else ending up with permanent eye trouble, may very well tell and prove the truth of this writer's argument all right here! Along with everything making up the Creation, did not God create the sun too? Would that not make him greater than even it, as well as all the rest he created? Quite a thought!

The only person who came close to seeing God as he really looks was Moses, who requested to do so. Exodus 33:18-23 says the following: "And he said, I beseech thee, show me thy glory. And he said, I will make all my goodness pass before thee; and will be gracious to whom I will be gracious, and will show mercy on whom I will show mercy. And he said, Thou canst not see my face: for there shall no man see me and live. And the Lord said, Behold, there is a place by me, and thou shalt stand upon a rock: And it shall come to pass, while my glory passeth by, that I will put thee in a clift of the rock, and will cover thee with my hand while I pass by: And I will take away mine hand, and thou shalt see my back parts: but my face shall not be seen."

These verses make it plain to you and me. While Jehovah God allowed Moses to see what he looked like from the back, he would not allow him to see his face. Had that happened, Moses would have perished right then and there on the spot! God told him, "there shall no man see me and live." One might as well accept the fact that "no man hath seen God at any time." Whether one wishes to argue that God refused Moses to view his face because it was too bright for Moses to see and continue living, or whether this refusal was due to God's not wanting Moses to tell others what our Creator looked like, or whether both, either way, God has never allowed any human being to see his true facial features. The one writing this book, therefore, will believe the Bible over any of *man's* testimony. Man is so often mistaken, but what God says is gospel!

As it was, seeing as much of God as Moses *was* allowed to see affected his physical appearance, showing all the more the omnipotence of the Almighty Jehovah. Exodus 34:29-35 says, "And it came to pass, when Moses came down from Mt. Sinai with the two tables of testimony in Moses' hand, when he came down from the mount, that Moses wist (knew—PN) not that the skin of his face shone while he talked with him. And when Aaron and all the children of Israel saw Moses, behold, the skin of his face shone; and they were afraid to come nigh him. And Moses called unto them; and Aaron and all the rulers of the congregation returned unto him: and Moses talked with them. And afterward all the children of Israel came nigh: and he gave them in commandment all that the Lord had spoken with him in Mt. Sinai. And till Moses had done speaking with them, he put a veil on his face. But when Moses went in before the Lord to speak with him, he took the veil off, until he came out. And he came out, and spake unto the children of Israel that which he was commanded. And the children of Israel saw the face of Moses, that the skin of Moses' face shone: and Moses put the veil upon his face again, until he went in to speak with him."

The concept of someone's very appearance being so shiny and glowing that it changes the appearance of the one merely *looking* at that being should make us all hold God not only in respect, but in the highest of *awe*, as well! How would it impact you as the reader to be in the presence of someone whose countenance was so powerful and bright, it changed *your* very appearance? What kind of an impression would it leave on you? You certainly would never forget it! Such would for sure stay on your mind the rest of your earthly life! Knowing this is all the more reason to reverence God! What an *essence!*

Jehovah's might is above and beyond all powers, both on earth and in Heaven. He is the first and the last cause of all that exists, and has ever existed in the way of strength and vitality. There is none who can deliver themselves from God's hand, as has been quoted from the "good book." To have all power means to have all control. God displayed his power in the Bible from time to time by using the very elements he created—fire, thunder, lightning, wind, the sun, etc. The sound of his very *voice* shows his strong, unbeatable, unmatchable, independent greatness. To take any of it lightly is to only fool oneself and be in for a rude awakening somewhere in some way at sometime. Respect and obey your Maker. Any power you may be able to conjure up, individually or collectively, will be as weak, powerless, and helpless as physical death itself, when competing with the endless strength of God. His perfect power is not to be compared with that of any being or force, because it *cannot* be compared! Our Creator is truly a great, big, wonderful personality! God is *omnipotent*!

**Questions**

1. "Omnipotent" means "______________________________."
2. "Let the sighing of the prisoner come before thee; according to the __ ____________________________________ preserved thou those that are appointed to die."
3. "And the sun _________________ and the moon ____________, until the people had avenged themselves upon their enemies."
4. "He stretcheth out the north over the __________ place, and hangeth the earth upon _____________________."
5. "And the people saw the ______________, and the ________________, and the ____________ of the _____________, and the mountain _____________: and when the people saw it, they ____________, and stood _______________. And they said unto Moses, Speak thou with us, and we will hear: but let not _________ speak with us, lest we _________."
6. "Behold, the nations are as a _______________________________ _, and are counted as the _________________________________:

behold, he taketh up the isles as a ________________________."

7. Name the ten plagues that came upon Egypt, showing but one example of God's total control even of Nature: (1) ___________ (2) ____________ (3) ____________ (4) ____________ (5) ____________________ (6) ____________ (7) _____________ (8) _______________ (9) _________________ (10) __________________________________

8. Anytime in the Bible that a word ends with "eth," it always shows ______________.

9. The Ten Commandments, written on two tables of stone, were "written with the ________________ of God."

10. "There is _____________ that can deliver out of thine hand."

11. Since God CREATED all, he has the _______________ over all.

12. The word "omnipotent" itself is used ________ times in the Bible. It is in _________________________.

13. "And the flood was __________ days upon the earth."

14. God, being the "power of powers," is not only mighty in his strength and ability, but also in his very _________________________.

15. "There shall no man see me and ___________."

16. After Moses finished talking to God and came down from Mt. Sinai, we read, "And when Aaron and all the children of Israel saw Moses, behold, the skin of his face ____________: and they were _________ to come _________ unto him." Moses then "put a _________ on his face."

17. "For out God is a _________________________________."

18. "And Moses stretched out his hand over the sea; and the Lord caused the sea to _____________ by a ____________________ all that night, and made the sea _________________, and the waters were _________."

19. "The Spirit of God hath _________ me, and the _____________ of the Almighty hath given me _______________."

20. "Hast thou an arm like __________? Or canst thou _______ with a ______ like him?"

Chapter 10

# God Is Omnipresent

Remember we said in the last chapter that the prefix "omni" meant "all." Hence, God's being "omnipresent" means that he is "everywhere." This would mean everywhere *at the same time*! The "how" and the "why" of his being able to *know* all is clearly seen, explained, and understood by the fact that he can *see* all. Just like his being *omniscient* shows that in God's case we have no privacy, as before stated, the same thing obviously applies to his being *omnipresent*. God sees and hears all that you and I do, along with everywhere we go. There is nothing that escapes his all seeing eye. There is nothing we can speak, but what God will not hear it. There is no place where we can travel, but what God will not see and know all about it. Wherever we go, God will be present. This applies to everybody, everywhere, every day, and every time. No being of any type can get away from Jehovah God. It cannot be done, no matter who you are or what is attempted. God is present wherever mankind dwells. God is present wherever mankind *does not* dwell! All that we say and do is made manifest to him. There is no such thing as "putting one over" on God, for one can never, ever escape his sight.

This baffles a lot of people, no doubt. How can God be in St. Louis, Missouri and Los Angeles, California all at once? How can his presence exist in Denver, Colorado and Miami, Florida at the same time? How can he be present in Europe, Asia, Africa, North America, South America, on and in every body of water, and all other areas of the world *simultaneously*? Many people, by their own finite reasoning, judge all this as an utter impossibility. "You must to be kidding," many will say! "You are crazy," some will avert! "There is no way that this is possible," others will exclaim! However, remember this: Since God is the Creator of all that has ever existed, exists now, and ever *will* exist, that makes his mind, strength, and abilities to be "far beyond those of mortal men," (as the slogan is stated in the comic strip character of *Superman*).

Somebody greater than you or I would naturally have higher and more superior capabilities in every area of life. That would include the know-how to be in more than one place at a time. After all, God is *present* over all because he *created* all. The entire chapter of Psalm 139 tells of the everlasting presence and power of God by King David. Notice particularly verses 7-12: "Whither shall I go from thy Spirit? Or whither shall I flee from thy presence? If I ascend up into heaven, thou art there: if I make my bed in hell, behold, thou art there. If I take the wings of the morning, and dwell in the uttermost parts of the sea; even there shall thy hand lead me, and thy right hand shall hold me. If I say, Surely the darkness hideth not from thee; even the night shall be light about me. Yea, the darkness hideth not from thee; but the night shineth as the day: the darkness and the light are both alike to thee."

David is saying in the above verses that it is impossible to get away from God. Just read the book of Jonah in the Old Testament and see how old Jonah himself learned that the *hard* way! Psalm 94:7-9 tells us the following: "Yet they say, The Lord shall not see, neither shall the God of Jacob regard it. Understand, ye brutish among the people: and ye fools, when will ye be wise? He that planted the ear, shall he not hear? He that formed the eye, shall he not see?" How can God not be omnipresent when he was the one who formed the very first *eye*? All eyes belonging to the human race, the fowls, the animals, and the sea creatures are limited as to how much and how far they can see at one time. God's eye is not so! He sees everything and everyone collectively! Walk, run, crawl, hide, drive, ride, fly, do whatever you like! God will be present at every moving moment and every still moment. Where you go, he follows, for he has such an ability to do so. What you do and to whom you visit, he sees it. What you say, he hears it. This is due to the fact that he was—and is—*already there!* This explains his being omnipresent.

King Solomon declared in Proverbs 15:3, "The eyes of the Lord are in every place, beholding the evil and the good." All that is said and done in the way of right, wrong, or questionable is witnessed by God because all that is said and done is witnessed by God, *period*! His eyes miss nothing. (Let us note that the singular word "eye" appearing in the Bible sometimes applies in the plural sense, too). Solomon also stated in chapter 5:21, "For the ways of man are before the eyes of the Lord, and he pondereth all things."

Nobody can say that profane word, tell that lie, commit that crime, or do that evil act behind another person's back without God's catching it. Nobody can voice that compliment, tell that truth, or do that good deed without God's seeing or hearing it because of his omnipresence. The verse says, "The eyes of the Lord are in every place." This means what it says. God is in the wide and the narrow, the light and the dark, the big and the little, the closed and the open, the near and the far, and so this means every place, inclusively and conclusively!

In II Chronicles 16:9, Hanani the seer rebukes Asa, king of Israel, by saying, "For the eyes of the Lord run to and fro throughout the whole earth, to show himself strong in the behalf of them whose heart is perfect toward him. Herein thou has done foolishly: therefore from henceforth thou shalt have wars." The eyes of God are not merely present in a few small places in this world, but "to and fro throughout the whole earth." His eyes fall on all and miss nothing, whoever, whatever, whenever, and wherever. The same thought is mentioned in Zechariah 4:10, where the prophet says, "For who hath despised the day of small things? for they shall rejoice, and shall see the plummet in the hand of Zerubbabel with those seven; they are the eyes of the Lord, which run to and fro through the whole earth." Since God is omnipresent, that means he sees, and thus, knows where you are and what you are doing this very second. (Yes, he knows you are reading this book because he sees you doing it right now!) He sees what *everyone* is doing right this very moment and during each second that passes. He knows all our activities, past and present.

While King Solomon was praying to God, he said this of him in I Kings 8:27: "But will God indeed dwell on the earth? behold, the heaven and heaven of heavens cannot contain thee; how much less this house that I have builded?" Solomon shows us the ever presence of God by attempting to show illustratively how big God is; which, he says, cannot be done, as he explained when saying, "the heaven of heavens cannot contain thee." Solomon realized this even through all the great empire he owned, along with the enormous power and authority he had at his disposal. Because of God's size, he *must* be omnipresent. Let us refer to Jeremiah 23:23-24 where the text has the prophet declaring of God, "Am I a God at hand, saith the Lord, and not a God afar off? Can any hide himself in secret places that I shall not see him? saith the Lord. Do I not fill heaven and earth? saith the Lord?" It does not matter if this self-description refers to God's stature, or if the words make a mere statement of God's ability to see all that goes on at once, or both. No matter how you slice it or dice it, figuratively or literally, these verses show that God is omnipresent. The fact that he can "fill heaven and earth" would show that point to be irrefutable from any angle.

In Isaiah 59 we quote again where the prophet tells of Israel's corruption. Verses 1-2 say, "Behold, the Lord's hand is not shortened, that it cannot save; neither his ear heavy, that it cannot hear: But your iniquities have separated between you and your God, and your sins have hid his face from you, that he will not hear." There is nothing limited about God, as it is told especially here of his hand not having the ability to reach out and save, for it easily can, nor his ear not being capable of hearing Israel's pleas and prayers, for it is able to do so with no problem. The sad truth is, as said elsewhere in this book, that many prayers and petitions are not answered by God, nor are so much as even pondered by him, because many who pray are not living as God commands them. He will not condone or tolerate the presence of sin. To have one's life not right in the sight of God, but still expect one's prayers to be answered, is to expect the impossible; as impossible as an unlisted telephone number in a department of civil law! Be that as it may, still, God does see and hear all. Make no mistake about it. His being omnipresent enables him to know which prayers to answer, for he definitely knows if that person is living as he directs, or not.

Jehovah sees that person shoplift. He watches that burglar break into that house or building. His eyes note that spouse who is unfaithful. He catches and spies on that murderer in the very act. He observes that dishonest employee. He did not miss that driver greatly exceeding the speed limit. He knows about all cover-ups, conspiracies, and connivance, for his very presence was there to *take in* all such plans and deeds.

On the other hand, God views those who do right; that obedient employee; that faithful spouse; that honest banker; that generous helping hand given by someone(s) to those less fortunate than many of us. The list of right and wrong here is practically endless, gentle reader. God is everywhere. He sees when you eat, sleep, bathe, answer the calls of nature, travel in any form, make phone calls, shop, and on and on it goes with anything and everything else said and done.

The *truth* on anything and everything cannot be concealed from God, unlike it can often be from mankind. He knows every complete fact and flaw about all history written, for he has seen the *whole* of it during its very making, as he does so now, and continues to do so. Hence, he knows what historical writings are wrong, right, or even *half* right. None of us need try to escape God's sight or existence. Just look straight up at anytime, and *automatically* God will be looking straight down at you, even though you cannot or will not see him, as said in the last chapter. He is *omnipresent*!

## Questions

1. The prefix "omni" means "________."
2. The eyes of God miss ________________.
3. "Behold, the ___________ and ___________ of ___________ cannot contain thee."
4. "Behold, the Lord's hand is not _____________, that it cannot save; neither his ear _____________, that it cannot hear."
5. Just look ______________________ at anytime, and God will be looking ______________________ at you.
6. "___________ shall I go from thy ___________? Or ___________ shall I flee from thy ___________? If I ascend up into heaven, __________________________: if I make my bed in _________, behold, ______________________________."
7. "Yea, the darkness ______________________________; but the night ____________________________: the ______________ and the __________________ are both ______________ to thee."
8. "He that planteth the ________, shall he not __________? He that formed the ________, shall he not _____________?"
9. Since God is omnipresent, he has to have powers and abilities "far beyond those of _______________________."
10. "The eyes of the Lord are in ________________, beholding the __________ and the ______________."
11. "For the eyes of the Lord run ______ and ________ throughout the _________________________."
12. Since no one can ever escape God's sight, there is no such thing as "putting one ________" on God.
13. "For the ways of ________ are ___________________ of the Lord, and he pondereth __________________."
14. "Am I a God ________________, saith the Lord, and not a God _____________? Can any _________ himself in _________________ that I shall not _________ him? saith the Lord. Do I not fill ___________ ______________________? saith the Lord?"
15. "They are the eyes ___________________, which run ______ and

__________ through the ________________________."

16. God's being omnipresent enables him to know EXACTLY what __________________ to answer.
17. Wherever we go, God will be _________________.
18. The word "eye" in the Bible sometimes refers to God's omnipresence in the _________________ sense.

Chapter 11

# God Is Independent

Jehovah God is not dependent on anybody or anything to survive. Since he is the Creator of all things past and present, and since he existed before any food, water, or living creature, that would show his independence to be *eternal*. Therefore, his self-reliance has always been within just that--himself. God needs nothing to maintain his eternal body, if for no other reason, because he is a *spirit*, as we discussed a few chapters back. All of this being so, it would mean that nobody or no force can be in control over him. It is stated again that he cannot be taught, advised, counseled, assisted, or regulated in any manner. God is *self-sustaining*, so he is his own free moral agent, thus, solely making his own decisions and judgments. He needs no aid from any member of the human race to keep him going. He is his own provider, guide, and supervisor. The very fact that God is omniscient, omnipresent, and omnipotent, as discussed and defined in the previous three chapters of this book, bear impeccable and unfailing proof as to how he is altogether independent, for possessing all of those three traits combine to make him that way. We need him. He does not need us.

King David said of God in Psalm 8:3-4, "When I consider thy heavens, the works of thy fingers, the moon and the stars, which thou hast ordained; what is man, that thou art mindful of him? and the son of man, that thou visitest him?" Some of these words are also recorded in Hebrews 2:6. While somewhat expressing God's independence, David is likewise manifesting his amazement at the attention given to him and the rest of the human race by our Creator. While God does not need us to maintain his existence, by the same token, he does love us very much. I wanted to mention that in this paragraph, so the reader will understand that God loves and cares for us all ever so fervently, in spite of his being an *independent* God. His being self-existent does not keep him from deeply loving us. The chapter on God's love will elaborate on this point.

King David also stated in Psalm 24:1, "The earth is the Lord's, and the fullness thereof; the world, and they that dwell therein." As stated earlier in this book when citing this passage, many of the same words are spoken by the Apostle Paul in I Corinthians 10:26 and 28. God thought to create this marvelous universe *on his own!* There was no help or suggestions from so much as *one* member of the host of Heaven, let alone the entire compilation.

All that our eyes fall upon originated from God's infinite mind, one of total independent thinking and planning. Psalm 50:10-13 has the writer Asaph repeating these words from God to Israel: "For every beast of the forest is mine, and the cattle upon a thousand hills. I know all the fowls of the mountains: and the wild beasts of the field are mine. If I were hungry, I would not tell thee: for the world is mine, and the fullness thereof. Will I eat the flesh of bulls, or drink the blood of goats?" This is God saying in so many words, "Even if I had to eat and drink in order to survive, which I do not, I would not tell you, for I still would not need your help in doing so. I would just simply live off the land that I created." David further declared in Psalm 89:11, "The heavens are thine, the earth also is thine: as for the world and the fullness thereof, thou hast founded them."

Since God has unconditional ownership of all that he brought about, (minus any lien, as said before) including you and I, what could we possibly give to him that he needs and wants of which he does not already possess, or has not already created? What could we in any way do for him that he could not do, and has not done, for himself?

Job 38:4-6 shows God's rebuking of Job by telling him, "Where wast thou when I laid the foundations of the earth? Declare, if thou hast understanding. Who hath laid the measures thereof, if thou knowest? Or who hath stretched the line upon it? Whereupon are the foundations thereof fastened? Or who laid the corner stone thereof?" God created the heavens and the earth without any assistance from mankind, for the very simple reason mankind was not present then and there to help him, for the very simple reason mankind was not yet brought into the picture, and for the very simple reason mankind was created by God *himself*! We find some more of that rebuke in Chapter 40:2: "Shall he that contendeth with the Almighty instruct him? He that reproveth God, let him answer it." What can you and I teach God that he *does not* already know and *did not* already know? (The reader will recall that this was covered in the chapter on God's being *omniscient*). That is precisely why we should listen to him, and why he has no reason to heed anything we say.

Notice some more of God's independence, as he says to Job in Chapter 41:11, "Who hath prevented me, that I should repay him? Whatsoever is under the whole heaven is mine." Again, no other being can make such a claim as this! God *owns* all and *controls* all! When God finishes his say-so to Job, we find Job's reply in Chapter 42:2-3, "I know that thou canst do every thing, and that no thought can be withholden from thee. Who is he that hideth counsel without knowledge? Therefore have I uttered that I understood not; things too wonderful for me, which I knew not." Job appears to be acknowledging God's power, wisdom, and independence collectively here. He humbly says in verse 6, "Wherefore I abhor myself, and repent in dust and ashes." Who with a sane and rational mind would dare tell an independent God what to do, what to speak, what to think, in what manner to think anything, or what he needs? No man, woman, boy, or girl has this inept an ability or such a *right* as that! (Some act it, though!) The Creator needs to be told *nothing!* Having all power, all knowledge, and all wisdom are what make Jehovah *independent* of anything, everything, anybody, and everybody.

When Stephen was preaching to the Jews just before his stoning, he spoke the following words about God in Acts 7:49-50: "Heaven is my throne, and earth is my footstool: what house will ye build me? saith the Lord: or what is the place of my rest? Hath not my hand made all these things?" Stephen was quoting from Isaiah 66:1-2. What on earth can you and I say or do to help someone who is in absolutely no *need* of help to begin with here? What house can we build for God? What throne or piece of furniture must he require to obtain from us? What food or drink can we provide for him? What clothing can we manufacture and/or purchase for our Maker? What *support* does he possibly need from anyone? He did without all of these things before the world was made. The fact is, even if he needed any of the material things which you and I must have in order to stay alive, they would have already existed in Heaven before the creation of the earth, for God has the ability to create and make anything he so desires.

Paul made God's independence perfectly clear when speaking his sermon to some men on Mars Hill in Athens, Greece. Let us return to this sermon we have commented on a number of times. Paul says in Acts 17:24-25, "God that made the world and all things therein, seeing that he is Lord of heaven and earth, dwelleth not in temples made with hands; Neither is worshipped with men's hands, as though he needed any thing, seeing he giveth to all life, and breath, and all things." Note that Paul declared, "as though he needed any thing." God *does not* need anything! He possesses everything in Heaven itself, because it was every bit created by him. The same goes likewise with all things we find on this earth, including the earth itself and everything existing in all the heavens. "All things" Paul spoke of here mean *all things*! That means no exceptions, be it physical, material, or spiritual.

No human being should have the unimaginable audacity and gall to dare try and tell God what to do, what to say, or how to conduct himself. He does not need lessons on how to talk, act, and make decisions. Such was already everlastingly contained in his infinite, sinless, flawless, matchless, and perfect mind. Complaining about what he says in his Bible is not only fruitless, it yields no positive assistance in one's eternal destiny. While the good Lord loves us too profoundly for words to describe, notwithstanding, he does not need anything or any type of aid from us to carry on his existence. We are dependent on him for every last tiny bit of our survival, but he has no reason to rely on us. He is not a helpless being in any shape, form, or fashion. Jehovah God is an *independent* God!

**Questions**

1. God is dependent on ________________ or ________________.
2. God is ________-sustaining.
3. "The earth is _____________, and the _______________________: the ___________, and they that ___________________________."
4. "The heavens are ______________: as for the _________ and the __________________ thou hast ___________________."
5. "For every _____________ of the ___________ is mine, and the ________ upon ________________. I know all the ________ of the ______________________: and the _________________ of the __________ are ___________. If I were ____________, I would not ______________ thee: for the __________ is __________, and the _ _____________________________."
6. "Shall he that condendeth with the Almighty ______________ him? He that _________________ God, let him _____________ it."
7. "Who hath ____________________ me, that I should __________ him?

Whatsoever is under the ____________________ is ___________."

8. "Where wast thou when I laid the ______________ of the __________? Declare, if thou hast _______________________."
9. The Creator needs to be told _____________________.
10. "God that made the _____________ and ______________ things therein, seeing that he is ___________ of _____________ and __________, dwelleth not in ____________________ made with ____________; Neither is worshipped with ________________, as though he needed ___________________."
11. "Heaven is _______ throne, and earth is ________ footstool: what house will ye ________________ me? Saith the Lord: or what is the place of my ___________? Hath not _______ hand made _______ these things?"
12. "When I consider the heavens, the works of ________ fingers, the _______________ and the _______________, which _________ hast ordained; what is ___________, that thou art ______________ of him? and the ___________ of man, that thou _________________ him?"

Chapter 12

# God Is Everlasting

The word "everlasting" explains itself by its very pronunciation. Play with the word a little, and this writer's point is made; last forever; lasting ever; lasting forever; forever lasting. Any way one investigates this word, it has to mean "never ending." The words "everlasting" and "eternal" are used interchangeably in the Bible, as the reader will see in the verses quoted in this chapter. They appear to mean the exact same thing. Everlasting actually means, "Never to end; indeterminate as to duration." Such is the existence of Jehovah God. His life never, ever ceases. It does not come to an end. God does not die, age, or even so much as diminish. He is the same, identical God *now* that he was at the Creation. I will lay you one more: He is the same, identical God *now* that he was *before* the Creation! He is changeless, tireless, and limitless. He knows no variation, altering, or boundary lines. He always was, which means he presently is, and thus, ever will be.

Such baffles and blows many a person's mind, no doubt. After all, we as humans *measure* everything by a *beginning* and an *end*. All pertaining to physical life has *limitations*. Based on our own individual biological and chemical makeup, along with time and chance, we are born at a given moment and only live so long. After a certain amount of time, which is different in length for each of us, we all must die—whether of natural or unnatural causes. We only grow to a limited height, stay awake the given number of hours our bodies can endure, when the body then becomes tired, and hence, we must sleep for awhile. We work for a spell, and then we need to take a break. We get hungry, so we have to eat and drink in order to stay alive. We travel from point A to point B, which takes a specific amount of time. On the subject of time, we have but a short amount of it in our lives to do with what we want and need to do. Time exists in seconds, minutes, hours, days, weeks, months, years, centuries, and millenniums. Buildings and other structures wear out, making it necessary either to demolish them or renovate them. Clothes wear out. The things we must buy such as food, drink, cosmetics, toilet supplies, and so on, are eventually consumed. Automobiles, planes, trains, boats, and other vehicles of transportation wear out with the passing of time. One has to only look around to see death, decay, and the passing away of every physical and material thing. Nothing and nobody in this world lasts forever. Fads and clothing styles come and go, some of which return, only to faze out again.

However, Jehovah God has always been around. He is one being in which no person or force can reduce or annihilate. He is the everlasting God.

When speaking of "everlasting," the word carries with it more than the idea of never having an *end* to it. Where *God's* existence is concerned, there was no *beginning*, as well. In Moses' prayer to God, he said in Psalm 90:1-2, "Lord, thou hast been our dwelling place in all generations. Before the mountains were brought forth, or ever thou hadst formed the earth and the world, even from everlasting to everlasting, thou art God." Moses shows us two things in this text about the everlasting existence of God: (1) He has existed ever since the world began, for the text reads "all generations;" and (2) He existed prior to anything created or made, for it also reads, "from everlasting to everlasting."

Before anything or anyone came into being, God was there. (This is all the *more* reason to believe that God is the Creator of all things). He is a God without beginning or end. He did not *come* from anywhere, and he is not *going* anywhere. This is where our finite minds have no choice but to draw the limit and simply accept some things such as this by *faith*. None of us need make ourselves frustrated, angry, confused, or miserable in trying to figure out the so-called *beginning* of God, for there is none. Why endlessly search out a question to which there can be *no* answer? It is as useless as fighting the wind! Such a thing is vain and vexing to one's spirit, as King Solomon so attests to periodically in the book of Ecclesiastes.

Our minds are *finite*, which means they are *limited*, as said in discussing God's *omniscience*. If our minds were *infinite* like God's, which means, again, "without limits," then we could argue deeper on the existence of God. Since we cannot go any farther back than the Creation, it is best to just leave some things *alone*! Just think of God's forever existence as being his own "finished product." If God did have a beginning, the only halfway sensible answer one could give was that he created *himself!* Hardly makes any logic, though, does it not? Well, do you see my point? In Psalm 90:10, in speaking of man's limited life on earth, Moses points out, "The days of our years are threescore years and ten; and if by reason of strength they be fourscore years, yet is their strength labor and sorrow; for it is soon cut off, and we fly away." That is the life of the human race.

Now back to God. In Psalm 93:2 the writer says, "Thy throne is established of old: thou art from everlasting." Like Psalm 90:1-2 previously cited, this verse does not just use the term "everlasting," but instead, says, "*from* everlasting." Similar words are penned by King David in Psalm 41:13: "Blessed be the Lord God of Israel from everlasting to everlasting. Amen and Amen." Much of the same terminology is echoed in Psalm 106:49. A little boy once said he wished he had a piece of peppermint candy with only one end on it. For us as human beings containing a soul that will live on forever somewhere after this earthly life, that is a pretty good definition of "everlasting." It will have only one end on it, that being the starting point. From that moment on, life will be *timeless,* because life will be *everlasting* for us.

Speaking of being timeless, this commodity known as *time* means absolutely nothing to God. In speaking of the end of the world, the Apostle Peter said in II Peter 3:8, "But, beloved, be not ignorant of this one thing, that one day is with the Lord as a thousand years, and a thousand years as one day." With Jehovah, time does not mean frost on a bucket! When something or someone is everlasting, they are, as stated at the end of the last paragraph, *timeless.* There is no measuring of time, for there are no limitations on anything or anyone. There are no schedules to meet; no "race against time," as the saying is; no deadlines; no "beating the clock." That which is everlasting stays identically the same always, never to end, never to erode, and never to fade. This is the life of God, for this is God himself. He knows no set years, because he has none. The passing of time does not affect God in the least. Time puts no strain on him. Therefore, God has no birthday, for he was never born, which means he was never conceived, meaning God has no parents. So, due to God's being everlasting, there are no clocks in Heaven to measure time, for in every last way, God is timeless.

Genesis 21:33 says, "And Abraham planted a grove in Beersheba, and called there on the name of the Lord, the everlasting God." Our Maker and Creator lasts *forever*, gentle reader! He is not a "has been." He is, as earlier stated in this chapter, an "always was." In speaking of his own everlasting existence, Jesus told a group of unbelieving Jews in the last part of John 8:58, ". . .Verily, verily, I say unto you, Before Abraham was, I am." Jesus did not word it, "I was, am now, and always will be." He showed his everlasting Deity by saying, "I am." That is a strong term, packing a lot of *wallop*! The term "I am" would show no beginning or end, either one, but instead, illustrates always having been in existence. God has Moses tell this about his perennial life to Israel: "For I lift up my hand to heaven, and say, I live for ever" (Deuteronomy 32:40). This is quite plain and elementary, is it not? God lives on and on, never to cease, never to decease, and never to end being God, for he will never end *being!* In speaking of a future hymn of praise to be sung by Judah, the prophet Isaiah exhorts, "Trust ye in the Lord for ever: for in the Lord Jehovah is everlasting strength" (Isaiah 26:4).

As we discussed earlier in this book, God is *omnipotent*, which means he is all-powerful. If his *strength* is everlasting, then so must be his *existence*, for any way one studies it, anything or anyone everlasting has unequivocally no end. The prophet Isaiah also spoke these words in Chapter 40:28: "Hast thou not known? hast thou not heard, O Israel, that the everlasting God, the Lord, the Creator of the ends of the earth, fainteth not, neither is weary? there is no searching of his understanding." In Chapter 63:16 he says directly to God, "Doubtless thou art our father, though Abraham be ignorant of us, and Israel acknowledge us not: thou, O Lord, art our father, our Redeemer; thy name is from everlasting." We see that God's own *name* is everlasting. That is because his very *reputation* and *authority* are the same. Since he is everlasting, there is no way God grows the least bit exhausted in his energy and power, or becomes liquidated with any of his characteristics. Hence, his *existence* being one of everlasting calls for all his abilities to be likewise.

Now we will note some Bible passages using the word "eternal." In blessing one of the tribes of Israel, Asher, Moses says in Deuteronomy 33:27, "The eternal God is thy refuge, and underneath are the everlasting arms: and he shall thrust out the enemy before thee; and shall say, Destroy them." In this verse, God is called "eternal" with "everlasting arms," showing his existence to always be present and his protection to forever be there for those who obey him. In Habakkuk 1:12, we read where the prophet declares concerning God's using of the wicked to punish his own people, "Art thou not from everlasting, O Lord my God, mine Holy One? we shall not die. O Lord, thou hast ordained them for judgment; and, O mighty God, thou hast established them for correction." Habakkuk, like some of the other writers quoted, uses the term "from everlasting," then he refers to God as being the "Holy One" and "mighty God."

Nothing about God's being everlasting shows any deterioration in his strength and sinless nature. One may very well say God is just as "fresh" now as he was before, during, and after the Creation. There is no wearing down or ebbing away of him. He is not "losing it," as we often joke.

The mind is overwhelmed when trying to come up with the innumerable amount of people who have died since Adam and Eve were created--person after person after person. No matter how long anyone lives on this planet, somewhere along the way, from some cause, all must leave this earthly life. The oldest person recorded in the Bible was Methuselah, who lived 969 years (Gen. 5:27). However, he too died, as that same verse denotes.

There is no such thing as "physical immortality," (as there used to be before sin entered into the world) so none of us need act egotistical about growing old, even though it is fully realized that this is often a touchy subject, especially with the fairer sex. Touchy or not, though, let us all face reality! Whether slow or fast, aging will happen, for it is happening now to you and to this writer, even as you read. You can throw old age a curve, and you can slow it down, but you will not ever *stop* it. The year that you quit *aging* is the year you will quit *breathing*! All birthdays will then come to a complete halt. So enjoy every birthday you are able to see, for that is another year of life given to you by our good Jehovah. The only way one can avoid growing old is to die young; but young, old, or anywhere in-between, physical death comes to all people. In Hebrews 9:27 the writer states, "And as it is appointed unto men once to die, but after this the judgment."

God told Adam and Eve after they sinned in the Garden of Eden, "In the sweat of thy face shalt thou eat bread, till thou return unto the ground; for out of it wast thou taken: for dust thou art, and unto dust shalt thou return" (Gen. 3:19). Then we read the ever so sad but true words of the wise King Solomon in Ecclesiastes 3:19-20: "For that which befalleth the sons of men befalleth beasts; even one thing befalleth them: as the one dieth, so dieth the other; yea, they have all one breath; so that a man hath no preeminence above a beast: for all is vanity. All go unto one place; all are of the dust, and all turn to dust again." No human being has ever been, or will ever be, immuned to physically dying. All of us will at one point pass away, except for those who will live to see the end of time.

It is a most sobering thought to realize that everyone of us are going to quit the walks of life one day, say goodbye to all the world, everything contained in it, and bid farewell to every member of mankind who is still alive at that time; those known to us, as well as those unknown. We will then be reduced to only a memory. For us, life is limited. However, Jehovah God will still be around after our departure *from* this life, just as he was before our entry *into* this life. We all come and go, but God stays. He does not expire. He never, ever sees the end of his life. What a God we have! He is *everlasting*!

**Questions**

1. "Everlasting" means, "________________________________________________ ________________________________________________."
2. "Lord, thou hast been our ________________ place in ______ generations."
3. God has ________ beginning.
4. "The days of our ________ are ____________ and ______; and if by reason of ____________ they be ________________ years, yet is their strength ___________ and ___________; for it is soon ____________, and we _________________."
5. "Blessed be the Lord God of Israel from ___________________ to ____________________."
6. God did not ________ from anywhere, and he is not _________ anywhere.
7. "Thy throne is established of _____: thou art from ___________."
8. Time means _______________ to God.
9. God existed not only SINCE the world began, but also _________ the world began.
10. All pertaining to physical life has _______________.
11. "But, beloved, be not ____________ of this one thing, that _________ is with the Lord as __________________, and ________________ as _______________."
12. "And Abraham planted a grove in Beersheba, and called there on the name of the Lord, the ______________________ God."
13. Concerning Himself, Jesus said, "Before Abraham was, ________."
14. "The _____________ God is thy _______________, and underneath are the ___________________ arms."
15. "Art thou not from __________________, O Lord my _______, mine __________________ One?"
16. There is no such thing as "________________ immortality."

17. "And as it is _______________ unto men once to __________, but after this the ____________________."
18. "For that which befalleth the ________ of ________ befalleth ____________; even one thing befalleth them: as the ______ dieth, so dieth the _____________; yea, they have all _______ breath; so that a man hath no ______________________ above a __________: For _______ is vanity. _____________ go unto one place; ______ are of the _____________, and ______ turn to _____________ again."
19. "Trust ye in the Lord ___________: for in the Lord is _______________ strength."
20. Nothing about God's being everlasting shows any _______________ in his _________________ and _________________ nature.

Chapter 13

# God Is Gracious

The word "gracious" spans a lot of varied territory. It is defined as: "(1) pleasing; acceptable (2) marked by kindness and courtesy; graceful; marked by tact and delicacy; urbane; characterized by charm, good taste, and generosity of spirit (3) merciful; compassionate—used conventionally of royalty and nobility." This covers ever so well another area of Jehovah God, for he is the very height of "royalty and nobility." He is a God of *grace*, therefore, he is *gracious*. He is more gracious than any words can phrase, for there is not a part of him that is not this way. This makes him all gracious, with "no holes barred." Not only has he generously supplied us with all the *necessities* of life, a lot of us are equipped with either a few or a good number of *luxuries,* as well.

When one sees all the many, many different types of food and drink existing, one must realize all of such came from God. Take a look at the vast numbers of fabrics in this world responsible for the manufacturing and tailoring of our clothes, along with the abundance of clothing. God has also provided a huge variety of raw materials such as wood and various metals for the construction of our homes, furniture, vehicles, and businesses. Then there is the soil of "Mother Earth" herself, growing the foods and grains. There are innumerable wells and springs flowing from underground, supplying us the water we need so desperately for our drinking, bathing, washing, along with various uses in commerce and industry. God sends us the sunshine and rain, very pertinent for not only the survival and irrigation of the farmer's crops and the maintaining of the ground, but also for the replenishment of this world's water bodies. Too, how perpetually hot and unbearable it would be without the presence of any wind! To say that God is *good* is to barely *begin* describing his generosity. It is hardly scratching the surface.

Remember this writer said before that every trait possessed by God is of a very large nature. So being a big God, he is also big in every way, whatever it be. This graciousness of God, like all the aforementioned definitions tell, is quite complex. Imagine containing every one of those qualities and talents in the biggest way possible. This should take one's breath away! God is ever so gracious to you and I, no matter who or what we are. He often provides so much more than what we ask of him. This not only makes him ever so generous, this makes him a God of limitless *versatility*. Truly, the words "many," "abundance," "vast," "liberal," "accommodating," "great," and "bountiful," just to name a few describing God's generosity, make up the gracious side of him.

Now! Some people who think God is so stingy and tight should look around at the countless physical and spiritual blessings that accompany human life. True, there are people who are more blessed than others, but how many times do we realize that since God has *placed* so many things in this world for us to use, perhaps one has not taken the possible and necessary steps to *reach out* to them? Yes, this writer speaks of the old adage, "Go for it!" Set goals! Then work towards reaching them. While some things are definitely impossible, not *all* things are, we very much know—and should accept! Do not cheat yourself in life, even though you will most probably never get *everything* you desire in the way of accomplishments and material gain. God's graciousness, however, has enabled you to, as they say, "do something with your life." So, do something with your life! Take advantage of opportunities, some of which either come seldom to you or only once in a lifetime. Sensibly pursue all that your heart desires. If God did not mean for you to *use* the things contained in this world, he would not have *placed* them here.

However, no matter how successful or blessed an individual becomes, one should always express *thanks* to God for his being gracious in every way, along with his receiving the glorification for having brought about those very things sought. After all, everything *good* and *right* achieved in life results from the help, grace, and provisions of God. They would not be in the world, were it not for God. He is the Maker of all good and worthwhile opportunities.

King David, being the very thankful person he was, says in Psalm 86:15, "But thou, O Lord, art a God full of compassion, and gracious, long-suffering and plenteous in mercy and truth." David praises God in a number of ways here, one of which is that of being "gracious". On all these words of praise, he says that God is "full of" them all. When one is "full," one cannot contain anymore. It is at the point of total completion and capacity. God could not be any more "full of" graciousness than what he is! Quite similar words are expressed by David in Psalm 103:8 where it reads, "The Lord is merciful and gracious, slow to anger, and plenteous in mercy." One could hardly be "plenteous in mercy" without having the trait of being gracious. Chapter 111:4 says, "He hath made his wonderful works to be remembered: the Lord is gracious and full of compassion."

How could God's "wonderful works" be in any way "remembered," or how could he be "full of compassion" without his being "gracious?" After all, when one person is gracious to another person, or to a group, such is usually never forgotten—nor should it be. Chapter 116:5 declares, "Gracious is the Lord, and righteous; yea, our God is merciful."

God's graciousness—his generosity—his thoughtful manner—his consideration—his concern—ought never to go unnoticed. Why? For one thing, it never ceases. Asaph declared in Psalm 77:9, "Hath God forgotten to be gracious? Hath he in anger shut up his tender mercies? Selah." ("Selah" is a pause—not said, but done.) Even when displaying anger, God's graciousness still comes through, as we will note later on in this chapter. King David elaborates on God's being gracious when he says in Psalm 145:8-9, "The Lord is gracious, and full of compassion; slow to anger, and of great mercy. The Lord is good to all: and his tender mercies are over all his works." Along with possessing all knowledge and all wisdom, as previously discussed, God also manifested his gracious side even in his works.

Who could be so thoughtful as to create all that has been created with such, as this writer already said, versatility? Observe every one of the large varieties God put into the shapes, sizes, colors, and depths of everything? Only a supreme mind could be supreme in his works; and you know something else, gentle reader? This makes God's graciousness "icing on the cake!"

In Psalm 136:25 the writer tells us of God, "Who giveth food to all flesh: for his mercy endureth for ever." Without God's provision of the food, each and every last fleshly being would starve to death! ("Oh really,"you may jest!) In Chapter 146:7-9 it says of Jehovah, "which executeth judgment for the oppressed: which giveth food to the hungry. The Lord looseth the prisoners: the Lord openeth the eyes of the blind: the Lord raiseth them that are bowed down: the Lord loveth the righteous: the Lord preserveth the strangers; he relieveth the fatherless and widow: but the way of the wicked he turneth upside down." What a lesson here! Look how much *more* God would do for mankind if more of mankind would do for God—just *obey* him! While his graciousness extends to *all* people as it is, needy or prosperous, it extends all the more to the *righteous*; to those who *heed* his commands. Think about it, you who read this! (So should this writer!)

In Exodus 34:6-7, God says this of himself while passing before Moses: "And the Lord passed by before him, and proclaimed, The Lord, The Lord God, merciful and gracious, long-suffering, and abundant in goodness and truth, Keeping mercy for thousands, forgiving iniquity and transgression and sin, and that will by no means clear the guilty; visiting the iniquity of the fathers upon the children, and upon the children's children, unto the third and unto the fourth generation." No being, God or whoever, could possibly have goodness, mercy, long-suffering, or be willing to forgive all wrongs unless one has the trait of being *gracious* inside oneself. In II Chronicles 30:9, King Hezekiah says to Israel concerning God's willingness to forgive, "For if ye turn again unto the Lord, your brethren and your children shall find compassion before them that lead them captive, so that they shall come again into this land: for the Lord your God is gracious and merciful, and will not turn away his face from you, if ye return to him." God is always standing by to forgive all sin. He *wants* to do so, but forgiveness must be—and will only be—done on *his* terms. God *forgives*, everybody! The trouble with too many people is that they just do not *let* him!

On the other side of the table, what about those who *truly* want him to forgive? In Isaiah 30:18-19, we see the prophet saying to Israel, "And therefore will the Lord wait, that he may be gracious unto you, and therefore will he be exalted, that he may have mercy upon you: for the Lord is a God of judgment: blessed are all they that wait for him. For the people shall dwell in Zion at Jerusalem: thou shalt weep no more: he will be very gracious unto thee at the voice of thy cry; when he shall hear it, he will answer thee." God is actually *standing by* to forgive anybody who comes to him repenting, but only as *he* would have that person do. We just read where he will be "very gracious" to the righteous, for they are the ones who follow his commandments. After all, does not graciousness beget yet more graciousness?

While there are a number of Old Testament passages of God's promise to the Israelite nation that they would inhabit the land of Canaan, I would like to cite a vast amount of scripture from one Bible chapter. These verses show God's graciousness to Israel, along with Israel's history, as a whole, of returning all too often a *lack* of graciousness to God. Gentle reader, as you note the following words, let this be a valuable lesson to you and to this one writing as in how *not* to act. In Nehemiah 9:7-31 the prophet says this:

> Thou art the Lord the God, who didst choose Abram, and broughtest him forth out of Ur of the Chaldees, and gavest him the name of Abraham; And foundest his heart faithful before thee, and madest a covenant with him to give the land of the Canaanites, the Hittites, the Amorites, and the Perizzites, and the Jebusites, and the Girgashites, to give it, I say, to his seed, and hast performed thy words; for thou art righteous: And didst see the affliction of our fathers in Egypt, and heardest their cry by the Red Sea; And showdest signs and wonders upon Pharoah, and on all his servants, and on all the people of his land: for thou knewest that they dealt proudly against them. So didst thou get thee a name, as it is to this day. And thou didst divide the sea before them, so that they went through the midst of the sea on the dry land; and their persecutors thou threwest into the deeps, as a stone into the mighty waters. Moreover thou leddest them in the day by a couldy pillar; and in the night by a pillar of fire, to give them light in the way wherein they should go. Thou camest down also upon mount Sinai, and spakest with them from heaven, and gavest them right judgments, and true laws, good statutes and commandments: And madest known unto them thy holy sabbath, and commandest them precepts, statutes, and laws, by the hand of Moses thy servant: And gavest them bread from heaven for their hunger, and broughtest forth water for them out of the rock for their thirst, and promisedst them that they should go in to possess the land which thou hadst sworn to give them. But they and our fathers dealt proudly, and hardened their necks, and hearkened not to thy commandments, And refused to obey, neither were mindful of thy wonders that thou didst among them; but hardened their necks, and in their rebellion appointed a captain to return to their bondage: but thou art a God ready to pardon, gracious and merciful, slow to anger, and of great kindness, and forsookest them not. Yea, when they had made them a molten calf, and said, This is thy God that brought thee up out of Egypt, and had wrought great provocations; Yet thou in thy manifold mercies forsookest them not in the wilderness: the pillar of the cloud departed not from them by day, to lead them in the way; neither the pillar of fire by night, to show them light, and the way wherein they should go. Thou gavest also thy good spirit to instruct them, and withheldest not thy manna from their mouth, and gavest them water for their thirst. Yea, forty years didst thou sustain them in the wilderness, so that they lacked nothing; their clothes waxed not old, and their feet swelled not. Moreover thou gavest them kingdoms and nations, and didst divide them into corners: so they possessed the land of Sihon, and the land of the kind of Heshbon, and the land of Og king of Bashan. Their children also multiplidest

> thou as the stars of heaven, and broughtest them into the land, concerning which thou hadst promised to their fathers, that they should go in to possess it. So the children went in and possessed the land, and thou subduedst before them the inhabitants of the land, the Canaanites, and gavest them into their hands, with their kings, and the people of the land, that they might do with them as they would. And they took strong cities, and a fat land, and possessed houses full of all goods, wells digged, vineyards, and oliveyards, and fruit trees in abundance: so they did eat, and were filled, and became fat, and delighted themselves in thy great goodness. Nevertheless they were disobedient, and rebelled against thee, and cast thy law behind their backs, and slew thy prophets which testified against them to turn them to thee, and they wrought great provocations. Therefore thou deliveredst them into the hand of their enemies, who vexed them: and in the time of their trouble, when they cried unto thee, thou heardest them from heaven; and according to thy manifold mercies thou gavest them saviours, who saved them out of the hand of their enemies. But after they had rest, they did evil again before thee: therefore leftest thou them in the hand of their enemies, so that they had the dominion over them: yet when they returned, and cried unto thee, thou heardest them from heaven; and many times didst thou deliver them according to thy mercies; And testifiedst against them, that thou mightest bring them again unto thy law: yet they dealt proudly, and hearkened not unto thy commandments, but sinned against thy judgments, (which if a man do, he shall live in them;) and withdrew the shoulder, and hardened their neck, and would not hear. Yet many years didst thou forbear them, and testifiedst against them by thy spirit in thy prophets: yet would they not give ear: therefore gavest thou them into the hand of the people of the lands. Nevertheless for thy great mercies sake thou didst not utterly consume them, nor forsake them; for thou art a gracious and merciful God.

Is not this terribly sad? As many might word it, "This is the pits!" The more Jehovah God did for his people, even giving them large amounts of land and whole kingdoms, neither of which they worked to obtain, the less most of them showed in the way of thanks and appreciation. Such is behaving like spoiled brats! (And acting bratty does not solely apply to young children!) As we read in these passages, and as stated before, though Israel received punishment from God due to their unbelief by having to wander 40 years in the wilderness, he still provided for them adequately. As just quoted in Nehemiah, the clothes and shoes of the Israelites were kept fresh and new. They had plenty of food and water to sustain their lives. They were not treated like *hardened prisoners* by their Maker. Israel was still, in spite of that nation's sinful ways, treated, yes, most *graciously*! Even witnessing all the great and miraculous works of God right before their very eyes did not humble many of them, increase their faith, or spur them on to maintain their obedience to Jehovah. How little Israel *thanked* God! How little they *obeyed* him! How little *gratitude* this nation felt! Indeed, God was so often gracious to them even in his times of anger, rebuke, and retribution. What a careless and despicable way to treat such a loving God!

Let us return still again to the Apostle Paul's sermon on Mars Hill preached to some men of Athens, Greece. He says in Acts 17:24-25, "God that made the world and all things therein, seeing that he is Lord of heaven and earth, dwelleth not in temples made with hands; Neither is worshipped with men's hands, as though he needed anything, seeing he giveth to all life, and breath, and all things." Isaiah said virtually the same thing as Paul when he told Israel, "Thus saith God the Lord, he that created the heavens, and stretched them out; he that spread forth the earth, and that which cometh out of it; he that giveth breath unto the people upon it, and spirit to them that walk therein" (Isaiah 42:5).

This gracious being you are reading about in this particular chapter, along with all his other characteristics contained in this entire book, is the God that made every part of the heavens and the earth! This is the same God that constantly gives breath and every possible thing needed and wanted to mankind, as well as all of nature! You have *all* that you have because of him! You would not have *anything*, bar none, necessity or luxury, without his gracious consent and loving provision! When was the last time you acknowledged God's graciousness? How often do you do it? What about your very *existence*? As said previously, you are alive right now—breathing—moving—because of God's bringing you into this world through that certain couple known as your parents. You accomplish all the *good* in your life through God's grace. May we never take any of this for granted, but be thankful each and every day of our lives.

When the prophet Joel was calling Israel to repent and fast, he said to them, "And rend your heart, and not your garments, and turn unto the Lord your God: for he is gracious and merciful, slow to anger, and of great kindness, and repenteth him of the evil" (Joel 2:13). Rending (tearing) one's garment was a sign of grief back in those times. Joel was saying these people needed to rend their *hearts* instead! They should feel completely broken inside, thus, sad, and driven to tears, for the way they treated God. If they felt penitence and returned to him, God, in all his wonderful graciousness, would forgive them and take them back. However, this kind of behavior has and does represent much of the entire human race. It was not just shown in the hearts of the Jews of this day and time. Let it not be said in the least that this writer is singling out one particular race.

It is a shame and a disgrace how much of mankind has mistreated God! Many, I mean to say, untold numbers, ought to bow their heads in embarrassment and cry their hearts out right this split second in repentance, for their often lack of remembering who has provided them with all the blessings they enjoy in this life, both temporal and spiritual!

In speaking of *spiritual* things, we must remember once more, as already written in this book, that not only the *tangible* things originate from God, but so do the *intangible* things. One such of many, discussed in God's omniscience, is *wisdom*. James 1:5 once more informs us, "If any of you lack wisdom, let him ask of God, that giveth to all men liberally, and upbraideth not; and it shall be given him." We cannot overlook the fact again that God is a *liberal* giver. It is no different with spiritual things, as well as those physical and material. We must, however, also state yet again that God only answers the prayers of those who do his complete will, for that is what his Holy Word says. The whole point here is that God's graciousness extends to those things we both see and *not* see. One should be deeply moved inside when considering how gracious God is to us.

The Apostle Peter tells the following in his first epistle written to Christians in several countries: "Wherefore laying aside all malice, and all guile, and hypocrisies, and envies, and all evil speakings, As newborn babes, desire the sincere milk of the word, that ye may grow thereby: If so be ye have tasted that the Lord is gracious" (I Peter 2:1-3). The person who habitually practices all the sins listed in these verses (or any sin, for that matter!) has yet to fully "taste" of God's gracious "milk of the word," for had they *fully* done so, they would find that "taste" of God much better than that "taste" of Satan. Since God's graciousness went into giving a "taste" to all *physical* food, the same would apply to the "taste" of all *spiritual* food. None of God's Bible, in other words, has a *bitter* taste to it, although many view it in that manner. This is for sure, because they do not want to give up some of their wrongdoings.

God's graciousness would not and could not allow any of his statutes to be offensive, so the "taste" resulting in obeying him is nothing but *sweet*! That is how far in depth God is in being gracious. Each and everything in the Bible is for our enjoyment, tranquility, and good, not for our detriment.

Jehovah is not a God of deprivation. He is not a "stick in the mud!" God knows all around what is best for us. Spiritually speaking, he does not give us "junk food!"

Of course, we must never forget the greatest example of God's graciousness. This was when he sent his one and only Son Jesus to die for sinful man. In John 3:16, we see again where Jesus says to the young Pharisaic ruler Nicodemus, "For God so loved the world, that he gave his only begotten Son, that whosoever believeth in him should not perish, but have everlasting life." No greater gift was ever given to man than Jesus Christ. Without his coming to earth, nobody would have a chance to live with God in Heaven for all of eternity. Each of us would perish in sin. This part of God's graciousness will be covered at length in the final chapter.

When we stop and consider all we need in life to get by, the extras many of us have, along with any happiness and success we experience, it ought to bring us to our knees in thankfulness, appreciation, humility, and awe to God for his being so gracious to us. It is ineffable. It is so abundant. It can scarcely be taken in without one's emotions welling up inside. We should stand in *amazement* before God on this! His generosity toward us is too wonderful and so undeserved. How so little we are able to give in return for all God has given to us for survival and enjoyment, for we must lean solely upon him in all ways. God is so wonderful a God because, among many other things, he is a *gracious* God!

## Questions

1. Define "gracious," as it is stated in this chapter: "________________

   ________________________________________

   ________________________________________

   ________________________________________

   ________________________________________

   ________________________________________"

2. Name the seven words I used to describe God's graciousness, even though one could find more: (1) ________ (2) ____________ (3) _________ (4) ______________ (5) ______________________ (6) __________________ (7) ________________

3. "But thou, O Lord, art a God full of ________________, and ____________, ______________________ and ______________ in ________________ and ________________."

4. "He hath made his _________________ works to be _________________: the Lord is _________________ and full of _________________."
5. "The Lord is _________________ and _________________, slow to _________________, and _________________ in _________________."
6. "Who giveth __________ to all __________: for his __________ endureth _________________."
7. "But thou art a God ____________ to pardon, _______________ and _____________________, slow to _________________, and of great _________________, and forsookest them __________."
8. "Nevertheless for they great ______________ sake thou didst not utterly _________________ them, nor ______________ them; for thou art a _______________ and __________________ God."
9. "And rend your _____________, and not your _____________, and turn unto the Lord your God: for he is _____________ and ____________, slow to ______________, and of great ____________________, and ___________________ him of the evil."
10. "If any of you lack _______________, let him ask of _________, that giveth to all men _______________, and _______________ not; and it shall be _____________ him."
11. "As newborn babes, desire the sincere ___________ of the _________, that ye may _____________ thereby: If so be ye have tasted that the Lord is _____________."
12. "For God so loved the _____________, that he gave his _____________, _____________, that _______________ believeth in him should not _______________, but have ________________ life."
13. You as the reader fill in your own blank here: "When we count our blessings given to us by God, we find our baskets ________________.
14. Concerning the earth: "He that giveth _______________ unto the _____________ upon it, and __________ to them that walk therein."
15. "And therefore will the Lord ________, that he may be ______________ unto you, and therefore will he be ___________, that he may have __________ upon you: for the Lord is a God of _____________: blessed are ______ they that ___________ for him. For the people shall dwell in __________ at ________________: thou shalt weep ______________: he will be very ______________ unto thee at the voice of thy ________; when he shall _____________ it, he will ________________ thee."

16. "_______ is the Lord, and _______; yea, our God is _______."
17. God FORGIVES, everybody! The trouble with too many people is that they just do not ___ him.
18. God's graciousness has enabled you to, as they say, "do _______ with your ____!"
19. If "tasting" of the Lord is "gracious," then "tasting" of Satan must be "_______."
20. Pertaining to God's graciousness, no greater gift was ever given to man than _________.

Chapter 14

# God Is Merciful

Mercy, like grace, is something that cannot be merited. It is given through pity and compassion to someone who has committed one or more wrongs. It is either granted or it is not, depending on the circumstances and the decision of the one(s) in authority. We find mercy extended a lot in the courts of our land to first time offenders, along with those offenders involved in what is called "extenuating circumstances."

During the reign of Napoleon Bonaparte, a soldier in his army was sentenced to die before a firing squad for desertion. The mother of that soldier pleaded to Napoleon for mercy on behalf of her son. The leader replied to her in words something like, "Why should I grant him mercy? He does not deserve it." The mother replied, "If he deserved it, it would not be mercy." The life of her son was spared. Is it not so true that no one can love like a mother! Mercy, of course, is given by people making up every walk of life, as well, and not just in the area of authority.

Jehovah God is a *merciful* God. We should be ever so thankful for this, or none of us would have any hope of Heaven during this earthly life. The Apostle Paul said in Romans 3:23, "For all have sinned, and come short of the glory of God." All individuals of an accountable age and mind are guilty of sin, or the Bible would not say, "*all* have sinned." It was through God's grace and mercy, due especially to his great love for all of mankind, that he sent his only Son, Jesus Christ, to die for our sins. Paul also stated in Romans 6:23, "For the wages of sin is death; but the gift of God is eternal life through Jesus Christ our Lord." The fact that something has "wages" attached to it would indicate it is *earned*, and thereby, *deserved*!

When a job is performed in any field of employment, the employee has the right to *expect* that paycheck when the time comes. Well, that is on the same level as sin. It "comes with a price," as we often hear it said. A "gift," on the other hand, is something that is not--and cannot be--earned. When a gift is given to somebody, for whatever special occasion, or even if the gift is given on no particular occasion, it is given to the recipient because the giver *wants* to give it, and not because that giver is *obligated* to give it. That "gift of God" was given like any other gift--because God *wanted* to give it. He did not *have* to do so. That is where the subjects of grace and mercy come to the forefront, along with God's being gracious, as was the subject of the last chapter. Were it not for God's mercy, we would all be doomed to Hell eternally. Because "all have sinned," this would mean forthright that none responsible for their sinful actions deserve mercy. Paul further says of God's being merciful, "Blessed be God, even the Father of mercies, and the God of all comfort" (II Corinthians 1:3). The fact that mercy *originated* from God should not surprise us much to read here of his being called "the *Father* of mercies." This title would also indicate the greatness and vastness of God's mercy. Many an individual in the Bible must have recognized the need for mercy in their lives, either when they sinned, or when some unwarranted calamity came their way, for they begged before God that mercy be given to them. You and I have been no different from time to time in our own lives.

The various uses of this word under consideration are mentioned far too much in the King James Version to quote every last one of them. However, we will note a few verses to make our point. In Hebrews 8:12, the writer quotes God: "For I will be merciful to their unrighteousness, and their sins and their iniquities will I remember no more." This was a quote from Jeremiah 31:34. God despises sin of any kind. He does not measure it in *degrees* like much of mankind does. He will punish, and has punished, any person who refuses to repent of their wrongs. He has every right to do so, for man had the *choice* to sin or not sin in the Garden of Eden. It is sad to say, but man chose to sin. God never intended for the human race to stray from his law. The *merciful* part comes in when God said he would "be merciful to their unrighteousness, and their sins." He would forgive anyone if the request was made on his terms, and thus, remember one's sins no more.

All 26 verses of Psalm 136 vividly show God's mercy extending to all in the human race. Every one of the verses end with no exception by saying, "for his mercy endureth for ever." God is merciful to you and I more than we may realize, considering all the blunders, wrongs, and shenanigans we have pulled. Along with being exercised in the courtroom often, as said before, mercy is likewise shown in practically all forms of authority; home, school, employment, military, etc. How could we make it through our lives like we do if no mercy whatsoever were extended to us? We simply could not. This would apply to making an honest mistake, as well as to deliberately doing wrong. How many direct punishments a lot of people have *escaped* because of mercy being extended to them! How many consequences have been made *lighter* due to mercy! How many times one has received a "tongue" lashing, instead of the other type, again, due to mercy!

Actually, a lot of the Bible mentions God's mercy, whether by a *direct* statement or an *indirect* statement. In Psalm 86, containing some of the verses quoted in previous chapters, we find that all 17 of them contain a prayer of King David *asking* for mercy, (along with his recognizing that God has *given* him mercy in the past) by keeping his enemies from taking his life. How much sooner David would have died without mercy from God! In another Psalm David wrote, he takes up the better part of the chapter speaking of God's mercy. Notice verses 8-18 of Psalm 103: "The Lord is merciful and gracious, slow to anger, and plenteous in mercy. He will not always chide: neither will he keep his anger for ever. He hath not dealt with us after our sins; nor rewarded us according to our iniquities. For as the heaven is high above the earth, so great is his mercy toward them that fear him. As far as the east is from the west, so far hath he removed our transgressions from us. Like as a father pitieth his children, so the Lord pitieth them that fear him. For he knoweth our frame; he remembereth that we are dust. As for man, his days are as grass: as a flower of the field, so he flourisheth. For the wind passeth over it, and it is gone; and the place thereof shall know it no more. But the mercy of the Lord is from everlasting to everlasting upon them that fear him, and his righteousness unto children's children; to such as keep his covenant, and to those that remember his commandments to do them."

How *great* is God's mercy? Note that King David said, "For as the heaven is high above the earth, so great is his mercy toward them that fear him." How *long* is it? David declared, "from everlasting to everlasting upon them that fear him." What a comparison!

It always falls back on *obeying* God if one expects, in this case, full mercy from him. In Psalm 100:5, the writer there says in his song of praise to God, "For the Lord is good; his mercy is everlasting; and his truth endureth to all generations." How awesome and wonderful to know that God's mercy never ends! It endures everlastingly to those who follow his commands! Praise be to that!

Look again at the mercy of God expressed by Paul when writing to the Christians at Ephesus: "And you hath he quickened, who were dead in trespasses and sins; Wherein in time past ye walked according to the course of this world, according to the prince of the power of the air, the spirit that now worketh in the children of disobedience: Among whom also we had all our conversation in times past in the lusts of our flesh, fulfilling the desires of the flesh and of the mind; and were by nature the children of wrath, even as others. But God, who is rich in mercy, for his great love wherewith he loved us, Even when we were dead in sins, hath quickened us together in heavenly places in Christ Jesus: That in the ages to come he might show the exceeding riches of his grace in his kindness toward us through Christ Jesus" (Ephesians 2:1-7).

In spite of God's ultimate hatred for sin, he "is rich in mercy," due to his warm and unfailing love for us. He gives you and I every chance to repent of all sin and come to his Son before our physical life screeches to a halt. Without God, we would *have* no mercy. What is even more to consider is that without God's perfect makeup being what it is, there would *be* no mercy!

This writer does not want to leave out something very necessary here. If we *want* mercy from God and our fellowman, then we had better *give* mercy in return! Jesus said in his Sermon on the Mount, "Blessed are the merciful: for they shall obtain mercy" (Matthew 5:7). The old saying goes so true, "You get what you give." People generally act the way they are treated and are treated the way they act. Those who do not *give* mercy to others will not *get* mercy from God, and at times, will not get it from their own fellowman, either. (Even though two wrongs do not make a right, this is what occurs from time to time, nonetheless!)

King David surely had observed what happens to those who give mercy to others, along with his *own* need for mercy. He stated in Psalm 41:1-4, "Blessed is he that considereth the poor: the Lord will deliver him in time of trouble. The Lord will preserve him, and keep him alive; and he shall be blessed upon the earth: and thou wilt strengthen him upon the bed of languishing: thou wilt make all his bed in his sickness. I said, Lord, be merciful unto me: heal my soul; for I have sinned against thee." The individual who practices mercy on those around him is likely to receive it in return when he needs it. This would, of course, include forgiving others who wrong us, for we ourselves have wronged others, be it often or seldom.

After teaching his listeners to pray in what has become known as "The

Lord's Prayer," Jesus said in Matthew 6:14-15, "For if ye forgive men their trespasses, your heavenly Father will also forgive you: But if ye forgive not men their trespasses, neither will your Father forgive your trespasses." It is cut and dried! Forgive others and God will forgive you. Do not forgive others, and you will not be forgiven by God until you decide to forgive others. Mercy and forgiveness go hand in hand quite a lot, and always with God. Referring to the Christians at Ephesus again, Paul told them, "And be ye kind one to another, tenderhearted, forgiving one another, even as God for Christ's sake hath forgiven you" (Ephesians 4:32). He informed the Christians at Colossae, "Forbearing one another, and forgiving one another, if any man have a quarrel against any: even as Christ forgave you, so also do ye" (Colossians 3:13). We not need claim any mercy to be inside us if we do not forgive others—especially when they come to us *asking* our forgiveness.

The Bible records a self-explaining parable of Jesus that teaches the absolute *necessity* of forgiving others, and what will result if mercy and forgiveness are not practiced. In Matthew 18:21-35 it says, "Then came Peter to him, and said, Lord, how oft shall my brother sin against me, and I forgive him? till seven times? Jesus saith unto him, I say not unto thee, Until seven times: but, Until seventy times seven. Therefore is the kingdom of heaven likened unto a certain king, which would take account of his servants. And when he had begun to reckon, one was brought unto him, which owed him ten thousand talents. But forasmuch as he had not to pay, his lord commanded him to be sold, and his wife, and children, and all that he had, and payment to be made. The servant therefore fell down, and worshipped him, saying, Lord, have patience with me, and I will pay thee all. Then the lord of that servant was moved with compassion, and loosed him, and forgave him the debt. But the same servant went out, and found one of his fellow servants, which owed him a hundred pence: and he laid hands on him, and took him by the throat, saying, Pay me that thou owest. And his fellow servant fell down at his feet, and besought him, saying, Have patience with me, and I will pay thee all. And he would not: but went and cast him into prison, till he should pay the debt. So when his fellow servants saw what was done, they were very sorry, and came and told unto their lord all that was done. Then his lord, after that he had called him, said unto him, O thou wicked servant, I forgave thee all that debt, because thou desiredst me: Should not thou also have had compassion on thy fellow servant, even as I had pity on thee? And his lord was wroth, and delivered him to the tormentors, till he should pay all that was due unto him. So likewise shall my heavenly Father do also unto you, if ye from your hearts forgive not every one his brother their trespasses."

There is no "monkeying around" with Jehovah God, gentle reader! Mercy definitely cannot be present unless one has a true forgiving heart. Jesus said, "from your *hearts* forgive." Here was a servant whose Lord forgave him of a large debt he owed, but he was unwilling to forgive his own fellow servant of a much smaller debt owed him. The *amount* of the two debts are not so much the main point of the parable, but rather, the necessity of always practicing *forgiveness* here. Of course, the fact that the servant owed much more to his Lord than his fellow-servant owed him made the unmerciful servant look pretty *small*, did it not? Show mercy to others, just as God and others have shown mercy to you. One who says, "I will forgive, but I will not forget," well, that person has not the least bit forgiven. Such a false-hearted remark tells on itself, and the person uttering it reveals one's "true colors!" No such thing as "half forgiveness" exists. (That is like saying a woman is "half pregnant!") An individual either sincerely forgives or does not do so. Positively no deceiving can be done here, or seeing how much one can "get away" with, where Jehovah is concerned. There is no "looking for a way out," for it is just not there!

How very sad and hopeless it would be for all of us if God had no merciful side to him. Our eternal souls would not stand a ghost of a chance for salvation in this life or in the next life. It would be like trying to store up snow and ice inside an active blast furnace. If you as the reader will just be honest with yourself, you will recall many a time when mercy was shown to you. Did you appreciate it? Were you not greatly relieved? Was it not very comforting? Then do likewise to others. Do not be one-sided. This writer has *certainly* received mercy in the past, to be sure!

Since we can all remember how much we needed mercy, or else we would not have asked for it at one time or another, let us then imagine ourselves in somebody else's shoes as much as possible and, as far as we can see fit to do so, without being a pushover or placing our lives or other's lives in jeopardy, non-begrudgingly render mercy to one another. Let us also not take undo advantage of our fellowman and hence, abuse this thing known as mercy, by repeating the same offenses, and that means to anybody, then turn around and dare ask for mercy for the umpteenth time. Such is "using" people, "playing on their sympathy," and so, brings to the surface an unfair, insincere, and malicious heart. This harbors a rotten attitude! God does not approve of mankind's "playing games" with his mercy, nor anybody's else's mercy!

In concluding this chapter, we should all face up to the fact as to how much we need mercy from God ourselves, for he has to deal with us and all the rest of mankind every day he allows the earth to stand. So, we all should be merciful to others. What a soothing spiritual balm it is to know that Jehovah God is a *merciful* God!

**Questions**

1. "For the ____________ of sin is ____________; but the ____________ of God is ____________________ through Jesus Christ our Lord."
2. "Blessed be God, even the ___________ of _____________, and the God of all _________________."
3. At the end of every verse in Psalm 136, it says, "for his ____________ endureth __________________."
4. "O thou ___________ servant, I ____________ thee all that ________, because thou ______________ me: Should not thou also have had ______________ on thy _____________, even as I had ____________ on thee?"
5. "For if ye _______________ men their ____________________, your heavenly Father will also ___________ you; But if ye _______________ ______ men their __________________, neither will your Father forgive your _________________."
6. "But God, who is _________ in _________, for his great _________ wherewith he _____________ us, even when we were dead in ________, hath _______________ us together in _____________ _________________ in ______________________________."
7. "I said, Lord, be ____________ unto me: heal my ______________; for I have ____________ against thee."
8. "And be ye __________ one to another, _______________________, ___________________ one another, even as God for _____________ sake hath _________________ you."
9. "Lord, how oft shall my brother _______ against me, and I ____________ him? till _____________ times? Jesus saith unto him, I say ______ unto thee, Until ______________ times: but, Until ______________ times _______________."
10. __________________ definitely cannot be present unless one has a true ______________________ heart.
11. "__________________ one another, and ____________________ one another, if any man have a ____________ against any: even as Christ

_______________ you, so also do _______."

12. "The Lord is _______________ and _______________, slow to _____________, and plenteous in __________. He will not always ___________: neither will he keep his ___________ forever."
13. "For I will be _________________ to their __________________, and their ________ and their __________________ will I remember no more."
14. Mercy is deserved. Right_____ Wrong_____
15. "Blessed are the _____________, for they shall obtain __________."
16. "Blessed is he that considereth the _______________: the Lord will _____________ him in time of ____________. The Lord will ____________ him and keep him ___________; and he shall be _______________ upon the earth; and thou wilt _________________ him upon the bed of ___________________: thou will make all his ________ in his ___________________."
17. One who says, " I will forgive, but I will not ___________," has not truly forgiven.
18. "For as the _____________ is high above the ___________, so great is his ___________ upon them that ___________ him."
19. "For the Lord is __________; his ____________ is _________________; and his ______________ endureth to all generations."
20. The old saying goes so true: "You ________ what you _________."

Chapter 15

# God Is Just

Although plenty is mentioned in the Bible about Jehovah's being a God of *mercy*, as the reader noted in the last chapter, he is also a *just* God. He could not be the sinless, flawless, and perfect being he is if he were not one to practice *justice*. No doubt, we all have heard such phrases as, "Justice was served," and, "Is there no justice?"

How so very often questions such as the following are asked: "How can God punish if he is such a loving God?" It is also heard, "How can such a loving God send someone to Hell eternally?" Others exert, "I do not believe God would do such a thing as *eternally* punish!" This writer has to say here, in all humility, that when someone utters such remarks as these, that person: (1) Has not *read* all the Bible, or (2) Has *ignored* what the Bible says about God's many punishments being carried out to so many people listed there. (Besides, why would God bring about a place such as Hell if he did not plan on utilizing it? After all, did he not create Heaven for a purpose too?)

Quite obviously, people often allow their emotions to rule them, regardless of what the Word of God teaches. As the saying is, they "let the heart rule the mind." Those in business will tell you that allowing this kind of reasoning and guidance to reign is just plain outright unwise, more often than not! Justice in many forms is practiced every passing day of our lives, and this has always been the case, not only since God established the first form of civil law, but prior to that. There had to be other examples of justice taking place before the flood—not just those that are recorded in the Bible. Oh yes! Justice came into the world when sin first arrived!

However, let us notice the first establishment of civil law. In Genesis 9:6, after God brought on and completed the great Flood, he told Noah following his family's exit from the ark, "Whoso sheddeth man's blood, by man shall his blood be shed: for in the image of God made he man." This is *punishment* our Creator speaks of here! This is a *penalty*! This is *retribution*! This is God's *revenge* meted out to all wrongdoers! This is *payback!* This is *justice*!

When any type of fine is paid, when that jail or prison sentence is served, when that reprimand is given by that judge or officer of the law, when that death sentence is carried out, this is all under the name of *justice*! There was a law broken; a wrong committed. Even many professed "pacifists" understand a lot of civil justice. If there were no justice, how much *more* crime would continually be committed? How much *less* safe would it be anywhere—outdoors or indoors? How much *more* frustration, misery, fright, antagonizing, agony, and horror would there be among all people? How much shorter would many lives be? This writer refers again to more questions that contain the answer themselves.

Here is some food for thought for any who feel that one can get by in life, thus, enjoy peace, happiness, and prosperity without *ever* retaliating in some way against wrong: *When force threatens, talk is no good!* This writer cares not how one argues it. The more you let some people mistreat you, the longer it will continue and the worse it will get. How far must it go before a *stop* is put to it? How many more physical and emotional scars would result if lawlessness was *not* dealt with in some way? While there is a right way and a wrong way to fight evil, still, it must be battled. Otherwise, many evil doers would never, ever quit or be taken out of society! In Isaiah 26:10, the entire chapter records the prophet singing a hymn of praise to God. He says, "Let favor be showed to the wicked, yet he will not learn righteousness: in the land of uprightness will he deal unjustly, and will not behold the majesty of the Lord." In praying to God for the wrongdoer to be overthrown, the writer of Psalm 10 says of the wicked in verse 6, "He hath said in his heart, I shall not be moved: for I shall never be in adversity." This is how hardened and heartless many godless people feel! No excuses whatsoever will hold water here. Justice is necessary!

How many of you would want every prison cell all over the world to be completely emptied of its inmates simultaneously, especially since a lot of prisoners admit they will never change? This writer certainly does not wish such a thing! Such an atrocity would be equivalent (or maybe worse!) to releasing all zoo inhabitants to run rampant, along with transferring all residents of the jungle to this country, then turning them loose to roam about with no control! What a panic! What a fiasco! Think of the results here! Take away justice, and you have a *madhouse!* King Solomon says ever so truthfully in Ecclesiastes 8:11, "Because sentence against an evil work is not executed speedily, therefore the heart of the sons of men is fully set in them to do evil." When it comes to a lack of justice, or not believing in it, Satan has himself a heyday!

Since nearly everybody of a mind to reason understands many degrees of justice, it has to follow that God is the one who *brought* it into this world due to sin. If sin had never come into the picture, justice would not have been necessary, for where there is no *wrong* done, there is no *need* for justice. Justice only warrants being exercised when laws and rules are broken. The Apostle Paul makes that clear when writing to the church at Rome. He says to them, "Let every soul be subject unto the higher powers. For there is no power but of God: the powers that be are ordained of God. Whosoever therefore resisteth the power, resisteth the ordinance of God: and they that resist shall receive to themselves damnation. For rulers are not a terror to good works, but to the evil. Wilt thou then not be afraid of the power? do that which is good, and thou shalt have praise of the same: For he is a minister of God to thee for good. But if thou do that which is evil, be afraid; for he beareth not the sword in vain: for he is the minister of God, a revenger to execute wrath upon him that doeth evil. Wherefore ye must needs be subject, not only for wrath, but also for conscience sake" (Rom. 13:1-5).

God originated and instituted civil law. It did not come from nowhere, nor was mankind responsible for its commencement. One passage just listed in the last paragraph reads, "the powers that be are ordained of God." Paul said that to resist *them* is to resist *God*! The use of the word "sword" would symbolize authority, along with some sort of punishment for lawbreaking. While there are, and have been in the past, "rulers" who *have* been "a terror to good works," those are the ones who most always are done away with sooner or later. On the other hand, if those in rule practice their authority even in the *least* way that God would have them to do, they will not upset "good works." Justice is not justice when innocent people are punished or mistreated. Justice is only justice when retribution is rendered to those individuals who have done wrong. So when wrongs are committed, justice is necessary. If God is not a God of justice, if he did not mean for any and all sin to be recompensed, why under the very name of "common sense" did he *establish* civil law?

As already said, many were the persons listed in the Bible who received punishment because they disobeyed God, either by doing so directly to him, or by wronging others. Read about Adam and Eve in all of Genesis 3. Notice the great Flood, briefly mentioned already, that God brought upon the entire (then) world in Genesis 6-8. Observe King Saul from I Samuel 9 to the very end of that book. Study on Nadab and Abihu in Leviticus 10:1-7. Look at the numerous times God punished Israel for their idolatry, murmuring, complaining, and other sins told in so much of the Old Testament. There are too many instances recorded in the Word of God concerning Israel's disobedience to cite them all in this book. Then read about one of the King Herods in Acts 12:20-23. See what happened to Ananias and Sapphira, a married couple, in Acts 5:1-11. Jesus mentions punishment in a number of his parables, especially the one on the rich man and Lazarus in Luke 16:19-31, where one example of Hell's existence is given. He speaks of *eternal* punishment in all clarity and detail in Matthew 25. Notice in particular verses 41-46, where Jesus describes the end of time. Read about the vengeance God took upon untold numbers of individuals in Revelation, particularly in chapter 18. *Again,* this writer says that someone has either not read *all* the Bible, or else has *ignored* what its pages say many times on injustice.

All of the aforementioned incidents are but very few examples of God's justice being rendered throughout the Bible. For that matter, many, many promises and warnings are made in both the Old Testament *and* the New Testament of God's saying he will punish those who disobey him. The punishments afflicted upon those disobedient people told of in the last paragraph were recorded in the Bible for a reason. What is that reason? Paul answers this question for us in Romans 15:4: "For whatsoever things were written aforetime were written for our learning, that we through patience and comfort of the scriptures might have hope." Those many examples of punishment penned in God's Word were intended to be *lessons* for us to learn; learn how *not* to live, learn how *not* to think, and learn what kind of an attitude one should *not* have before and about God. In speaking of Hell, the Bible has a lot to say on the subject, to be sure! Such a place does exist! It is all there! Justice! That is another side to God.

In Hebrews 2:1-3, the writer admonishes all who claim to serve God, "Therefore we ought to give the more earnest heed to the things which we have heard, lest at any time we should let them slip. For if the word spoken by angels was steadfast, and every transgression and disobedience received a just recompense of reward; How shall we escape, if we neglect so great salvation; which at the first began to be spoken by the Lord, and was confirmed unto us by them that heard him." God excuses no sin! He punishes all wrongs that are not repented of, as the above verses and many others clearly state. It says, "*every* transgression and disobedience received a just recompense of reward." Hebrews 10:29-30 warns that those who began to follow God, but fell away, will have justice given to them on a larger scale: "Of how much sorer punishment, suppose ye, shall he be thought worthy, who hath trodden under foot the Son of God, and hath counted the blood of the covenant, wherewith he was sanctified, an unholy thing, and hath done spite to the Spirit of grace? For we know him that hath said, Vengeance belongeth unto me, I will recompense, saith the Lord. And again, The Lord shall judge his people." The last verse was taken from Deuteronomy 32:35-36. Hebrews 12:29 says, "For our God is a consuming fire."

God *punishes* sin because he *hates* sin! He has made that very clear in the Bible, as this writer has tried to do in this book. God has the prophet Isaiah also make it clear to Israel: "Behold, the Lord's hand is not shortened, that it cannot save; neither his ear heavy, that it cannot hear: But your iniquities have separated between you and your God, and your sins have hid his face from you, that he will not hear" (Isaiah 59:1-2). This, I say once more, is why Israel's prayers and petitions to God were not heard or honored. If God did not refuse so vehemently to absent himself from the presence of sin, he would not have established justice as his means of *dealing* with it. God must have wanted to get some clear message in his Word across to this world, or else he would have allowed all sin to go unpunished. If not, why not?

While on this subject of justice, let it be known that this writer fully believes in capital punishment. While being a much controversial topic containing intelligent arguments on both sides, that is my position. There are at least 39 examples of capital punishment in the Old Testament. Where the New Testament is concerned, not one place is it stated where Jesus spoke against the death penalty in any way, unlike he taught against so many other things. Nor do you read where God himself condemned it. It goes back to Genesis 9:6, mentioned earlier in this chapter: "Whoso sheddeth man's blood, by man shall his blood be shed: for in the image of God made he man." The argument many give in their disapproval of this particular punishment is by citing John 8:1-11, where Jesus kept a certain woman from being stoned to death who was caught in the act of adultery. However, a careful reading of this story does not show that Jesus abolished capital punishment. When he told the woman in verse 11, "go, and sin no more," he had granted her a *pardon* from her sin, so she received no punishment for it, whatsoever. Pardons have been--and are--granted in our own justice system from time to time for all types of wrongs. Too, Jesus had a point to make here as to how those people in his presence were handling the Law of Moses. It is all shown by the way their consciences worked on them, as verse 9 clearly states. No, this story does not mention Jesus' *repealing* the death penalty. He is merely showing an act of mercy to the defendant. Too, the thing to keep in mind about this accused woman is that she was caught committing *adultery*, not *murder!*

Another thing here: How can any opponent *or* proponent of capital punishment rightfully call the method of lethal injection, "cruel and unusual punishment?" What is so "cruel and unusual" about drifting off into death by a virtually painless means? The only way of passing from this life easier than that is to die in one's sleep—which therefore makes for a very thin and fine line drawn between the two. Besides, it has been most often the case that no "painless means" was used when these convicted killers took the lives of their victims now, was it? I hold no animosity against any of those who are against capital punishment, but again, I do endorse it. I feel I have stated clearly as to why, and that is all I will say on the matter.

Anytime a law officer, or simply a citizen of this country, should swear out a warrant for somebody's arrest, is not *justice* being sought? Yes, it is! If you are suing someone, are you not after *justice*? You are, most definitely so! That is why prosecutors exist, and again, that is why civil law is with us. However, many of us sincerely feel that justice is sorely lacking a lot of times in the judicial system. Laws are at times passed to protect the guilty more than the innocent. Some defendants are released on a mere, minute "technicality," while others are let go for lack of evidence. Too, many has been the time we feel it was a grave error when some proposed evidence was suppressed. No so with the Creator of the heavens and the earth. He merely recognizes pure, unadulterated truth. He only views sin as being wrong, and it is either repented of, or one must "pay the piper!" (Even with repentance, there is still some kind of punishment involved, due to the very nature of sin itself!) Because God is all wise, all knowledgeable, all controlling, and all seeing, and due to the fact that he hates sin to the maximum, he not only judges fairly, he renders his judgments justly! Therefore, he is not wrong in whatever decisions he makes. Justice is a part of his makeup.

Let us not paint God as some sort of being who is so nice, so sweet, so warm, so merciful, so kind, so passive, so understanding, so permissive, so giving, so patient, and so tolerant, that he lets sin go undone without some sort of *infliction* being given in return! The very laws of nature itself are not by any means that way—which God created, as we discussed before. To think of God in such a light is to make him a *pushover*, and one is only sadly being deceived when reasoning this way. God is not one to be "run over." He is not a "patsy." God pours out his wrath on all sinners refusing to repent. He knows no *degrees* of sin. All sin is alike to him. While God's merciful side, as elaborated on in the previous chapter, gives all accountable people everywhere more than enough fair chances to change their lives from sin to righteousness, while he does forgive those who repent on his terms, by the same token, God also has a side of "pay back" he displays to those who will not obey his will. In Galatians 6:7-8, Paul tells the Churches written to, "Be not deceived; God is not mocked: for whatsoever a man soweth, that shall he also reap. For he that soweth to his flesh shall of the flesh reap corruption; but he that soweth to the Spirit shall of the Spirit reap life everlasting." On that same thought, the first part of Hosea 8:7 has God saying to the prophet about Israel's disobedience, "For they have sown the wind, and they shall reap the whirlwind:" Please do not ever kid yourself, gentle reader! For every wrong done, there is a *consequence* to be received by God as a result of it, sooner or later. Jehovah is a God of *justice*!

**Questions**

1. We are familiar with the following phrases: "___________ was served," and, "Is there no ________________?"
2. "Whoso sheddeth man's ______________. By man shall his ________ be _________: for in the __________ of God, __________ he man."
3. Even many professed "pacifists" understand a lot of _______ justice.
4. "Let __________ be shown to the _____________, yet he will not learn _________________: in the land of _________________ will he deal ____________, and will not ____________ the majesty of the Lord."
5. Concerning the wicked, the Psalmist said, "He hath said in his ________, I shall not be _____________: for I shall never be in adversity."
6. "Because sentence against an ___________ work is not executed ________________, therefore the _____________ of the sons of men is fully ___________ in them to do ___________."
7. "Whosoever resisteth the __________, resisteth the ______________ of ____________."
8. "For _________ things were written _________________ were writ-

ten for our _______________, that we through ____________ and ____________ of the _________________ might have _________."

9. "For if the ___________ spoken by angels was _______________, and every _________________ and _________________ received a _____________________ of _________________; How shall we _______________, if we _____________ so great ____________; which at the ____________ began to be spoken by the ___________, and was ______________ unto us by them that ___________ him."
10. While God is a MERCIFUL God, he is also a ______________ God.
11. Why would God bring about such a place as ___________, if he did not plan on utilizing it?
12. "For rulers are not a ___________ to __________ works, but to the _________."
13. God only views sin as being __________, and it is either ___________ of, or one must "pay the ___________."
14. Even with ______________, there is still some kind of ______________ involved, due to the very ___________ of sin itself.
15. All sin is _________ to God.
16. "For he is the ____________ of God, a _______________ to execute ____________ upon him that doeth __________."
17. Name as many examples of justice as you can think of found in the Bible, in addition to those mentioned in this chapter: Include both the Old and New Testaments: (1) ________________ (2) ______________ (3) _______________ (4) _________________ (5) ___________________ (6) _________________ (7) _______________ (8) _________________ (9) _________________ (10) _______________ (11) _________________ (12) ________________
18. Take away justice, and you have a _________________.
19. Justice is not justice when _____________ people are ____________ or ___________________.
20. "Wherefore ye must needs be ___________, not only for __________, but for ____________________ sake."

Chapter 16

# God Is A Rewarder

Our Creator *rewards* those who do his will. This shows Jehovah God to be absent from any degree of *favoritism* in his judgments and decisions, as we will discuss in the chapter on his not being a respecter of persons. This would also have a hand in making God a most *fair* personality. While he punishes for wrongdoing, as we spoke in the last chapter, he also rewards those who do *right*! One may call it "six of one and half a dozen of the other." Since God is equal in *all* things, his rewarding is no different. Like all other sides of God, this area of him is very great, and should be ultimately appreciated by us all.

Hebrews 11 is labeled by some as, "The Bible's Hall of Faith." Many Old Testament characters are listed in this chapter as examples of what comes from fully obeying God, no matter what the situation. These people were highly rewarded for doing so. Verse 6 declares, "But without faith it is impossible to please him: for he that cometh to God must believe that he is, and that he is a rewarder of them that diligently seek him." Faith is necessary to please God, and one cannot read the second half of James 2 without seeing that faith must accompany works! One must *do* if one is to be rewarded by Jehovah, and not just *say* or *mentally accept!* Along with first believing that God exists, that person must "diligently seek him." That requires wholehearted work, for "diligently" means, "honestly; thoroughly; completely; fairly." No stone is to be left unturned. No Bible command can be discarded. God does not reward those who are *selective*, in other words, when it comes to obeying him. God wants *all* or he wants *none* of us. The whole point of Hebrews 11:6 is that God most assuredly rewards. Hebrews 6:10 says, "For God is not unrighteous to forget your work and labor of love, which ye have showed toward his name, in that ye have ministered to the saints, and do minister."

Since there is nothing "unrighteous" about God, that means he has the perfect memory in regards to whom he will reward, making it, therefore, always right. He never forgets anything said or done in his name; that is to say, what is done according to his will. Hence, being as he never forgets, that means he always rewards. We must remember, however, that while many rewards for obeying him are given in this earthly life, the highest reward, and the one for which we should seek the most, is a home in Heaven that is eternal. Just like every sin has its consequence, so does every obedience of God contain some type of a reward.

It should be pointed out here that from time to time in the Bible, the word "reward" is also used to describe consequences and punishments for doing wrong. One may call a "reward" a "result" in the most elementary of terms. So, this writer will use the word in this section of the book as we mostly understand it--that which is a "result" from doing good and right. It is always a refreshing feeling to receive some kind of reward from our fellowman for doing what God sanctions. A reward can be a compliment--verbally or in writing. It can be in the form of a "thank you" by card, by note, or simply orally. It may be a simple nod and/or smile of approval. It may be a monetary gift, or some other type of gift, or token. A reward can as well be a satisfied feeling one experiences when doing a good deed, even if no human recognition stems from it. I merely speak of *feeling* good about *doing* good. There is nothing wrong with that. Whatever, wherever, whenever, and from whomever, we all like to be recognized and acknowledged by others for saying and doing helpful things, along with solving any problems. It is good medicine to the soul. It gives us peace of mind. A reward makes us feel warm inside. It both nourishes and uplifts the spirit.

God is by all means and in all ways no different when it comes to being a rewarder of his commands. The first mentioning in the Bible of the word "reward" is in Genesis 15:1, where God is talking to Abram before his name was changed to Abraham: "After these things the word of the Lord came unto Abram in a vision, saying, Fear not, Abram: I am thy shield, and thy exceeding great reward." God must reward in a very big way, or he would not have referred to his very *self* as that "exceeding great reward." Such was given to Abraham plentifully, as one sees while reading of his life farther on in God's Word. This type of reward will be no different for you and I if we faithfully obey God. In Psalm 19:7-11, King David says, "The law of the Lord is perfect, converting the soul: the testimony of the Lord is sure, making wise the simple. The statutes of the Lord are right, rejoicing the heart: the commandment of the Lord is pure, enlightening the eyes. The fear of the Lord is clean, enduring forever: the judgments of the Lord are true and righteousness altogether. More to be desired are they than gold: sweeter also than honey and the honeycomb. Moreover by them is thy servant warned: and in keeping of them there is great reward." There is nothing more rewarding than obeying our Maker, for his commands are perfect in all ways. They are every one given for our own good, and they are right every time to follow. Here, David calls the benefits of honoring "The law of the Lord" as that of "great reward."

Remember that God is *gracious*, as previously studied, hence he is most *generous* with his rewards. In Psalm 58:10-11 David says, "The righteous shall rejoice when he seeth the vengeance: he shall wash his feet in the blood of the wicked. So that a man shall say, Verily there is a reward for the righteous: verily he is a God that judgeth in the earth." We note here "vengeance" given to the wicked, but "there is a reward for the *righteous*." This shows how fair and just God is. Like everything else about God, he is the top best in rewarding. In Psalm 18:20, the writer tells us, "The Lord rewarded me according to my righteousness; according to the cleanness of my hands hath he recompensed me. The word "recompense" means, "to give in return." In return for having, as the Psalmist says here of himself, "cleanness of my hands," God rewarded him. David said the same words in his song of deliverance in II Samuel 22:21after God protected him from the Philistines and King Saul.

Whatever we do and say, right or wrong, something is given in return. Something is "recompensed." So, why not seek rewards instead of punishments? (Of course, let it be made perfectly clear on this matter that one should not be *self-seeking* when it comes to rewards from mankind, but instead, ought to give God the glory, and hence, should seek being rewarded only from him). Do we want to be "recompensed" for obeying Satan, or do we want to be "recompensed" for obeying God? The choice is ours. No one can "twist our arm" either way.

The wise King Solomon takes up several chapters in the book of Proverbs contrasting the wise and the foolish. Let us notice some of those verses: He tells us in chapter 11:18, "The wicked worketh a deceitful work: but to him that soweth righteousness shall be a sure reward." There is no *guessing* about those who live righteous as to whether or not they will receive a reward. It "shall be a *sure* reward." God will not overlook it or look upon that reward as feeling, "Well, that is not really necessary." Solomon tells us it is "either-or" in chapter 13:13 when he says of God's laws, "Whoso despiseth the word shall be destroyed: but he that feareth the commandment shall be rewarded." That Bible can either *destroy* you or *reward* you, depending on your attitude towards it, which will mean that if one *sincerely* has the right attitude, one will both read and obey that book. In chapter 24, Solomon gives the same contrast cited earlier comparing God's law with sweetness when he says in verses 13-14, "My son, eat thou honey, because it is good; and the honeycomb, which is sweet to thy taste: so shall the knowledge of wisdom be unto thy soul: when thou hast found it, then there shall be a reward, and thy expectation shall not be cut off." If there is a reward for being wise, then there must be a punishment for being foolish, for a reward is the exact opposite of a punishment, as is being wise the exact opposite from being foolish. Therefore, let us be wise. How? By obeying God! Notice verses 19-20: "Fret not thyself because of evil men, neither be thou envious at the wicked; for there shall be no reward to the evil man; the candle of the wicked shall be put out." There can be no possible reward for living wicked. It is solely of a *consequential* nature.

Let us notice another *irony* here, if one really wants to stretch out this subject on being rewarded from God. Why not give it a whole new label? What happens when good is returned for evil? So oftentimes, doing this will blow the enemy's mind! That person will ever so much of the time feel befuddled as to how to handle it! (Admittedly, there are those individuals who, if permitted to continually do so, will *endlessly* play someone for a sucker and a pushover, as some people never, ever quit!) In reading some more in the book of Proverbs, look at chapter 25:21-22, where King Solomon says, "If thine enemy be hungry, give him bread to eat; and if he be thirsty, give him water to drink: for thou shalt heap coals of fire upon his head, and the Lord shall reward thee." Paul expressed the same thought as Solomon in Romans 12:20-21: "Therefore if thine enemy hunger, feed him; if he thirst, give him drink: for in doing so thou shalt heap coals of fire on his head. Be not overcome of evil, but overcome evil with good." Previously in verse 17 Paul declared, "Recompense to no man evil for evil. Provide things honest in the sight of all men." The Apostle Peter said, "Not rendering evil for evil, or railing for railing: but contrariwise blessing; knowing that ye are thereunto called, that ye should inherit a blessing" (I Peter 3:9).

The old saying is applied here that says, "Kill them with kindness." No, it is not a perfect record every time that one's enemy will "soften" when good is returned to that individual for evil, but doing so causes it to occur as a general rule. The really important thing stressed here in this chapter is that God recognizes and rewards those who treat one's enemies this way. This has happened in all walks of life; home, employment, business, society, or whatever! The one who has wronged somebody is treated the exact opposite in return, and the wrongdoer often ends up with a burning conscience!

In his Sermon on the Mount, Jesus speaks of being rewarded after withstanding persecution. He tells the people present there in Matthew 5:10-12, "Blessed are they which are persecuted for righteousness' sake: for theirs is the kingdom of heaven. Blessed are ye, when men shall revile you, and persecute you, and shall say all manner of evil against you falsely, for my sake. Rejoice and be exceedingly glad: for great is your reward in heaven: for so persecuted they the prophets which were before you." The Saviour is closing out those verses many of us have come to know as the "Beatitudes," which is Latin for "blesseds," as he phrases in verses 1-11. "Blessed" means, "Happy; God-sanctioned." We are told here that if we endure and overcome persecution while continuing to pursue and obey God's commands, we will be rewarded. Jesus also stated in Luke 6:35, "But love ye your enemies, and do good, and lend, hoping for nothing again; and your reward shall be great, and ye shall be the children of the Highest: for he is kind unto the unthankful and to the evil." Matthew's version of this is recorded in chapter 5:44: "But I say unto you, Love your enemies, bless them that curse you, do good to them that hate you, and pray for them which despitefully use you, and persecute you." Since God himself is kind, both to those evil and to those righteous, and since we should try and live like God, then this is how we should be as much as possible.

The life of *right* must be sought after, regardless of circumstances—peer pressure, politics, pride, prodding, pounding, plundering, pestering, punching, you name it! No reward or any "peace on earth" is so worth sacrificing one's soul in Hell for all of eternity! The price is much too great, no matter what the enemy threatens and does. God indeed rewards all those who obey him.

Jesus again speaks of being rewarded by God in Matthew 10:40-42 when he says the following to his newly chosen apostles: "He that receiveth you receiveth me, and he that receiveth me receiveth him that sent me. He that receiveth a prophet in the name of a prophet shall receive a prophet's reward; and he that receiveth a righteous man in the name of a righteous man shall receive a righteous man's reward. And whosoever shall give to drink unto one of these little ones a cup of cold water only in the name of a disciple, verily I say unto you, he shall in no wise lose his reward." Mark's account of this says in chapter 9:41, "For whosoever shall give you a cup of water to drink in my name, because ye belong to Christ, verily I say unto you, he shall not lose his reward."

Belonging to Christ is the same as belonging to Jehovah God, seeing as Jesus said in John 10:30, "I and the Father are one." As one lives, so shall one be rewarded. Be absolutely *certain* of one thing, gentle reader: All rewards by God are more important, profitable, and endearing than any *material* reward mankind can give! Please meditate on that thought.

Those who promote New Testament Christianity will be rewarded, as well. Paul tells the Christians at Corinth, "Now he that planteth and he that watereth are one: and every man shall receive his own reward according to his own labor" (1 Cor. 3:8). Those who work according to God's will--not man's--will receive their due reward. Therefore, the reward will be *fair and complete*! In the matter of fully obeying Jesus, Paul said in verse 14, "If any man's work abide which he hath built thereupon, he shall receive a reward." All will be rewarded from God who submit to his will word for word, for his efforts will "abide;" that is to say, remain; stay; endure; last. This means, again, that one's *attitude* will be right, for such an attitude will seek only a "thus saith the Lord," a phrase found many times in the Bible, all in the Old Testament, which means, "God said it." Paul encourages these same people in chapter 15:58 by saying, "Therefore, my beloved brethren, be ye steadfast, unmovable, always abounding in the work of the Lord, forasmuch as ye know that your labor is not in vain in the Lord." This verse reads that the only way a person's "labor" will not be "in vain" is for it to be "in the Lord." The term "in the Lord" means according to the way *he* directs.

Paul exhorts all servants who are Christians at Colossae how to properly treat their masters: "Servants, obey in all things your masters according to the flesh; not with eyeservice, as menpleasers; but in singleness of heart, fearing God: And whatsoever ye do, do it heartily, as to the Lord, and not unto men; Knowing that of the Lord ye shall receive the reward of the inheritance: for ye serve the Lord Christ" (Colossians 3:22-24). The same command is written by Paul in Ephesians 6:5-8: Servants, be obedient to them that are your masters according to the flesh, with fear and trembling, in singleness of your heart, as unto Christ; Not with eyeservice, as menpleasers; but as the servants of Christ, doing the will of God from your heart;

With good will doing service, as to the Lord, and not to men: Knowing that whatsoever good thing any man doeth, the same shall he receive of the Lord, whether he be bond or free." The modern day application we always point out here is in the field of employment where one should work all the time--both when the boss *is* around and when the boss *is not* around. When a person is diligently following God, he will be rewarded in all areas of life, whatever that area be, for how to *conduct* oneself in every walk of life is written in the Bible.

When it comes to endurance and *knowing* you are right with God, the Hebrew writer urges the Christians to whom he is writing for them to, as this writer has stated elsewhere in this book, "keep on keeping on." He warns us, "Cast not away therefore your confidence, which hath great recompense of reward. For ye have need of patience, that, after ye have done the will of God, ye might receive the promise" (Hebrews 10:35-36). We are not to have that "Oh, what's the use!" type of thinking. Like Moses, we are to have *forethought*! This same writer says of him in the chapter on faith already mentioned, "By faith, Moses when he was come to years, refused to be called the son of Pharaoh's daughter; Choosing rather to suffer affliction with the people of God, than to enjoy the pleasures of sin for a season; Esteeming the reproach of Christ greater riches than the treasures in Egypt: for he had respect unto the recompense of reward. By faith he forsook Egypt, not fearing the wrath of the king: for he endured, as seeing him who is invisible" (Hebrews 11:24-27).

This lesson is easy to draw here. Moses *looked ahead*! He weighed the importance of the *eternal* reward against the importance of an *earthly* reward, and guess as to what conclusion he came? The answer is obvious. Moses got his *priorities* straight! When it comes to really worthwhile rewards, where are *our* priorities?

What you do on earth will follow you into the next life. We all write our own *book* in life, and whatever type of *pages* are in its contents is left up to us, for the most part. Again, the latter part of Psalm 90:9 tells us by Moses, "...we spend our years as a tale that is told." Just as a police record follows the criminal all during his life, so does a good record follow the one who "straightens up and flies right," as the teaching goes. In Revelation 14:13, the Apostle John says in his vision, "And I heard a voice from heaven saying unto me, Write, Blessed are the dead which die in the Lord from henceforth: Yea, saith the Spirit, that they may rest from their labors; and their works do follow them." God is keeping a *record* on you and I, and none of us need think otherwise. The text reads, "and their works do follow them." Where did their works follow them? They followed them into Heaven. Why did their works follow them into Heaven? It is because their works were the works of God, and not as much of mankind would otherwise direct. They received their *reward* because they lived *right*! That is why they made it to *Heaven*! So, those who do not live as God directs can only go to one other place—that place already mentioned which is full of nothing but *punishment*! Where will our "works" in this earthly existence "follow" us? Are you and I going to be eternally *rewarded* or eternally *punished*?

When it comes to being rewarded by God, let us not be under a false impression. These rewards from the Almighty are not *merited*. That is to say, we cannot *earn* them. So, we are not to think we *deserve* them. This being the case, we should not have that frame of mind which tells us to see how many "notches" we can have on our belt. Another way of putting it is how many "brownie points" we can collect. Such would make us *vain* individuals in the eyes of God. Paul told the churches at Galatia, "Let us not be desirous of vain glory, provoking one another, envying one another" (Galatians 5:26). He told another group of Christians, "Let nothing be done through strife or vainglory; but in lowliness of mind let each esteem other better than themselves" (Philippians 2:3). When doing God's work, one should not be saying, "Look what *I* am doing!" It should not be the disposition of "me, me, me!" Do not put the spotlight on yourself, for the glory must be given to God, not you.

Going back to Jesus' Sermon on the Mount, he said in Matthew 5:16, "Let your light so shine before men, that they may see your good works, and glorify your Father which is in heaven." Christ did not say to "*shine* your light." He said to "*let* your light so shine." There is quite a difference in *pushing* something to the forefront as opposed to allowing it to reveal itself *on its own*. When receiving praise from others, there is also a difference in "tooting one's own horn," and someone else's "tooting" it for you. Just obey God, and people will automatically see your efforts. You will not have to conduct a "show and tell" for them.

Jesus taught that *grandstanding* is a sin, when he spoke against the scribes and Pharisees in Matthew 6:1-4, saying, "Take heed that ye do not your alms before men, to be seen of them: otherwise ye have no reward of your Father which is in heaven. Therefore when thou doest thine alms, do not sound a trumpet before thee, as the hypocrites do in the synagogues and in the streets, that they many have glory of men. Verily I say unto you, They have their reward. But when thou doest alms, let not thy left hand know what thy right hand doeth: That thine alms may be in secret: and thy Father which seeth in secret himself shall reward thee openly."

Note what Jesus says on individual prayer in verses 5-6: "And when thou prayest, thou shalt not be as the hypocrites are: for they love to pray standing in the synagogues and in the corners of the streets, that they may be seen of men. Verily I say unto you, They have their reward. But thou, when thou prayest, enter into thy closet, and when thou hast shut thy door, pray to thy Father which is in secret; and thy Father which seeth in secret shall reward thee openly."

As many of you know, it was a custom to *fast* in the Bible times. In verses 16-18, Jesus said this on the subject: "Moreover when ye fast, be not, as the hypocrites, of a sad countenance: for they disfigure their faces, that they may appear unto men to fast. Verily I say unto you, They have their reward. But thou, when thou fastest, anoint thine head, and wash thy face; That thou appear not unto men to fast, but unto thy Father which is in secret: and thy Father, which seeth in secret, shall reward thee openly."

God does not want *performers* doing his work, for those who perform do so to get attention, and this is wrong—in the area of religion. Leave performing where it rightfully belongs and was correctly made for--in the area of show business. God does not like a *showoff*! Jesus said, "do not sound a trumpet." Instead, let somebody else do it, as someone will, sooner or later. God expects those to have *humility* when doing his work. The real reward is coming from him, not from mankind. The purpose of doing God's will is to please *him*, not to gain the praise of one's fellowman. Besides, if those watching you possess the right kind of heart that God wishes them to, they, on their own, will praise you for your deeds; but do not *look* for praise. This kind of thing *repels* God. Let *him* do the praising, for when it is given by God, that is where it really matters.

As I stated before, there is a difference between a *gift* and a *wage*. It is the wage that is *merited*, while the gift is *unmerited*. That difference is shown clearly in Romans 6:23 where once more Paul teaches, "For the wages of sin is death; but the gift of God is eternal life through Jesus Christ our Lord." While one rightfully has wages coming—the payback—the recompense—for the job that has been done, this person does not earn a gift. It is handed forth through one's own *free will*, not out of *necessity*. Hence, God does not reward us because we have *obligated* him to do so. How then are we rewarded? How do we inherit eternal life?

Paul tells the Christians composing the church at Ephesus, "For by grace are ye saved through faith; and that not of yourselves: it is the gift of God: Not of works, lest any man should boast" (Ephesians 2:8-9). God knows the tendency lies in much of mankind to boast—brag—gloat—be pompous—over one's achievements and rewards, and he will not let anyone take the glory away from him that he rightfully deserves. It is "by grace" that a person is saved by God, and thus, rewarded in the hereafter. Paul said that this grace was "through faith."

Going to James 2, we find that this must be a *working* faith. This working faith, however, is not a *meritorious* faith, although we still have to practice works in order to be rewarded by God. James says by way of example in verses 14-17, "What doth it profit, my brethren, though a man say he hath faith, and have not works? can faith save him? If a brother or sister be naked, and destitute of daily food, And one of you say unto them, Depart in peace, be ye warmed and filled; notwithstanding ye give them not those things which are needful to the body; what doth it profit? Even so faith if it hath not works, is dead, being alone." Verse 14 begins by asking another question answering itself? In verse 17, it is "spelled out," shall we say, once more, for it reads, "Even so faith, if it hath not works, is dead, being alone." After giving a few more examples of how faith must accompany works, verse 24 reads, "Ye see then how that by works a man is justified, and not be faith only." Then, after another example follows this verse, we note verse 26: "For as the body without the spirit is dead, so faith without works is dead also." James tells us in no misunderstanding terms that faith and works are *inseparable* when it comes to pleasing God, and thus, being rewarded by him. One cannot be without the other.

So, do Ephesians 2:8-9 and James 2:24, along with the surrounding verses *contradict* one another, as many seem to claim? They do not in the least! The key word in James 2:24 is "justified." That word means, "made right." This very definition shows that mankind cannot *earn* his rewards from God, because is it God who does the justifying of man—not man doing the justifying of himself. No individual can make himself right with God by thinking up and exercising his own good works. Only God can do such a thing. That means these two sets of scripture very much *harmonize* with one another. Justification is a *gift*, not a *wage*. It is therefore given by the grace of God, and not because any of us have merited it. However, justification is still needed, for without it, we would not stand the faintest chance of inheriting Heaven.

If I told you I would give you half a million dollars (no, I do not have that kind of money!) for painting my house, that would not be something you earned, because painting my house would not *merit* that much money being paid to you for that kind of job. That would, again, be a *gift*, not a *wage*. However, if you *refused* to paint my house, you would not *receive* that half a million dollars, would you?

Let us always remember to be humble in God's sight when doing his will and conducting his work. While works done for God are not earned, they still must be done in order to receive access into his grace, hence, receiving the Maker's justification. His grace is not handed out to us on "a silver platter." Full obedience is mandatory.

Referring once again to the Sermon on the Mount, may our hearts be as Jesus said in Matthew 5:5, when he spoke the very first beatitude: "Blessed are the poor in spirit: for theirs is the kingdom of heaven." Insert some antonyms into that verse, and you see the very opposite of how to think: "Cursed are the rich in spirit: for theirs is the kingdom of Satan." Jesus told his apostles in regards to the duty of a servant in Luke 17:7-9, "But which of you, having a servant plowing or feeding cattle, will say unto him by and by, when he is come from the field, Go and sit down to meat? And will not rather say unto him, Make ready wherewith I may sup, and gird thyself, and serve me, till I have eaten and drunken; and afterward thou shalt eat and drink? Doth he thank that servant because he did the things that were commanded him? I trow not. So likewise ye, when he shall have done all those things which are commanded you, say, We are unprofitable servants: we have done that which was our duty to do." (The word "trow" means "think; believe") All rewards from God come as a gift for doing right, but that gift will not be given unless one *does* right, does so with the proper attitude, and unless one *does*!

God overlooks nothing that has ever been said or done. He punishes all wrong and rewards all right. That is his demeanor, for he is a sinless God, as already discussed. He is fair to all. No good deed escapes his eye. Whatever you do in the way of his commands will not be overlooked or even half-rewarded. What a wonderful God we have! Among all the other positive traits he possesses, Jehovah is not a God to *cheat* anybody from receiving good for obeying him. He is not a *tightwad*! He is a most generous *rewarding* God!

### Questions

1. Our Creator ________________ those who do his will.
2. "But without __________ it is ______________ to ___________ him: for he that cometh to God must ____________ that he is, and that he a ______________ of them that _____________ seek him."
3. "For God is not _____________ to ____________ your __________ and ___________ of __________, which ye have ____________ toward his _____________, in that ye have _______________ to the ________________ and do _______________."
4. One may call a "reward" a "______________."
5. "Fear not, Abram: I am thy __________, and thy exceeding great ________________."
6. In speaking of obeying God's commands, King David said, "and in ________________ of them there is great _____________."
7. "For ________________ shall give you a ________ of __________ to drink ____________________, because ye belong to ____________, verily I say unto you, he shall not lose his _______________."
8. "Now he that ______________ and he that ______________ are _______; and every man shall receive his own ______________."
9. One mandatory point in the way of being rewarded from God is to have a "thus saith the ____________" attitude.
10. "Let your light so ____________ before _________, that they may ________ your good __________, and ___________ your __________ which is in _______________."
11. There is quite a difference in _________________ something to the forefront as opposed to allowing it to reveal itself ______________.
12. "That thine __________ may be _________________: and thy _____________ which __________ in ___________ himself shall ________________ thee openly."
13. "But thou, when thou _______________, enter into thy ___________, and when thou hast ________________________, pray to thy ________ which is in ______________; and thy __________________ which

is in ______________ shall ____________ thee __________."

14. God does not want ________________ doing his work, for those who ________________ do so to get ____________, and this is wrong.
15. All ____________ from God are a ____________ for doing right.
16. "For the wages of ________ is ____________; but the ________ of God is ______________ life through ______________ our Lord."
17. "Justified" means, "______________________."
18. So, justification is a ___________, not a _____________.
19. "Ye see how that by ____________ a man is _______________, and not by ________________ only."
20. "Blessed are the __________ which ________ in the ________ from henceforth: Yea, saith the __________, that they may _________ from their ____________; and their ________ do __________ them."

Chapter 17

# God Is No Respecter of Persons

When someone is a "respecter of persons", that individual shows favoritism to some people. (If this were not "favoritism," it would not be practiced just on "some people!") Special allowances are made in various areas, as well. To put it simply, *exceptions* are made to the rule. *Partiality* is practiced. Some *slack* is cut. As well, all of us have at one or more times in our lives been unfairly and wrongfully "singled out."

God is not this kind of being. He shows no preference to people when it comes to suffering the consequences for sin, nor does he render special protection to any age group of those who have been wronged in whatever way, including those who are victims of crime. God does not recognize *isolated* cases. If such an innocent one as a baby ingests poison, that baby will suffer, just as anybody else. If a young child is shot, there will be the wounding of the flesh, like all other people. Whoever has one's skin pricked or cut is going to bleed. Whether someone is a law-abiding citizen or an outlaw, they still fall under the same laws of nature. Hence, God does not know any "privileged characters." This applies to *nepotism* as well, a.k.a. family favoritism. God treats *every* part of what and whom he brought into this world as equal, people or otherwise. All laws of nature apply to each part of his Creation. God is not one to break from his set pattern.

Sadly, and sometimes disgustingly, respect of persons is practiced by the human race in every phase of life. There are those who are allowed to get away with some things for which others are disciplined. In the job market, some employees are terminated for breaking certain rules which other employees are let off from with a lesser disciplinary method. Still yet, other employees, when violating company policy, are not disciplined at all! There are individuals who consider themselves "above" civil law. There are some who think they are non-applicable to the rules of employment. There are those who become angry if not *allowed* to be that "exception" to the rule, and this calls for whatever area of life one wishes to bring into the picture. Existing are people who act so brazen as to *demand* special treatment, such as some customers patronizing a business. The attitude is, "I am not like everybody else! I am different! I am better! I am *above* the rules!" As we know the age-old saying, this person is grouped into that "one in every crowd" breed of characters! A number of these so-called "special" people are at times "on the take." There also exists the ones who are known as "sue crazy."

To break down the title of this chapter, individuals such as this want "out of the way" favors for themselves. Grant you, there are cases where exceptions and special allotments must be made, and are. We know these are either "extenuating circumstances," (as spoken of in the chapter on God's being just), or, it may simply be that the one(s) in authority wish to make a once in awhile exception to the regular policy. This is to be understood, for we all have done such during our lives, as well as having been subjects ourselves in this matter under consideration.

However, when some people *demand* to be treated differently to a rule or law simply because they do not *like* that rule or law, or if they think they are "better" than a particular rule or law, or if they think that special treatment rendered to them will bring about some kind of extra gain, these are the ones who cause a low morale in the home, employment, society, and all other avenues of life. If these contrary individuals do not get their way, they badmouth the business and those in authority in an attempt to hurt them, thereby, getting their "revenge!" Some people get a real "thrill" if they can persuade a business or someone in any form of authority to treat them, as said at the beginning of this chapter, as "privileged characters."

This writer has witnessed some who feel like they must "control" the rules of an establishment, along with other people's lives. While oftentimes claiming to want *equality*, this class of persons possessing such nerve instead are really after *superiority*! This brand of conduct disgusts others who try to live by the rules and obey the law. Many times, a bad reflection is cast upon those in the seats of authority who cede to this kind of behavior. (The word "politics" undoubtedly enters into the scene a lot!) In fact, some in authority, in trying to manage and/or own a business honestly, but cannot because of "politics," as said, find their hands tied, or else end up wringing them tightly with frustration and dismay! It is then no wonder why some employees and supervisors seek work elsewhere, why some sons and daughters become estranged from various of their family members, why some couples end up in divorce court, why some friendships end, why some partnerships in business dissolve, and why some people make enemies the way they do. It is often due to this menace known as "respect of persons."

Jehovah God, it is said again, is not this way with the human race or in any other areas of his Creation. If he were, he would not be, as numerously argued aforetime, a sinless being. God makes or allows no exceptions to his commands, and as said, to his laws of nature. There are plenty of Bible verses to show that God does not give preferential treatment to you and I. There are eight passages proving this and stating directly so, beyond any shadow of doubt. We will notice them in the chronological order they appear.

In Deuteronomy 10:17, Moses exhorts Israel by saying, "For the Lord your God is God of gods, and Lord of lords, a great God, a mighty, and a terrible, which regardeth not persons, nor taketh reward." (One cannot *bribe* God to alter his commands!) In II Samuel 14:14, we note where an unnamed wise woman from Tekoah, sent to King David by Joab as a plan to get David's son, Absalom, to return to Jerusalem, says, "For we must needs die, and are as water spilt on the ground, which cannot be gathered up again; neither doth God respect any person: yet doth he devise means, that his banished be not expelled from him." II Chronicles 19:7 has King Jehoshaphat talking to a group of appointed judges: "Wherefore now let the fear of the Lord be upon you; take heed and do it: for there is no iniquity with the Lord our God, nor respect of persons, nor taking of gifts." (Another example of not being able to bribe God!) In Acts 10:34-35, we find a certain apostle speaking to a group of Gentiles: "Then Peter opened his mouth, and said, Of a truth I perceive that God is no respecter of persons: but in every nation he that feareth him, and worketh righteousness, is accepted by him." The Apostle Paul told the Roman Christians, "For there is no respect of persons with God" (Romans 2:11). In Ephesians 6:9, Paul instructs an authoritative group to display good will toward their servants: "And, ye, masters, do the same things unto them, forbearing threatening: knowing that your Master also is in heaven; neither is there respect of persons with him." Paul gives the same instructions to another group of masters when he tells them in Colossians 3:25, "But he that doeth wrong shall receive for the wrong which he hath done: and there is no respect of persons." Then Peter says, "And if ye call on the Father, who without respect of persons judgeth according to every man's work, pass the time of your sojourning here in fear" (1 Peter 1:17).

Now, let us review the phrase and terminology in each of these verses respectively: "a great God, a mighty, and terrible, which regardeth not persons;" "neither doth God respect any person;" "for there is no iniquity with the Lord our God, nor respect of persons;" "God is no respecter of persons;" "For there is no respect of persons with God;" "your Master also is in heaven; neither is there respect of persons with him;" "and there is no respect of persons," and, "the Father, who without respect of persons."

Ladies and gentlemen, to find such a phrase this many times in the Bible and still *disregard* it is to simply *discard* it! God recorded it all in black and white. Some people act like they want it in *color*! God does not show respect of persons to those of any race, gender, occupation (employer or employee), or social standing. In the eyes of the Almighty, being poor does not make one *less* of a person ! Also, in his eyes, being rich does not make one *better* than anybody else! Jehovah sees us all identically the same. That is because we *are* the same in every basic way.

Let us refer again to the universal rules of being human. We all must eat and drink to live. We must all answer the calls of nature. Too, each of us put our clothes on the same way. Civil law applies to every one of us in any jurisdiction where we live or visit. Everybody gets sick from time to time in life, without exception. Everyone of us laugh, cry, mourn, become angry, and hurt (in any way you wish to apply the last word). We must all, if we act as *responsible* adults when on our own, pay debts. Then, we discussed before that nobody is immune to death. People of notoriety die, just as do all others. It is foolish reasoning and wishful thinking for any human beings to think God is going to show respect of persons to them or any of their acquaintances, be that a friend or relative, simply on the grounds that such an individual is special to them, or because that person has reached a particular status or rank in life. God's commands apply to all of an accountable age and mind. Too, remember again that every law of nature applies to everybody and everything, period!

Pertaining to God's commands applying to all who know right from wrong, there are no exceptions even to the angels in heaven. (The word "angel" means, "messenger"). In II Peter 2:4, the apostle says, "For if God spared not the angels that sinned, but cast them down to hell, and delivered them into chains of darkness, to be reserved unto judgment." The same thing is stated by Jude: "And the angels which kept not their first estate, but left their own habitation, he hath reserved in everlasting chains under darkness unto the judgment of the great day" (Jude 6). The phrase "kept not their first estate," means some of those angels left their *domain* in which God had placed them. In Revelation 12, the Apostle John describes a conflict occurring in heaven with the devil and a group of angels who at one time followed God, but had now ceased to do so. Look at verses 7-9: "And there was war in heaven: Michael and his angels fought against the dragon; and the dragon fought and his angels, And prevailed not; neither was their place found any more in heaven. And the great dragon was cast out, that old serpent, called the Devil, and Satan, which deceiveth the whole world: he was cast out into the earth, and his angels were cast out with him."

All punishment told here in the verses cited in the above paragraph occurred because, as Jude stated, these angels "left their own habitation." Then Peter said, "God spared not the angels that sinned." How *permanent* was this loss? John says, "neither was their place found any more in heaven." If God so much as shows no respect of persons with any of the angels in Heaven, what makes any man, woman, boy, or girl think he will do so in regards to any member of humanity? Here were special creatures of God already *living* in Heaven, and yet, they acted against God and ended up being cast out! (Please excuse the dry humor here, but even angels could not "spread their wings!") God is without a doubt *absolute* in his not being a respecter of persons.

This truth applies both to the righteous and wicked when it comes to things in everyday life. We now refer to some verses discussed at length in a previous chapter. In Luke 6:35, Jesus says to a crowd of people during his Sermon on the Mount, "But love your enemies, and do good, and lend, hoping for nothing again; and your reward shall be great, and ye shall be the children of the Highest: for he is kind unto the unthankful and to the evil." (Such was expounded on in the last chapter about the argument of not rendering evil for evil). This may be quite tough to absorb for some individuals, but that is one area true of Jehovah God in regards to treating everybody the same way. Matthew's account of Jesus' same sermon states in chapter 5:44-45: "But I say unto you, Love your enemies, bless them that curse you, do good to them that hate you, and pray for them which despitefully use you, and persecute you; That ye may be children of your Father which is in heaven: for he maketh his sun to rise on the evil and on the good, and sendeth rain on the just and on the unjust." What did we just read? Jesus says first that God "is kind unto the unthankful and to the evil." Jesus then states that our Creator "sendeth rain on the just and on the unjust." God does not give what is called, "preferential treatment."

To say that a person is poor because of living evil is too many times not the case. To believe that somebody is rich because of being godly is to endorse folly. There are rich people who are good and rich people who are evil. There are poor people who are good and poor people who are evil. God does not restrict riches to the righteous and confine poverty to the unrighteous. His mind does not work that way. It is so often left up to the choice of the individual. With others, it is a matter of *chance* either way--that of being lucky or unlucky. Then at other times, one is rendered helpless due to one or more afflictions, sometimes as a result of their own fault, other times stemming from the fault of someone else. However one wishes to hash it, God states explicitly in his Word that he is no respecter of persons. He is totally impartial.

This trait of God must mean, as established before in this book and from the Bible, that he rewards all who obey him and punishes all who disobey him. There is no so-called "understanding" with God when it comes to sin. It is far too tragic that many think differently. Do not let Satan deceive any of you into thinking and believing otherwise. To do so sets one up for a shocking eye opener at the end of time when all will face God at the Judgment, and thus, these naïve people will eternally learn the hard way. Going back once more to Paul's sermon on Mars Hill in Athens, Greece, he told a group of men in Acts 17:30-31, "And the times of this ignorance God winked at; but now commandeth all men everywhere to repent: Because he hath appointed a day in the which he will judge the world in righteousness by that man whom he hath ordained; whereof he hath given assurance unto all men, in that he hath raised him from the dead." The term "this ignorance" Paul speaks of is the idolatry that Athens was deeply involved in, as an earlier part of the chapter tells. Paul also revealed to his audience that God "hath appointed a day in the which he will judge the world." How will he judge it? This apostle taught ever so plainly, "in righteousness."

*Every* way that God will judge will be without error, as have all his past judgments so been. Those rewarded an eternal home in Heaven from him will not receive it by any faulty discernment. By the same token, whomever Jehovah condemns eternally to Hell will not be issued that sentence unjustly. Whether one is lost eternally or eternally saved, that person will know exactly why, with no doubt left in the mind. No so-called "altered decisions" will take place when all souls stand before God at that last Great Day. Due to God's omnipotence, omniscience, and omnipresence combined, there is no way—no, not by any means—that all decisions made by God will not be 100% right, 100% fair, and 100% unchangeable, for they will be, yes sir and yes ma'am!

As with the other areas of his being, God will show all the more his never ending trait of being no respecter of persons. As we know the old saying, "the judge's decision is final." No more accepted cries for mercy will be forthcoming, along with any "plea bargaining" or "turning state's evidence." No gaps or loopholes will work. No apologies or repentance will be accepted from anybody who lived their lives for Satan, instead of to please God. This includes the backsliders--the ones who followed God's commands for awhile, then fell away. All last minute efforts to change any sinful ways will be rejected! No further chances for corrections, or, as previously worded in this book, "mending fences" will no longer be possible. Forget about any postponements, penalty reductions, sob stories, claims of ignorance, or defense lawyers to intercede and/or make excuses for an individual's incorrect conduct practiced in this earthly life, a really *big* one being that of often blaming others for the way one turned out. Forget about pleading for somebody else's soul because that person, as said earlier in this chapter, was cherished by you while living on earth—whether that loved one was your father, mother, sister, brother, grandparent, grandchild, aunt, uncle, cousin, niece, nephew, colleague, or close friend. Every one whose mind possessed the knowledge of right and wrong will be held responsible—completely on their own—for every uncorrected action done and every unrepentant idle word uttered. Nor will anybody be able to beg for your or my salvation. Our actions here on earth will determine our eternal destiny, and nothing else will be a contributing factor. No argument brought up by any soul soon to be cast into torment will be considered, however earnestly and fervently pleaded. No excuses for refusal to obey God will wash. The Creator of the heavens and the earth will not give special consideration to any race, social standing, popularity, or rank had during one's physical stay. Too, no "eleventh hour miracles" will be forthcoming.

Regarding each and every solitary judgment made by God on this day of days, there will be no turning back. Every unfortunate being on the wrong side of God will end up backed into a corner, as all failed attempts are made to talk one's way out of that dreaded eternal burning. As spoken on in the next chapter, all of God's long-suffering will totally, finally, and everlastingly cease! Gentle reader, both you *and* the writer of whose book you are now reading need to seriously think about all this!

God must not and cannot make special allotments to anyone if he is to be a *fair* God. For one thing, humankind is too big in number to expect such a thing. For another thing, God would be violating *his own commands* if he were to show even the slightest favoritism to any of us. He does not--and will not--say one thing, then do something else. Pro or con, God stands on his own will. His merciful side forgives, but his just side renders comeuppance. Neither scale tips the other. Nothing will overlap. When all is said and done, after everything is investigated by example and declaration in the Bible, it is made very clear with no way of misunderstanding it: *God is no respecter of persons.*

**Questions**

1. "God is no ________________ of persons."
2. When someone is a "________________ of persons," that individual shows ________________ to some people.
3. Name the eight known passages in the Bible showing that "God is no ________________ of persons: (1) ____________ (2) ________ (3) ____________ (4) ______________ (5) ______________ (6) ______________ (7) ________________ (8) ______________.
   If someone has discovered other passages, please write them down and cite them.
4. "For if God __________________ the angels that ___________, but cast them down to _____________, and delivered them into ________ of __________________, to be reserved unto _______________."
5. Even angels themselves could not "______________ their wings."
6. Some people, while claiming to want EQUALITY, really want ________________.
7. As especially with God, his decision is __________.
8. "And the times of this ______________ God ____________ at; but now commandeth _______ men ______________ to _____________: Because he hath __________________ a day in the which he will judge the _____________ in __________________ by that man whom he hath ________________; whereof he hath given ______________ unto ________ men, in that he hath ____________ him from the _____________."

9. The Creator of the heavens and earth will not give _____________ consideration to any ________, ___________________, _______________, or ______________ had during one's physical stay. Too, no "______ ________________________________" will be forthcoming.
10. Pro or con, God stands on ________________________.
11. There is no so-called "_________________________" with God when it comes to ______________.
12. "For he maketh his _________ to rise on the __________ and on the ____________, and sendeth ___________ on the ___________ and on the __________________."
13. In God's eyes, being ____________ does not make one better than being _____________.
14. People of ________________ die, just as do all others.
15. "But love your __________________, and do ________, and ________, hoping for nothing __________; and your ____________ shall be ___________, and ye shall be the _____________ of the ___________: for he is __________ unto the _______________ and to the __________."
16. If such an innocent one as a ___________ ingests poison, that ________ will _______________, just as anybody else.
17. When an individuals insists on "respect of ____________" being shown to him or her, they are saying, "I am not like ________________________! I am ________________! I am _______________! I am ___________ the rules." This makes such a person that "_________ in every _____________" type.
18. God does not restrict riches to the __________________ and confine poverty to the ___________________.
19. God would be _________________ his own commands if he were to show even the slightest _________________ to any of us.
20. Name some synonyms that apply to God's not showing preference to any person. Use your own judgment here: (1) _____________ (2) _______________ (3) ________________ (4) _______________ (5) __________________ (6)__________________

Chapter 18

# God Is Longsuffering

The term "long-suffering" means, "long and patient endurance of offense." One may contain patience, but patience only goes so far. This writer learned while serving in the military that there is a difference between strength and endurance. The same thing was also learned by "yours truly" in working out at a health club. To be able to *lift* a heavy barbell is one thing, but how long you are able to *keep it in the air* and curl it is quite another thing. Lifting that barbell is the strength, but holding onto it is the endurance. Hence, to be long-suffering is to possess a high level of *tolerance*.

Parents do not like some of the things their children say and do from time to time, (anymore than mine did!), but because of love for their own flesh and blood, they are long-suffering. They tolerate some or many shenanigans and wrongs, although, if they had their "druthers," those things they do not like would be discontinued. In any case, parents let some things be—some for a spell, some for always. Anytime, however, should their longsuffering of something disliked reach an end, a stop is put to it. I would venture to say that *no* generation of parents or legal guardians were any different. Being a parent myself, I can attest to that. An allowance was made for some things, even though there was no real endorsement of them. The same principle applies to all friendships.

This is the way God is with sin. It has to be so, or the world would have ended no telling how many centuries ago! While we have shown from the Bible in various parts of this book that Jehovah is totally against any kind of wrong living, the fact that the world is still standing indicates our Creator contains *oceans* of long-suffering! This writer will now use the same example stated earlier in this book: Just try to imagine in your own mind the number of people who exist now and have existed in this world since man and woman were first created in the Garden of Eden. Then attempt to multiply that by not only the number of sins committed past and present, but also by how many *times* each sin has been done! After all these estimated calculations, look at it from God's standpoint. If you have any respect and belief for the Bible, you cannot help but then ask yourself, "Why has God allowed the world to stand this long?" The answer lies in one word: Long-suffering. Otherwise, God would have brought all sinning to a head a long, long, long time ago. As stated when discussing the *merciful* side of God, that is why you and I have not always been directly and physically punished for wrongs we have committed, along with at times having received lighter punishments when being disciplined. We should, like many other sides that God possesses, be most thankful that he is long-suffering, or we ourselves would not have been given so much as a *frail* chance to correct our lives--like we have right now, this very moment, so long as we are alive and kicking.

Returning to Exodus 34:5-6, we find God talking to Moses: "And the Lord passed by before him, and proclaimed, The Lord, The Lord God, merciful and gracious, long-suffering, and abundant in goodness and truth, Keeping mercy for thousands, forgiving iniquity and transgression and sin, and that will by no means clear the guilty; visiting the iniquity of the fathers upon the children, and upon the children's children, unto the third and to the fourth generation." Very nearly the same words can be found in Numbers 14:18. We note here where God does not want sin in anyone's life, but he is long-suffering in giving a person many opportunities to correct it during one's earthly stay. Showing again God's generosity, the word "abundant" is used in the passages quoted from Exodus. Doubtless, he has an unthinkable amount of long-suffering within him. Mercy, grace, and goodness could not be extended from God for as long as it has been to you, me, others, and those who have lived in the past, without there being long-suffering. Is it not something how so many traits go hand in hand! When one is removed, the others either weaken or fall.

In Psalm 86:15 King David says, "But thou, O Lord, art a God full of compassion, and gracious, long-suffering, and plenteous in mercy and truth." God, being the loving Lord he is, wishes the *best* for his offspring. He wants us to be happy, contented, and wanting in nothing, be that of a temporal or spiritual nature. It is a hard lesson that many never learn, but *real* happiness is not found, nor *can* it be found, in material things. It comes from *within* a person! Some people can be happy and contented with having less physical possessions than others. Actually, many have been and are the individuals who are never happy, no matter how much goods or wealth they gain in life. God's Word states so many times that to *obey* him is real peace and contentment. His long-suffering to mankind exists, among other reasons, for the purpose of trying to get us to understand this.

God's longsuffering also extends to all people and to every one of their sins, for he wants nobody to be eternally lost. One example we will study is hypocritical judging of others. The Apostle Paul tells the Christians at Rome, "Therefore thou are inexcusable, O man, whosoever thou art that judgest: for wherein thou judgest another, thou condemnest thyself; for thou that judgest doest the same things. But we are sure that the judgment of God is according to truth against them which commit such things. And thinkest thou this, O man, that judgest them which do such things, and doest the same, that thou shalt escape the judgment of God? Or despisest thou the riches of his goodness and forbearance and long-suffering; not knowing that the goodness of God leadeth thee to repentance" (Romans 2:1-4)? Whether it pertains to one-sided judging mentioned here, or whether to anything else sinful, we find in this reading that God's long-suffering is a sure sign that all who make up humanity are given ample opportunity to *cease* doing so, before it is forever too late.

In the entire chapter of 2 Peter 3, the apostle is dealing with skeptics of his day and time who question whether there is such a thing as the end of time. Reading verses 3-9, we find this: "Knowing this first, that there shall come in the last days scoffers, walking after their own lusts, And saying, Where is the promise of his coming? for since the fathers fell asleep, all things continue as they were from the beginning of the creation. For this they willingly are ignorant of, that by the word of God the heavens were of old, and the earth standing out of the water and in the water: Whereby the world that then was, being overflowed with water, perished: But the heavens and the earth, which are now, by the same word are kept in store, reserved unto fire against the day of judgment and perdition of ungodly men. But, beloved, be not ignorant of this one thing, that one day is with the Lord as a thousand years, and a thousand years as one day. The Lord is not slack concerning his promise, as some men count slackness; but is long-suffering to us-ward, not willing that any should perish, but that all should come to repentance."

Time means nothing to God, as we just read and elaborated on in the chapter of his being *everlasting*. Peter, of course, spoke briefly in the above cited verses of the great Flood that God brought upon the earth in the days of Noah (Genesis 6-8). Everything was going on in life as normal when God's long-suffering ended. It was then that the rain came and drowned out all living things not inside the ark God had Noah to build. On that same parallel, Peter declares that the world has yet to be eternally destroyed—even to this very day and moment—because of God's long-suffering. The only reason that the world *exists* right now is not so life can go on as normal with all of its daily activities, be they right or be they sinful. All of the Creation still remains in order to give all of mankind a fair chance to discontinue listening to Satan and turn one's life over to God. Peter relays the same thought pertaining to God's long-suffering in the following verses: "For Christ also hath once suffered for sins, the just for the unjust, that he might bring us to God, being put to death in the flesh. but quickened by the Spirit: By which also he went and preached unto the spirits in prison; Which sometime were disobedient, when once the long-suffering of God waited in the days of Noah, while the ark was a preparing, wherein few, that is, eight souls, were saved by water" (I Peter 3:18-20).

All people in Noah's time, except eight persons, disregarded God's long-suffering until it was forever too late to do any changing. They did not listen, for these individuals did not care, because they did not *believe* Noah when he preached to them, fairly warning them of that truly upcoming rain of rains. God gave them 120 years to repent of their sins, but they flagrantly declined to do so. Proof of this time element is in Genesis 6:3: "And the Lord said, My spirit shall not always strive with man, for that he also is flesh: yet his days shall be a hundred and twenty years." Only Noah and his family ended up escaping those waters of death. Nobody else heeded Noah's words. Jesus himself said that very thing: "But as the days of Noah were, so shall also the coming of the Son of man be. For as in the days that were before the flood they were eating and drinking, marrying and giving in marriage, until the day that Noah entered into the ark, And knew not until the flood came, and took them all away; so shall also the coming of the Son of man be" (Matthew 24:37-39).

Just as life was going on in the usual way, and Noah's preaching was disregarded all the way up to the day of the great Flood, so it has been with so many people since then, and so it will be clearly up to the end of this world. People will continue to repeatedly *push* the long-suffering of God until he has taken enough. Then, he will put an end to it all forever.

How can we *specifically* define the long-suffering of God? Well, we already have, in a sense. Look, however, at the first part of II Peter 3:15 where the apostle remarks, "And account that the long-suffering of our Lord is salvation." There are those who have genuinely decided to come to God's obedience, and this was due to his long-suffering in waiting on them to cast aside their sinful lives. No long-suffering, and there is no chance for correction and reconciliation. We just read in the Bible, howbeit, that God's long-suffering does not continue on forever. As most any length of long-suffering ceases with all of us sooner or later, so it too comes to an end with God somewhere in time. There are other instances of this recorded in the Bible. So, on that same note, and even more sobering, this thing known as long-suffering will one day stop eternally with our Maker, where this world and sin are concerned.

If anyone is to be like God, then long-suffering must be a part of one's life as long as possible. Patience truly is a virtue, and patience will produce long-suffering. This is one of the fruits of the Spirit mentioned in Galatians 5:22. Think how your daily existence would be if *nobody* ever showed long-suffering to you and I! How merciless, unkind, and excruciatingly *tough* life would treat us! This would be even more the case when it comes to making amends with others; "mending fences," as it has been aforetime worded.

God is so unique, the more he is studied about in that great "book of books" known as the Bible. He has the greatest concern for all of us. Without God's containing all the colossal traits that he reveals of himself to us, how could we *succeed* as we do? The words "apology," "atonement," "reconciliation," and others of like nature could never be in one's daily walks of life, for God would not accept them or any other penitence for sin. God wants us to be with him in Heaven when our life on earth comes to a halt. That is why he is "*long-suffering* to us-ward!"

**Questions**

1. "Long-suffering" means, "______________________________________________ ______________________________________________."
2. "But thou, O Lord, art a God full of ______________, and ____________, and ____________________, and ________________ in __________ and ____________."
3. "Or despisest thou the ______________ of his _____________ and _______________ and ____________________; not knowing that the _______________ of God leadeth thee to ________________?"

4. "Which sometime were ______________, when once the __________ of God __________ in the days of ________, while the _______ was a preparing, wherein ______, that is, ____ souls, were saved by __________."
5. "And account that the _____________________ of our Lord is _________________."
6. "The Lord is not ___________ concerning his ______________, as some men count _______________; but is ______________ to usward, not willing that any should _____________, but that all should come to ________________."
7. "The Lord God, ______________ and ___________, ___________, and ______________ in ___________ and __________, Keeping _____________ for _______________, forgiving __________ and _________________ and ________, and that will be ____ means clear the ______________."
8. To be ___________________ means to possess a high level of _________________.
9. "And the Lord said, My _________ shall not always ___________ with man, for that he also is __________: yet his days shall be ____ _____________________________________________."
10. People will continue to repeatedly _______ the _________________ of God until he has taken enough.
11. "For as in the days that were before the _________ they were _______ and ______________, _______________ and ____________ in _________________, until the _________ that ________ entered into the ________, And knew _______ until the ___________ came, and took them _______ away."
12. Other than Noah and his family, ________________ heeded Noah's warning about the great Flood.

Chapter 19

# God Is Jealous

When coming upon the word "jealous" in the Bible as being another trait of Jehovah God, one may be surprised. After all, being jealous is nearly always looked upon in a negative way, so it could be very well believed by some to be a weakness. It is argued to be a characteristic in which many say cannot be helped. One is jealous of one's spouse. One sibling is jealous of another sibling. One friend feels jealousy towards another friend. Some people are jealous of somebody else's spouse, companion, friend, influence, popularity, wealth, possessions, success, occupation, authority, position of employment, etc. Whether relative, friend, co-worker, casual acquaintance, or even stranger, this matter of jealousy is manifested in all walks of life. Some of it is kept under control, and some is not. Some jealousy is hidden, while other times it is displayed—often quite openly. This of course depends on each person and how much self-control one has, along with someone's basic character.

Jealousy, in one sense, is on its way when people feel envy (known as that "green-eyed monster") for others in some way, and that "monster" is allowed to get the best of them. There are people who take leave of their senses, lose their composure, make fools of themselves around their fellowman, lose sleep, commit a crime(s), and exploit their victims when displaying their streaks of jealousy. This feeling of being jealous also rears its head whenever some individual or group suspicions that their territory, be it a person, object, or area, is either threatened to be taken away from them, or *has* been taken from them.

Then, as mankind is most always prone to *extremism*, there are those who are so jealous so often, if their jealousy were *cancer*, it would have killed them a long time ago! As with every family, so I too have witnessed this kind of behavior from those on both sides of my own kin. However, there have been times in all our lives when we have felt some degree of jealousy. We may as well admit this, (though some of us might be hesitant to do so) for it is the complete truth. Some individuals deliberately provoke jealousy in others as a means of spite and vengeance, while there are those who are honestly unaware they are doing so. Others cause jealousy in an effort to try and rekindle a relationship with, and/or "hook" someone of, the opposite sex.

Too, possessing some form of jealousy is right. Even those who have little or no jealousy in their nature feel it on occasions, due to their mistreatment, justifiable suspicion, and neglect. *Covetousness*, which is a strong desire to have something or someone, can and does lead to jealousy if not held in check. In fact, covetousness, one may word it, is a close "cousin" to jealousy. The very last of the Ten Commandments given to Israel directly told that nation in Exodus 20:17, "Thou shalt not covet thy neighbor's house, thou shalt not covet thy neighbor's wife, nor his manservant, nor his maidservant, nor his ox, nor his ass, nor anything that is thy neighbor's." Coveting often leads to other sins as well, such as adultery, stealing, and murder.

One more thing before I continue here: There is a difference in being "jealous" and simply "protecting one's own interests," of which I never hold against anybody for doing. You will find me no different in this area, I assure you! While I am not a jealous man, nonetheless, there have been some rare times in my life I have felt a need to step into a situation and speak out.

Since God is said to be a *jealous* God, there must be nothing wrong in his feeling that way. So, in his case, it has be justified. After all, we have spent this entire book on showing by the Bible how sinless and perfect God is. This writer just stated two paragraphs ago that one form of jealousy, I speak of covetousness, is a strong desire to have something or someone. This "strong desire" is not always out of place. In warning the Christians at Corinth against false teachers, the Apostle Paul said, "Would to God ye could bear with me a little in my folly: and indeed bear with me. For I am jealous over you with godly jealousy: for I have espoused you to one husband, that I may present you as a chaste virgin to Christ. But I fear, lest by any means, as the serpent beguiled Eve through his subtilty, so your minds should be corrupted from the simplicity that is in Christ" (II Corinthians 11:1-3). Paul uses the term "godly jealousy." So, not all jealousy is bad. Therefore, not all jealousy is sinful or *leads* to sin. Some of it must be right, or, again, jealousy would not be contained in the versatile makeup of God.

Paul further stated in Chapter 12:31, "But covet earnestly the best gifts: and yet show I unto you a more excellent way." These last two verses *plainly* inform us that not all areas of jealousy and covetousness are wrong.

God's being jealous goes as far back as his establishment of the Ten Commandments, the last one of which was already mentioned in this chapter. Hear what he has to say on commandment number one: "Thou shalt have no other gods before me. Thou shalt not make unto thee any graven image, or any likeness of any thing that is in heaven above, or that is in the earth beneath, or that is in the water under the earth: thou shalt not bow down thyself to them, nor serve them: for I the Lord thy God am a jealous God, visiting the iniquity of the fathers upon the children unto the third and fourth generation of them that hate me" (Exodus 20:3-5).

God is jealous because he does not wish to be, nor *will* he be, in competition with any idol, as was expounded on extensively in the chapter entitled, "God Is One." He wanted the Israelite nation to worship him *exclusively* and *conclusively*! You as the reader can note all throughout the Old Testament where God enforced this command quite repeatedly, and such is also recorded, not surprisingly, in the New Testament.

Just how much does the Almighty Creator *despise* idolatry? In Psalm 78:58-66, Asaph, in referring to those in Israel who were unfaithful to God, informs us, "For they provoked him to anger with their high places, and moved him to jealousy with their graven images. When God heard this, he was wroth, and greatly abhored Israel: so that he forsook the tabernacle of Shiloh, the tent which he placed among men; and delivered his strength unto captivity, and his glory into the enemy's hand. He gave his people over also unto the sword; and was wroth with his inheritance. The fire consumed their young men, and their maidens were not given to marriage. Their priests fell by the sword; and their widows made no lamentation. Then the Lord awaked as one out of sleep, and like a mighty man that shouted by reason of wine. And he smote his enemies in the hinder parts: he put them to a perpetual reproach."

Referring again to the chapter on "God Is One," it can very well be said that Israel had *poisoned* their minds, and thus, *polluted* themselves before their Maker, due to their worshipping of idols. These aforementioned verses should show us that God desires *all* of us, or he wants *none* of us, as argued elsewhere! What applies to an earthly marriage so applies to worshipping God, where *faith* and *fidelity* are concerned. Since Jehovah is the one and only true God, he has every sovereign and supernal *right* to be jealous of all the human race which he created when it comes to paying homage to him, for he *deserves* that homage. Most all of us are familiar with the saying, "Hell hath no fury as a woman scorned." Such is very right! (Is not that so, ladies?) Well, this is all the more true with God. We can say of him, "Hell hath no fury as GOD scorned!" Push him to jealousy, do not repent of it, and your fate will be the same, in a manner of speaking, as that which you just read about in those scriptures cited in the above paragraph. This case is multiplied numerous times in the Bible. God punishes all who bring out his jealousy.

God's jealousy was also displayed to the church at Laodicea, the sorriest of all the seven churches of Asia. Not one favorable thing was said about this particular congregation. The information on these churches cover the entire chapters of Revelation 2 and 3. Jesus, having dictated to the Apostle John what to write in each of the letters to them, said of Laodicea, "I know thy works, that thou art neither cold nor hot: I would thou wert cold or hot. So then because thou art lukewarm, and neither cold nor hot, I will spew thee out of my mouth. Because thou sayest, I am rich, and increased with goods, and have need of nothing; and knowest not that thou art wretched, and miserable, and poor, and blind and naked: I counsel thee to buy of me gold tried in the fire, that thou mayest be rich; and white raiment, that thou mayest be clothed, and that the shame of thy nakedness do not appear; and anoint thine eyes with eyesalve, that thou mayest see" (Revelation 3:15-18).

Here we just read about a group who saw themselves one way, but God saw them another way. Hence, the way God viewed them had to be the *right* way. Laodicea needed to make some crucial changes. They were fairly warned to face reality; to wake up; to *prove* themselves before God; to actually become what they *professed* to be, and that was followers of his Word. This church was living a *half-baked* religion. God called them "lukewarm." Just like any lukewarm water we drink makes for a bad taste, which then results in the expelling of it from our mouths, so it was likewise felt by God here in a figurative way, for he said, "I will spew thee out of my mouth." Being lukewarm carries with it the idea of half-doing something; half-pretending; half-hearted; being half-real; half there; half trying. This brings out the jealousy in God, for he wants us to give him our every effort.

The Israelites, I am sad to say yet once more, received punishment time and time again for provoking God to jealousy. In Ezekiel 39:25 the prophet says, "Therefore thus saith the Lord God; Now will I bring again the captivity of Jacob, and have mercy upon the whole house of Israel, and will be jealous for my holy name." The fact that God refers to his name as being "holy" would signify why he was almost constantly, *if* not constantly, jealous of Israel: They had profaned his name by being untrue to him, which had made them *un*holy. Their idolatry could be interpreted as *spiritual adultery*. If they would repent, and hence, return to worshipping and serving God only, he would "have mercy upon the whole house of Israel," pardon them, and take them back. How loving a Father he was to his one time chosen people! No matter how often they acted traitorous and spiritually adulterous to him, (which often led them to behave *literally* adulterous, too) he would always "forgive and forget" when they fully repented.

Grant you, some areas of God's jealousy may be hard to fathom. In Luke 14:26 Jesus said to a great number of people, "If any man come to me, and hate not his father, and mother, and wife and children, and brethren, and sisters, yea, and his own life also, he cannot be my disciple." "Hate my own *family* members," you may retort? Hold on, gentle reader! There is a sensible explanation that follows. Please here this writer out. The definition and application of many words centuries ago were different as to what they are now. When Jesus spoke this command, the word "hate" not only meant to "despise," it also meant to "love less." Being as several other passages in the Bible teach what the proper feeling, behavior, and respect must be toward one's family members, along with giving examples, one has to conclude that Jesus is not saying to "despise" your family members, but instead, to love them *less,* whenever it comes to following him. That is saying a lot for both Jesus and family alike, since we are to love them both very much. Where Jesus is concerned, however, he is to be "top priority." This is backed up and explained by another Bible passage, also spoken by Jesus. In Matthew 10:37, Jesus says to his apostles, "He that loveth father or mother more than me is not worthy of me: and he that loveth son or daughter more than me is not worthy of me."

It then stands to reason that "hate" would mean to love *less* in one area, while loving *more* in another area. By simple reasoning, what is contained less in one department will often be contained more in another department. Moses tells Israel in Deuteronomy 6:5, "And thou shalt love the Lord thy God with all thine heart, and with all thy soul, and with all thy might." When repeating these most nearly same words, Jesus adds in Luke 10:27, "...and with all thy strength, and with all thy mind..."

So, love your family members dearly, but know without reservation that only Jesus can save your soul eternally in Heaven when all else is said and done. (Furthermore, this force known as "peer pressure" will also not save you eternally!) We find the word "love," as it is used in the Bible, means more than just a *feeling*. The word also indicates a *priority,* as stated two paragraphs ago about how one should love Jesus, and as God ever so much desired Israel to recognize and practice before him.

Mankind is promised by God that those who fully live according to his commandments will not ever go without the necessities of life. (More will be said on God's promises in the next chapter). Jesus said in his Sermon on the Mount in Matthew 6:33, "But seek ye first the kingdom of God, and his righteousness; and all these things shall be added unto you." The word "first" can only point to that which is the greatest need; the top concern; that of being the most basic urgent requirement for one's spiritual guidance. The term "all these things" refer to the food and raiment (clothing) needed by everyone of us in verse 25. King David tells us in Psalm 37:25, "I have been young, and am now old; yet have I not seen the righteous forsaken, nor his seed begging bread." Hence, there is no need to provoke God's jealousy by worshipping other gods or by solely going after the things of this world, thus, leaving God out of your life totally, or treating him miscellaneously. Such is also a *figurative* form of idolatry.

We now come back to a word already used in this chapter when speaking of idolatry, and that is *covetousness*. Paul told the Christians at Colossae, "Mortify therefore your members which are upon the earth; fornication, uncleanness, inordinate affection, evil concupiscence, and covetousness, which is idolatry: For which things' sake the wrath of God cometh on the children of disobedience: In the which ye also walked some time, when ye lived in them" (Colossians 3:5-7). When you "mortify" something, you destroy it; deaden it. Paul said likewise in reference to covetousness to the church at Ephesus: "For this ye know, that no whoremonger, nor unclean person, nor covetous man, who is an idolater, hath any inheritance in the kingdom of Christ and of God" (Ephesians 5:5). This is the problem with too many people. They often do not know when to *mortify* or *fortify!*

To let anything or anyone else come first in one's life before Jehovah God is to be equally as guilty of idolatry as bowing down before a graven image. We just read it in the Bible. Either way that it is argued on idolatry, this makes God jealous. Treating him so shows the wrong attitude. To act in this manner brings out a half-giving heart, and God wishes our hearts to be *fully* given over to him.

The fact that God has a jealous side to him indicates not only his willingness for us to obey his every command, but also shows that he is a being who possesses *emotions*, as this writer expressed about our Creator in the "Foreword" section of this book. God could not have much, if any, of his other mannerisms listed in the Bible if he were not this way. He hurts inwardly just like you and I. God wants us completely devoted to him. He will settle for nothing less. He does not tolerate so much as *second* place, let alone, third, fourth, and so on. Jehovah will not be satisfied with wearing the title "runner up." He wants every part of you, and positively *nobody* has the right to think *ill* of God for his feeling as he does along this line. He will not stand for anything or anyone else coming between man and him. He is a *jealous* God!

**Questions**

1. "_______________" is nearly always looked upon in a _______________ way.
2. "_____________" is known as that "green-eyed ________________."
3. "Thou shalt not ___________ thy neighbor's __________, thou shalt not _________ thy neighbor's __________, nor his ________________, nor his _____________________, nor his _________, nor his _____, nor _________ that is thy neighbor's."
4. There is a difference is being "_____________" and simply "protecting one's own _________________."
5. "For I am _____________ over you with _____________________: for I have _________________ you to _________ husband, that I may present you as a __________________________ to Christ."
6. "But _________ earnestly the _________ gifts: any yet show I unto you a more ___________________ way."
7. Based on the two above quoted Bible passages, not ALL coveting and ________________ are wrong. Right ____ Wrong____
8. When you "mortify" something, you ______________ and ___________ it.
9. "But seek ye _________ the kingdom of _____, and his _______________; and all these things shall be _________ unto you."

10. "_______________ therefore your ______________ which are upon the ____________; _______________, ________________, ____________, and _____________, which is ___________: For which thing" sake the __________ of God cometh on the children of ____________________."
11. God wants us completely ______________ to him.
12. Jehovah will not be _________________ with wearing the title "____________________."
13. "For they _____________ him to _________________ with their __________________, and _________ him to _____________ with their ___________________."
14. "For I the Lord am a ______________ God, visiting the ___________ of thc _________________ upon the ______________ unto the ________ and __________ generation of them that _________ me."
15. Not only does "Hell hath no ___________ as a __________ scorned," but even MORESO, "Hell hath no ___________ as _______ scorned."
16. "Therefore thus saith the Lord God; Now will I bring again the captivity of __________, and have _________ upon the ________ house of Israel, and will be ____________ for my __________ name."
17. "If__________ man come to me, and __________ not his __________, and ________________, and ______________ and _____________, and _______________, and _______, yea, and his own __________ also, he cannot be my __________________."
18. "Hate," as it is used at times in the Bible means, "______________."
19. Numbers 17 and 18 above are explained and illustrated by Jesus in the following passage: "He that ___________ father or mother _________ than me is not _____________ of me: and he that _____________ son or daughter ____________ than me is not ______________ of me."
20. "For this ye know, that no ___________________, nor ___________ person, nor ________________ man, who is an _____________, hath any __________________ in the kingdom of __________ and of ______________."

Chapter 20

# God Is Keeper of All His Promises

All of us have made promises and not lived up to them. While we have definitely kept some, such has not always been the case. Even the best of people have gone back on their word, whether deliberately or unintentionally. While some promises were made that were impossible to fulfill, those stated of which the individual never intended to keep, or those pledged and were not kept due to unforeseen circumstances, there are promises that have been broken. When this happens, disappointment and/or hurt most always result. Anger at times shows itself, as well. Whatever the cause, we have not honored all our promises, we have known those who have not done so either, and they likewise have known others who have been the same. In reality, we do not believe in the saying, "Promises were made to be broken." We especially feel this way when someone breaks a promise made to us.

God, being the *sinless* personality he is (as studied in chapter 6), does not make any promise that is not carried out, those promises being good or bad. He is a faithful and true God, always living up to what he says he will do. This also applies to that promise being big or little, as mankind may so judge it. God never forgets, so his mind is sharp and alert every second. This is another reason he keeps all his promises, which accompanies his being perfect in every way.

First of all, God's promises are what we can fully label "tit for tat." His promises of *rewards* are just as sure as his promises for *punishments*, and vice-versa, both of which we have studied. Good or bad, Jehovah always upholds his vows. Make no mistake about it and never doubt it. Thus, whatever the Bible says about God's promises, we can just accept it to be genuine—pure—foolproof.

Let us notice first God's promises to Israel in the way of *punishment* for disobedience. Moses tells the people this in Deuteronomy 28:15-29: "But it shall come to pass, if thou wilt not hearken unto the voice of the Lord thy God, to observe to do all his commandments and his statutes which I command thee this day; that all these curses shall come upon thee, and overtake thee: Cursed shalt thou be in the city, and cursed shalt thou be in the field. Cursed shall by thy basket and thy store. Cursed shall be the fruit of thy body, and the fruit of thy land, the increase of thy kine, and the flocks of thy sheep. Cursed shalt thou be when thou comest in, and cursed shalt thou be when thou goest out. The Lord shall send upon thee cursing, vexation, and rebuke, in all that thou settest thine hand unto for to do, until thou be destroyed, and until thou perish quickly; because of the wickedness of thy doings, whereby thou hast forsaken me. The Lord shall make the pestilence cleave unto thee, until he have consumed thee from off the land, whither thou goest to possess it. The Lord shall smite thee with a consumption, and with a fever, and with an inflammation, and with an extreme burning, and with the sword, and with blasting, and with mildew; and they shall pursue thee until thou perish. And thy heaven that is over thy head shall be brass, and the earth that is under thee shall be iron. The Lord shall make the rain of thy land powder and dust: from heaven shall it come down upon thee, until thou be destroyed. The Lord shall cause thee to be smitten before thine emenies: thou shalt go out one way against them, and flee seven ways before them: and shalt be removed unto all the kingdoms of the earth. And thy carcase shall be meat unto all fowls of the air, and unto the beasts of the earth, and no man shall fray them away. The Lord will smite thee with the botch of Egypt, and with the emerods, and with the scab, and with the itch, whereof thou canst not be healed. The Lord shall smite thee with madness, and blindness, and astonishment of heart: And thou shalt grope at noonday, as the blind gropeth in darkness, and thou not prosper in thy ways: and thou shalt be only oppressed and spoiled evermore, and no man shall save thee."

While some of you readers may feel this is most *harsh* of God to punish in such a way, let those words quoted above serve as yet another reminder as to how much God hates sin; how much he loathes backpedaling away from him, which leads one back to Satan; how much he despises disobedience. The nation of Israel clearly heard here, as well as countless other verses in the Bible also state in so many words, that God "means business!" Misery, sickness, pestilence, destruction, and death would be the consequences of Israel's disobedience.

Next, let's read about God's promises of *rewards* to those who obey him. In that same chapter of Deuteronomy 28, verses 1-14 say, also by way of Moses, we read:

> And it shall come to pass, if thou shalt hearken diligently unto the voice of the Lord thy God, to obersrve and to do all his commandments which I command thee this day, that the Lord thy God will set thee on high above all nations of the earth: And all these blessings shall come on thee, and overtake thee, if thou shalt hearken unto the voice of the Lord thy God. Blessed shalt thou be in the city, and blessed shalt thou be in the field. Blessed shall be the fruit of thy body, and the fruit of thy ground, and the fruit of thy cattle, the increase of thy kine, and the flocks of thy sheep. Blessed shall be thy basket and thy store. Blessed shalt thou be when thou comest in, and blessed shalt thou be when thou goest out. The Lord shall cause thine enemies that rise up against thee to be smitten before thy face: they shall come out against thee one way, and flee before thee seven ways. The Lord shall command the blessing upon thee in thy storehouses, and in all that thou settest thine hand unto; and he shall bless thee in the land which the Lord thy God giveth thee. The Lord shall establish thee a holy people unto himself, as he hath sworn unto thee, if thou shalt keep the commandments of the Lord thy God, and walk in his ways. And all the people of the earth shall see that thou art called by the name of the Lord; and they shall be afraid of thee. And the Lord shall make thee plenteous in goods, in the fruit of thy body, and in the fruit of thy catttle, and in the fruit of thy ground, in the land which the Lord sware unto thy fathers to give thee. The Lord shall open unto thee his good treasure, the heaven to give the rain unto thy land in his season, and to bless all the work of thine hand: and thou shalt lend unto many nations, and thou shalt not borrow. And the Lord shall make thee the head, and not the tail; and thou shalt be above only, and thou shalt not be beneath; if that thou hearken unto the commandments of the Lord thy God, which I command thee this day, to observe and to do them: And thou shalt not go aside from any of the words which I command thee this day, to the right hand, or to the left, to go after other gods to serve them.

All of these things just quoted were promised by God to the children of Israel as *rewards* for following him. Happiness, peace, prosperity, safety, and life would be the fruits of their obedience. There was quite a contrast here. The Israelites would be bountifully *blessed* or bountifully *cursed*. The choice was up to them. No doubt, the reader caught the same wording in both readings: "Blessed" in those areas for doing right and "cursed" in those areas for doing wrong. While God is not a *cheater*, he is, I say again, not one to be played for a *sucker*, either! In reading all of the Old Testament, his promises—on both sides--are revealed. He is the same way today with you and I. If we obey him, we will be *blessed* fully. If we disobey God, we will be *cursed* fully.

Righteous Enoch made this prophecy pertaining to God's promise of punishment to all rebellion and wickedness: "And Enoch also, the seventh from Adam, prophesied of these, saying, Behold, the Lord cometh with ten thousands of his saints, To execute judgment upon all, and to convince all that are ungodly among them of all their ungodly deeds which they have ungodly committed, and of all their hard speeches which ungodly sinners have spoken against him" (Jude 14-15). Crossing God up must be very bad, as the word "ungodly" is mentioned four times here by Jude. All we have read in this particular book's chapter are not merely idle *threats*! They are *promises*! They will be carried out at the end of time, just as they are recorded in the Bible as having been done so in the past. Where the continual punishments for sin are concerned, they are meted out in everyday life everywhere upon this earth. Read all of Revelation 18 and see how sharp God's punishment was to the spiritual Babylon, believed by many scholars to be the Roman Empire. God will not let the impenitent persecution of his children go without his vengeance.

The same thing applies to any who, as stated before, obey him for a time, but quit doing so. In Hebrews 2:1-3, the writer tells the Christians, "Therefore we ought to give the more earnest heed to the things which we have heard, lest at any time we should let them slip. For if the word spoken by angels was steadfast, and every transgression and disobedience received a just recompense of reward; How shall we escape, if we neglect so great salvation; which at the first began to be spoken by the Lord, and was confirmed unto us by them that heard him." No promise by God goes unfulfilled. No sin goes without payback, especially those not repented of, gentle reader. None! The words say, "*every* transgression and disobedience received a just recompense of reward." Then came still another question that answers itself: "How shall we escape, if we neglect so great salvation?"

The Hebrew writer also says in chapter 10:23, "Let us hold fast the profession of our faith without wavering; (for he is faithful that promised;)." Chapter 13:5 tells us, "Let your conversation be without covetousness; and be content with such things as ye have: for he hath said, I will never leave thee, nor forsake thee." Similar words are spoken by God to Jacob in Genesis 28:15. God also spoke them to Joshua, the one who had succeeded Moses as leader of Israel after Moses' death (Joshua 1:5). Before that, Moses said to Joshua in Deuteronomy 31:6-8, in regards to Joshua's not having to fear the Gentile nations, "Be strong and of a good courage, fear not, nor be afraid of them: for the Lord thy God, he it is that doth go with thee; he will not fail thee, nor forsake thee. And Moses called unto Joshua, and said unto him in the sight of all Israel, Be strong and of a good courage: for thou must go with this people unto the land which the Lord hath sworn unto their fathers to give them; and thou shalt cause them to inherit it. And the Lord, he it is that doth go before thee; he will be with thee, he will not fail thee, neither forsake thee: fear not, neither be dismayed." King David told the same thing to his son, Solomon, who was to take over the throne as King of Israel, in 1 Chronicles 28:20. God makes promises on *both* sides of the coin—and keeps them! They work just as much for the side of righteousness as they do against the side of unrighteousness. Our Maker does not *bluff* either way.

A number of times from Genesis through Deuteronomy, God promised to those faithful in Israel access to and residency in the land of Canaan. They got it, as all of Joshua 3-4 proves. As a reminder to abstain from idolatry, along with Jehovah's being a forgiving God, Moses said to Israel in Deuteronomy 4:31, "(For the Lord thy God is a merciful God;) he will not forsake thee, neither destroy thee, nor forget the covenant of thy fathers which he sware unto them." The word "covenant" means, "A formal, solemn, and binding agreement." That is a sure *promise*, if this writer ever heard one! Big or little, God cannot lie in any way, the fulfilling of his promises included. Going to the book of Hebrews again, chapter 6:18-19 declares, "That by two immutable things, in which it was impossible for God to lie, we might have a strong consolation, who have fled for refuge to lay hold upon the hope set before us: Which hope we have as an anchor of the soul, both sure and steadfast, and which entereth into that within the veil." On the same note, where the apostle Paul said to the young preacher Titus, "In hope of eternal life," we note again, "which God, that cannot lie, promised before the world began" (Titus 1:2). We just read in no uncertain terms that God always tells the truth, as we, again, talked about in the chapter on God's being sinless. The verses read respectively, "it was impossible for God to lie;" "God, that cannot lie."

Do we really *believe* in all of God's promises? Then we will accept what the Bible says that all who follow him will be provided with the necessities of this life, as discussed in the last chapter. In returning to Jesus' Sermon on the Mount, he said to the people in Matthew 6:33, "But seek ye first the kingdom of God, and his righteousness; and all these things shall be added unto you." The words "these things" refer, again, to the necessary food and clothing mentioned in verses 25 and 30. Psalm 37:25 again bolsters what Jesus said, proving that God has always physically provided for those who obey his teachings. King David declared there, "I have been young, and now am old; yet have I not seen the righteous forsaken, nor his seed begging bread."

God has never let those who truly honor his laws go hungry or naked, for we just read where he so promised! Are we convinced, as the saying teaches, that "God helps those who help themselves?" If so, then there is no excuse for not abiding by his commands. As it is, there is no excuse, anyway! Besides, remember above and beyond all that living as God directs is what gives us a home in Heaven after this life.

While many claim to fully believe God to be without sin, why do some feel he does not keep his promises? First of all, if such were true, God would *not* be without sin. Second, the Bible, as we afore noted, says that lying is an utter impossibility with God. Do we really believe it? If we do, then Numbers 23:19 should "sew it up" for us, for when Balaam is talking to Balak, he says, "God is not a man, that he should lie; neither the son of man, that he should repent: hath he said, and shall he not do it? Or hath he spoken, and shall he not make it good?" Never doubt God's *word*, what is stated in God's *word!* If he promises, he will "make it good." If there is *no* promise, then he must have had a good reason not to make one. So, there will have been no promise made for God to "make it good," for if he was not going to "make it good," he would not make that promise to begin with now, would he? That is how sure his word is. The first part of Romans 3:4 has Paul telling the Christians there, "God forbid: yea, let God be true, but every man a liar..." Since God is true, there is not a promise made that *has not* been kept, nor any made which *will not* be kept.

Now back to you and I. In Proverbs 3:5-6, the wise King Solomon admonishes us, "Trust in the Lord with all thine heart; and lean not unto thine own understanding. In all thy ways acknowledge him, and he shall direct thy paths." God is saying, "Trust me all the way, for I will guide you right every time, and will never let you down. Do not depend on your own judgments. Listen to mine. Believe every word I say." In suffering much persecution for obeying God, Paul says to Timothy, "For the which cause I also suffer these things: nevertheless I am not ashamed: for I know whom I have believed, and am persuaded that he is able to keep that which I have committed unto him against that day" (2 Tim. 1:12). Paul said to the Christians at Corinth, "God is faithful, by whom ye were called unto the fellowship of his Son Jesus Christ our Lord" (1 Cor. 1:9).

When promises are made by people, I have no doubt but what many of those individuals intend to keep them. I have at least that much faith in my fellowman. Sometimes we hear those desperate terms, "I swear on a stack of Bibles"; "I swear on my dead mother's grave"; "I swear by the heavens above"; "With God as my witness"; etc. (Some such affirmations include a few *expletives*, as well!) However, the really *unique* thing about God's promises is the fact that God has nobody to promise or swear on but *himself*! His own oath is his gospel. So the truth is, he *needs* nobody but himself to tie up and secure his promises, for they are always there in his infinite mind. Referring to the Hebrew writer once again, he says of God, "For when God made promise to Abraham, because he could swear by no greater, he sware by himself, Saying, Surely blessing I will bless thee, and multiplying I will multiply thee" (Heb. 6:13-14). That promise was carried through, for it was from the seed of Abraham that the great Jewish nation began. Indeed, God swears by his own self on his promises. He can do that because he is totally absent of any possible sin. Since God has no faults, flaws, lapse of memory, or shortcomings to get in the way, we can rest not only our lives on his promises, but also our very *souls* on every last one of them. Do it! You will never, ever be disappointed. Remember though: God promises to punish all disobedience and reward all obedience. Make your choice, therefore, to heed his every command.

So many passages are contained in the Bible about the solidity of God's promises. You as the reader are challenged to investigate on your own and see for yourself. He never breaks even *one* of them. You can just "take it to the bank." Jehovah is not a "welsher." Unlike much of mankind already mentioned, he does not back-pedal. God says what he means and means what he says. He will always do what he says he will do, for that is how he has always been and will be everlastingly. I beg of you to trust in him all the days of your life. Read his Bible. Obey it. Keep all promises you make to God, for he keeps all he makes to you. (Try to keep all promises made to humanity, as well!) For any promises you have made to others and God that have been broken, please correct as many of them as possible and as soon as you can. Have an honest heart. Live up to your word, for God lives up to his. He cares for you so much. Carry it in your heart as long as you live that *God is keeper of all his promises.*

**Questions**

1. In reality, we do not believe in the saying, "______________ were made to be ________________."
2. God, being the _____________ personality he is, does not make any ________________ that is not ____________________, those ___________ being __________ or ___________.
3. The following verse paves the way for assurance of punishments: "But if shall come to pass, if thou wilt not ___________ unto the _________ of the Lord thy God, to ______________ to do ______ his commandments and his ______________ which I command thee this day; that all these __________ shall come ________ thee, and ___________ thee."
4. The following verse paves the way for assurance of rewards: "And it shall come to pass, if thou shalt _______________________ unto the _________ of the Lord thy God, to ____________ and to do _______ his commandments which I command thee this day, that the Lord thy God will set thee ____________________ above ______ nations of the ________________."
5. Depending on whether Israel obeyed or disobeyed God, they would be bountifully _________________ or bountifully ____________. The choice was up to _____________.
6. "Behold, the Lord cometh with ___________________________ of his ____________, To execute ______________ upon ________, and to convince ________ that are ___________ among them of all their _________________ deeds which they have ____________ committed, and of all their ____________ speeches which ___________ sinners have spoken ____________________ him."
7. "For is the word spoken by _____________ was _________________, and __________ transgression and disobedience received a __________ ________________ of ___________; How shall we ____________, if we ________________ so great __________________; which at the ________________ began to be spoken by the Lord, and was ________________ unto _______ by them that _________ them."

8. No _______________ of God goes __________________.
9. "Let us hold ________ the profession of our __________ without _____________; (for he is _____________ that _____________;)."
10. "For he hath said, I will never _________ thee, nor _____________ thee."
11. "For the Lord thy God, ______ it is that doth ________________ thee; he will not ___________ thee, nor ______________ thee."
12. God makes ______________ on __________ sides of the coin—and ______________ them!
13. "(For the Lord thy God is a _________________ God;) he will not ___________ thee, neither _____________ thee, nor ___________ the ______________ of thy ____________ which he ___________ unto them."
14. "That by two ________________ things, in which it was _____________ for God to _______, we might have a ________________________, who have fled for ____________ to _________________ upon the hope set before us."
15. "In hope of ________________ life, which God, that cannot ______, ______________ before the world ____________."
16. "But seek ye _________ the kingdom of ______, and his _____________; and all _________________________ shall be _________ unto you."
17. "I have been ___________, and now am __________; yet have I not seen the righteous ____________, nor his seed ____________ bread."
18. "God is not a _________, that he should _________, neither the _______ of man, that he should ______________: hath he ________, and shall he not _______ it? Or hath he ____________, and shall he not make it __________?"
19. "____________ in the Lord with ________ thine heart; and lean _____ unto _____________________ understanding. In _______ thy way ___________ him, and _____ shall direct thy ______________."
20. "For I ____________ whom I have ________________, and am ___________________ that he is ___________ to __________ that which I have _______________ unto him against that _________."

Chapter 21

# God Is Love

While love is said to be the same in all languages, love is also defined and expressed in so many ways. That love is a complex topic, there is no doubt. The only way this writer is able to *briefly* sum up love is by one generic definition: "An extraordinary feeling and admiration for something, someplace, or someone." Anybody reading this term can take it and go as soul-reaching as you know how to with this subject under consideration. No doubt many of you are able to define love in various depths, depending on your vocabulary, your experiences in life, along with what type of way you have with words, phrases, and terminologies. Especially is this true with you who have the ability to write poetry. The subject of love goes so very *deep*, and how deep one can go with it is based upon one's talents and abilities.

Love is spoken of in most every part of life. We speak of the foods we love; makes of automobiles; particular colors; shapes of furniture; cuts, designs, and fashions of clothing; forms and layouts of houses; certain towns; selected tourist attractions; a brand of music; particular songs; styles of writing; the beauty of some languages; and the list continues. Love is not limited to how we feel inwardly about some individuals. This wonderful subject is an attention-getter. Love tugs at the heartstrings. It brings back memories for all of us who have lived awhile—and one does not have to live long to chalk up memories of love; puppy love from grammar school; adolescent love from high school; young adult love from college; love felt at one's place of employment for a colleague; love of one's own job; *any* love we experience during our entire lifetime, for that matter.

Along with the terms just mentioned, there are other types of love expressed such as "tough love," "hard love," "deep love," "undying love," "matchless love," "Christian love," "unrequited love," "brotherly love," and so on. An insurmountable sum of poems have been penned on love.

An indescribable amount of songs have become vocalized on this topic. Too, we all very much cherish hearing the words " I love you" said to us, as well as saying it to others. This writer is no different. Love is universal in all forms of life—human, animal, fowl, and sea creature. With it accompanies affection, embracing, admiration, concern, compassion, devotion, provisions, consideration, and often, protection.

We could probably find an illustration for love using every letter of the alphabet! It truly *moves* all of those in different and various ways who are creatures of the flesh. Love is at the very *root* of all things consisting of life, as it *is* that very root. It gives birth to all kinds of *desire*, along with so many other things involved with motivation. Love makes us all say and do unusual things, as it does have a big hold on us. It causes us to perform more and greater things for some people than what we would otherwise do for others. Like electricity, love jolts both the mind and body.

When speaking of the love contained within Jehovah God, words cannot fully describe it, as is so frequently the case on love in all other areas. Since God is a being composed of nothing but right and good, trying to illustrate the entirety of his great love is to do so futilely. Love seems to hold an endless depth, no matter how loquacious, gifted, and eloquent one may be in trying to describe love and reach the bottom of it. Explore its contents as you may, but love can never be grasped in its entirety. The very *profound* thing about this mighty universal force is that, as stated in the chapter on the *intangible* things, God is not merely the *source* of love, God *is* love! John, often recognized as the apostle on love, has thus said much in his divinely inspired writings on this subject. In I John 4:8 he tells us, "He that loveth not knoweth not God; for God is love." John does not only say that God *produced* love, but, again, that "God *is* love." The same words listed at the very end of this verse just quoted are also found in verse 16.

Perhaps that is why love in most any form goes too deep for us to possess the ability to put it into words. It is such a "bottomless pit" to explore, so as to stifle the imagination. God is love *himself*! That is why he contains all those wonderful and majestic qualities this writer has been trying to convey to you as the reader in every page of this book! How could God be the origin of such traits as mercy, graciousness, rewarding, blessing, and long-suffering, as also mentioned in this book's pages, if he did not contain great love? The answer is elementary: He could not! Without love, there can *be* none of the above—or anything else in the way of tolerance or goodness. Love is the origin of it all. Love moves God to act, just as it does you and I. It is for sure a "force to be reckoned with," as the adage goes. It flutters the heart. Love brings about butterflies in the stomach. It gives mankind a reason to keep on living. How empty and dark life would be without it! As one of many tunes written about love declares, it is truly "a many splendored thing."

Concerning this beautiful subject, I think at times of the last verse contained in a hymn written by F. M. Lehman and arranged by Claudia Lehman Mays. It is appropriately titled, "The Love of God:"

> Could we with ink the ocean fill,
> And were the skies of parchment made;
> Were every stalk on earth a quill,
> And every man a scribe by trade;
> To write the love of God above
> Would drain the ocean dry;
> Nor could the scroll contain the whole,
> Though stretched from sky to sky.

What an awesome attempt at putting into words the boundless love of Jehovah God! The writer out and out states that such cannot be accomplished. God's love for you and I surpasses all boundary lines. That makes God's love too rich to stir and too big in circumference to fully embrace. Therefore, it must be *limitless*!

One ends up spellbound to try and imagine the love of God. The Apostle Paul tells the Roman Christians, "O the depth of the riches both of the wisdom and knowledge of God! how unsearchable are his judgments, and his ways past finding out! For who hath known the mind of the Lord? or who hath been his counselor? Or who hath first given to him, and it shall be recompensed unto him again? For of him, and through him, and to him, are all things: to whom be glory for ever. Amen" (Romans 11:33-36). These passages reveal to us that God is most *thorough* all the way. That makes him *complete* by every means. He is the most rounded being of all, figuratively speaking. So, he is equipped with full capacity in everything, being as he *is* everything, which is why all right and good *originate* from him. We just read, "how unsearchable are his judgments, and his ways past finding out!"

Exercise your wildest thoughts—those not against God's will. This writer means to say, *pull out all stops*! Go to each dictionary contained in this world, memorize the definition of every word in existence that is not wrong to utter, if you dare to accept such a humongous challenge. Compose all those words in the most profound sentences possible. Then, after every word has been said, when every application has been utilized, every analogy has been given, and thus, every effort depleted, you still will not have succeeded in reaching the complete *depth* of God's love! No sir! No ma'am! You will have missed it by a long shot! Such a thing as the richness of the love God feels for us pounds the heart, racks the brain, brings tears to the eyes, and stifles the imagination, when one attempts to really explore it! God's love cannot be comprehended! No bead can be drawn around it! One is left completely speechless! As a lady singer once crooned in the chorus of a love song, "Don't try to fight it, baby! It's bigger than the both of us!" Since so much love manifested even by the human race is such a mighty force, try to imagine the strong, assertive power behind the love of God!

In fact, while we are on this particular point, let us repeat again John 3:16, where Jesus is conversing with a Pharisee named Nicodemus: "For God so loved the world, that he gave his only begotten Son, that whosoever believeth in him should not perish, but have everlasting life." How can a *sinless* God (as spoken of in a previous chapter) love such a *sinful* world? Words cannot cut it in trying to reach the total depth of such a thing as God's love to and for sinful mankind! Why not ponder this amazing thought the next time you read the Bible or pray?

Let's now give some illustrations of nature and other things here in a further attempt to contemplate the love of God. An elm is not just the *representation* of a tree. It *is* a tree! A dog is not merely the *figure* of an animal. That dog *is* an animal! Any automobile is not just the *likeness* of a vehicle. It *is* a vehicle! Any road with a number labeled on a sign consisting of the colors red, white, and blue is not simply a *description* of an interstate. It *is* an interstate! Many other examples could be given here, but I believe the reader sees the point. God is not only the *representation* of what we know as love. Once again, he *is* love! God's love has no end in sight! Neither its beginning *or* end can be found! Its height is immeasurable! It cannot be weighed on any scale, so it cannot be recorded at all! We are unable to totally grab hold of God's love! Like all his other ways, it too is "past finding out." That which is "past finding out" cannot, obviously, be found out! We cannot find out the depth of God's love, no matter how hard we try, how long we investigate and research, or how big of a committee we may form to undertake the task. No single word or set of words in any language can succeed in such a feat. It is, nonetheless, a great challenge and a soaring, emotional lift for one to try. To do so would at least set a person to thinking. So, this writer challenges you, the reader, to try it!

When Paul wrote to the Christians at Corinth, he describes how love will and will not conduct itself. The word "charity" is used in the following verses to describe the word "love" in the King James Version of the Bible, the version used in this book, as stated in the "Foreword" section. Paul says, "Charity suffereth long, and is kind; charity envieth not; charity vaunteth not itself, is not puffed up, Doth not behave itself unseemly, seeketh not her own, is not easily provoked, thinketh no evil; Rejoiceth not in iniquity, but rejoiceth in the truth; Beareth all things, believeth all things, hopeth all things, endureth all things" (1 Cor. 13:4-7). The first part of verse 8 says, "Charity never faileth:" Verse 13 says, "And now abideth faith, hope, charity, these three; but the greatest of these is charity." Of course, Paul speaks here specifically of *Christian* love, but the same principles apply to the love we have for others—if it is true, genuine love.

All of these characteristics of love written by Paul fit Jehovah God to the "nth degree," as we sometimes say it, and as I have so stated before. We also use the phrase, "to a 'T'." Read over each clause in the verses just cited in the previous paragraph, and you will see every one of those features in God. His love is *perfect*, for his love, like another of his characteristics already explored, is *sinless*. Along with going deeper than we can ever realize, God's love is always in its proper place, it is always there, and always will be. God's love "never faileth." That tells us it cannot be killed, including when he chastises mankind for sin, as already said in another chapter. In fact, the Bible tells us just that. In Hebrews 12:6 the writer says, "for whom the Lord loveth he chasteneth, and scourgeth every son whom he receiveth." God's love never quits or diminishes. He forever loves you and I. Even though he punishes all sin, he still loves us with a true, unbeatable, and eternal love. What a God, everybody! Foolish is the person who refuses to take note of this!

When reading the Bible, we find the main reason that we should love God. Actually, it has been stated indirectly all the time in this book. I John 4:19 says of God, "We love him, because he first loved us." If that is not the first and foremost reason for loving God, what is? We should love him because he has so generously provided all our needs. We should love him for all that he has created, considering both the outward *and* inward beauty of every one of his works, along with the huge versatility they accompany. We should love him because he brought us into our very existence. Let us revert still again to Paul's speaking to a group of men on Mars Hill in Athens, Greece: "For in him we live, and move, and have our being; as certain also of your own poets have said, For we are also his offspring" (Acts 17:28). We should love God for the different seasons that come our way in most of the world. We should love him for all our close family members and friends whom we have in life to keep us company. We should love God for all the right and good opportunities he brings our way. If you are an animal lover like me, you should love God for the wonderful, loving, and faithful pets who have kept us company throughout life. This is only the beginning, however!

In turn, just how strong and unmovable should be our love for God? Paul tells the Roman brethren, "For I am persuaded, that neither death, nor life, nor angels, nor principalities, nor powers, nor things present, nor things to come, Nor height, nor depth, nor any other creature, shall be able to separate us from the love of God, which is in Christ Jesus our Lord" (Rom. 8:38). God loves us ever so fervently because he loves ever so fervently! How about our love for him? It has to work both ways if Heaven is to be our home in the next and final life. Love God with all your heart, as he truly loves you with all of his. Meditate upon this thought each day you live upon the good Lord's plentiful earth!

How many reasons we can indubitably find for loving God! They just keep on springing up in our thoughts, do they not? Love creates a fantastic amount of brainpower, gentle reader! Let us keep one main thing in mind, though: As quoted, we should love him, above and beyond all, "because he first loved us," as John said. That is what the Bible teaches. The *greatest* side of his love will be studied in the next chapter, which is the final one in this book.

One's breath should be taken away when we stop in our tracks and *really* consider the love of God, even though our minds cannot take in all of it. When was the last time we meditated upon it? When did we last thank God for his loving us so much more than we could ever know? Whoever you are, whatever you be socially, whatever occupation you have engaged in past or present, never forget or discount the enormous love Jehovah has for you. He loves you and all others no more or no less than he loves this writer. "For we are also his *offspring*," Paul declared. Such a wonderful truth as that should make us want to form an unbreakable, and so, eternal, bond with that great Creator and Maker. Without God, you would not be who and what you are in the way of good, right, abilities, and talent because all of that came from God, and so therefore, such is God through and through, such is God in you, and such are you in the eyes of others, with all the glory and praise returning right back to Jehovah God.

Your Creator cares for you. He cherishes you. You and I are a "term of endearment" to him. The biggest injustice for any individual to render is to *buck* God's love! God cares for your physical and spiritual welfare alike, so take *and* maintain proper care for both. Jehovah is big in every decent and righteous way. The top reason for it all is that God is *love*!

**Questions**

1. As the song goes, "________ is a many _______________ thing."
2. Name the eight different types of expressions of love listed in this chapter. Feel free to add any others that come to mind: (1) ___________ (2) _____________ (3) ___________ (4) ___________ (5) _____________ (6) _______________ (7) _______________ (8) ____________________
3. The three cherished words we all enjoy hearing are, "I _____________ you."
4. "He that ___________ not knoweth not _________; for ________ is _________________."
5. ____________ is at the very ______________ of all things consisting of _______________, as it ______ that very _____________.
6. Like all others traits of God, his great _________________ is a "______________________ pit."
7. "We ______________ him, because he first ________________ us."
8. God cares for your _____________ and ___________ welfare alike.
9. Our subject under consideration may be defined and summed up in one generic term: "An _________________________ feeling and admiration for ______________, ______________, or ________________."
10. In I Corinthians 13, the KJV uses the word _____________ to define Christian ________________.
11. "__________________ suffereth __________, and is ____________; ________ _______ not; "________________________ itself; is not

________________, Doth not behave itself ______________, seeketh not ____________, is not easily ________________, thinketh no _______________; _________________ not in _____________, but __________________ in the ________________; _____________ all things, ________________ all things, ____________ all things, ________________ all things."

12. "And now abideth ___________, ____________, ____________, these three; but the _______________ of these is charity."
13. "For whom the Lord _________ he _____________ and ___________ every ___________ whom he ________________."
14. God's love never ______________ or ______________. He forever _____________ you and I.
15. "For I am ______________, that neither ____________, nor _________, nor ____________, nor ___________________, nor _____________, nor ________________________, nor ___________ to come, Nor _______________, nor _____________, nor any other ______________, shall be able to ________________ us from the ________ of God, which is in ___________ our Lord."
16. "For God so ______________ the world, that he __________ his only begotten __________, that ______________ believeth in him should not ___________, but have ___________________ life."
17. "To write the _______ of God above would drain the ________ dry."
18. When it comes to God, "How __________________ are his judgments, and his ways past _____________________!" This accounts for his _____________ being too deep to fully contemplate.

Chapter 22

# God Is Giver of the Greatest Gift

When you and I are given a gift, it makes us (if our hearts contain any tenderness) show gratitude to the giver. We especially feel that way if the gift is big and/or costly. Many a woman has cried tears of joy when that engagement ring was slipped onto her finger and her male companion then "pops the question." If something else really major like an automobile or house is given through the generosity of a friend or family member, or if the vehicle is won in a contest, it definitely makes the recipient "take notice." (As for this writer, lockjaw would probably result!) Such a gesture is never forgotten as long as one lives. Yours truly for one can remember certain people (my wife included, of course!) whom I deemed most thoughtful when surprising me with something I either wanted but never expected to have, or else never dreamed would be given to me. (No hints attached to the reader, I promise you!) Too, this has happened not only on special occasions such as my birthday, Father's Day, or that time of the year we know as Christmas. On the contrary, someone thought enough of me to give me a gift, simply because they loved me or liked me to the extent they wanted to display that kind gesture. Gift giving touches and softens the heart.

One other point needing to be mentioned here was said earlier in this book: A gift, unlike wages received for services rendered, is not something that an individual *has* to give. It is something given because that person *wants* to give it! That is what makes a gift so nice; so thoughtful a gesture on the part of the giver; and thus, so much different from a paycheck! It is given out of *choice* instead of *necessity*!

Jehovah God, being the *gracious* God he is, as brought out in another chapter, and being so full of love for humankind, as mentioned in the last chapter, is the giver of the greatest gift to mankind. The generosity of this gift cannot be weighed. It cannot be valued in any dollar amount. Nor can any other gift even *equal* to it, let alone, be *topped*! It cannot so much as be compared to the old familiar saying, "worth its weight in gold."

*That gift was God's sending of his only begotten Son Jesus Christ to this earth.* Such love, thoughtfulness, and concern cannot be accurately and fully put into words. They cannot be assessed. In what has become known as the "Golden text of the Bible," I refer again to John the Apostle who records Jesus saying to the young Pharisaic ruler, Nicodemus, "For God so loved the world, that he gave his only begotten Son, that whosoever believeth in him should not perish, but have everlasting life" (John 3:16).

We need to meditate on the term "so loved the world." It is a *sinful* world in which we live. Crime and all forms of lawlessness are practiced every second this earth continues to exist. The list is too long to mention each and every wrong committed and law broken. Crime is occurring this exact moment, even as this very line is read by you now! How can God love a *sinful* world where there is every kind of bad thing happening around the clock? As argued before, why does not the Creator of the heavens and the earth call a *halt* to it all, and simply send every last member of mankind to the devil's torment—which includes you and I—for all of eternity? We just read why. It is because "God so loved the world." The word "so" would define God's love reaching its way to a certain degree. The way it is used in this verse means to a *great* degree. How great? So great is God's love for all people that "he gave his only begotten Son." God did not want to see the eternal destiny of anyone's soul become that of *condemnation*! That is how much he loves all human beings, even the most calloused and vile.

Look at something else here! John 3:16 states that Jesus was--and is--God's "only begotten Son." The word "begotten" is a form of the word, "beget," and that means, "born; brought forth; delivered." God's very own real, true, original Son is Jesus. Jesus is the only *genuine son* of God, where his actual *children* are concerned. That makes him God's "only *begotten* Son." The Bible does not record Jesus as having had any original spiritual brothers or sisters in Heaven who were begotten before or after him, although the Bible does record his having *earthly* siblings. Rightly, it must be brought out that he was born of a *virgin*, as was foretold in Isaiah 7:14 where the prophet says, "Therefore the Lord himself shall give you a sign; Behold, a virgin shall conceive, and bear a son, and shall call his name Immanuel." We know of course that this virgin was named Mary. These same words are repeated again by an angel to Joseph, Jesus' soon-to-be (adopted) earthly father, in Matthew 1:23. Immanuel was another name for Jesus, and it means in Hebrew, "God is with us."

What is difficult for some people to understand is that since Jesus was sent to earth by his Heavenly Father, Jehovah God, he must have already been around before that time. Someone or something cannot be *sent* that has not already *existed.* This argument is valid, due to the fact John 3:16 says that God "*gave* his only begotten Son." I cannot *give* you something unless it is *there* to give.

When Jesus spoke to a group of Jews, we read once more in John 8:57-58 where the apostle records: "Then said the Jews unto him, Thou are not yet fifty years old, and hast thou seen Abraham? Jesus said unto them, Verily, verily, I say unto you, Before Abraham was, I am." God identifies *himself* the same way in Exodus 3:14 and Isaiah 43:13. As more proof of Jesus' pre-existence to the birth of the world, he declared to God his Father while praying his famous prayer on unity not long before his death in John 17:5, "And now, O Father, glorify thou me with thine own self with the glory which I had with thee before the world was." Jesus says again that he was with God "before the world was." Going back to John 8:58, Christ, as aforetime said, did not say, "I was and still am." He said, "I am!" "God, who at sundry times and in divers manners spake in time past unto the fathers by the prophets, Hath in these last days spoken unto us by his Son, whom he hath appointed heir of all things, by whom also he made the worlds" (Hebrews 1:1-2). "And to make all men see what is the fellowship of the mystery, which from the beginning of the world hath been hid in God, who created all things by Jesus Christ" (Ephesians 3:9). "Who is the image of the invisible God, the firstborn of every creature: For by him were all things created, that are in heaven, and that are in earth, visible and invisible, whether they be thrones, or dominions, or principalities, or powers: all things were created by him, and for him" (Colossians 1:15-16). Using this term refers to his being *eternal*; to his always *having been in existence.*

There was never a moment when Jesus *was not*. He existed before the creation of the world, just like Jehovah God. Hence, Jesus took part in the formation of all things, too. John mentions these very same two things about Jesus which I just stated, and which was covered earlier: (1) He existed *before* the world was created, and, (2) He was the one who carried out the actual *execution* of all that was created: "In the beginning was the Word, and the Word was with God, and the Word was God. The same was in the beginning with God. All things were made by him; and without him was not any thing made that was made" (John 1:1-3).

Indeed, putting it facetiously, Jesus was around *long* before the world was formed. Like God, Christ saw the fall of man, due to his yielding to sin. That means he too, like his Father, has witnessed all of history, both secular and Biblical. This had to be, for it says of Jesus, "The same was in the beginning with God." Coming to earth was not the *beginning* of Jesus, for he *had* no beginning where the subject of *time* is concerned. He had aforetime been in Heaven with God, and still is, minus his some 33 years on earth, of course. Hard to imagine, grant you! Howbeit, this is what the Bible says, and I for one can only accept (based on that book's limited amount of revelation according to God's proper judgments) what it does tell in this area, or on any other subject.

Trying to grasp this whole concept, like God's love discussed in the last chapter, really cannot be done. It is as impossible as trying to fit all the water of any ocean into a teaspoon! Here is someone who hates and despises sin--Jehovah God. He formed a pure, sin-free world, mankind included. Here is one who created man as a free moral agent. That means God allowed him to *choose*. Man opted to sin against God instead of obey him. Yet, God loved the soul of man enough to want him rescued from the clutches of Satan. That love was so deep, it far surpasses understanding. So much a fact is this that God "gave his only begotten Son," causing Jesus to leave his ivory palaces of Heaven, and come to a heavy-laden earth of corruption. Compare leaving the White House in Washington, D.C. to go dwell in the jungle, and you might get a *fraction* of an idea as to what Jesus left behind for awhile in order to save mankind from his sins! However, such is only a very *mild* comparison! Jesus came to this earth to suffer, bleed, and die on the cross for the filthy stench of all sin!

The Apostle Paul said in Romans 6:23 to the church there, "For the wages of sin is death; but the gift of God is eternal life through Jesus Christ our Lord." As said before, so it is said yet once again, wages are *deserved.* Therefore, what is received in return for sin is *just*! It is what mankind has *coming* to him. Jesus, however, was not sent as an *obligation* from God. (God is not obligated to anybody in any way for anything, for that matter, as stated in the chapter on his being independent). Rather, Christ was sent as a "gift" to mankind, as the above text reads. His being a "gift" means that God *desired* to send his only son--the only one truly "begotten" of him. In

Romans 5:18-21 Paul also says, "Therefore as by the offense of one judgment came upon all men to condemnation; even as by the righteousness of one the free gift came upon all men unto justification of life. For as by one man's disobedience many were made sinners, so by the obedience of one shall many be made righteous. Moreover the law entered, that the offense might abound. But where sin abounded, grace did much more abound: That as sin hath reigned unto death, even so might grace reign through righteousness unto eternal life by Jesus Christ our Lord."

Paul tells us that what sin brought in, Jesus came to take out. Sin brought "condemnation," while Jesus brought "righteousness." Whatever sin marred, Jesus came to restore; renovate; correct; bind up; heal. It was God's "grace," as Paul said here, that brought about that "gift" to you and I, which was Jesus Christ. There is positively no greater gift that can be given by God or man, either one.

To further illustrate how much "God so loved the world," let us next go to Romans 5:6-8 where Paul says to the church there, "For when we were yet without strength, in due time Christ died for the ungodly. For scarcely for a righteous man will one die: yet peradventure for a good man some would even dare to die. But God commendeth his love toward us, in that, while we were yet sinners, Christ died for us." Sin *zapped* the human race of its physical immortality. That is what ushered old age and death into this onetime utopia world. Paul declared that one may die for a righteous individual. He went on to state that few would dare to die for a good person. Now, how much did God reveal his love to you and I? Paul says, "while we were yet *sinners*, Christ died for us!" In chapter 8:32 we find Paul teaching us, "He that spared not his own Son, but delivered him up for us all, how shall he not with him also freely give us all things?"

God "freely" gave Jesus. Nobody twisted God's arm, for nobody can. Nobody *forced* God, for nobody could succeed in doing so. ("No kidding," you may laugh and say, to the last two sentences!)

Unlike some people, along with those known as "fair-weather friends," God did not hit us when we were down! He sent Jesus into the world to *save* us, not shove us all the more *farther into* sin. When quoting John 3:16 near the beginning of this chapter, this writer did not want to leave out verse 17. Many, many people can quote verse 16, which is commendable, but verse 17 is what gives verse 16 it's meaning. It reads, "For God sent not his Son into the world to condemn the world; but that the world through him might be saved." I wish more people would remember that and think of this verse each time they are ready to "rub it in" so profoundly and proudly--or even in the least way--on someone who has paid for his wrongs, especially when that individual is a personal enemy of theirs.

No, this writer is not talking about excusing sin, for such an advocation would never, ever proceed from these lips! Instead, I speak of knowing—and accepting—the difference between rebuking someone in love, thus, trying to correct one properly, and then offering to help that person *overcome* the sin(s), as opposed to merely "chewing out" and "skinning alive" that precious soul, then desiring to ostracize that individual, instead of waiting, like a real New Testament Christian should, to see if *repentance* is shown or not! There is a difference in hating somebody and hating what that person has done.

Some people are really adept at scathing others! They give one the distinct impression they have either taken lessons on "cutting to the quick," have "rehearsed" their speech of scathe, or both! Scathing is one of those things which should very seldom have to be done. I say "seldom," because I recognize the fact that there are certain ones who will endlessly push a person, until finally, one can absolutely take no more. However, know that scathing can lead to railing, which it at times does, and the Bible directly condemns those who rail. This is found in I Corinthians 5:11, I Timothy 6:4, I Peter 3:9, and 2 Peter 2:10-11. A person tells on oneself when behaving this way, which often shows their lack of long-suffering. If God can show *his* long-suffering to the whole world for long, long periods of time, then you and I need to display it as much as possible to those who try our patience. We must remember that we too, yes, all of us, have been *trying* individuals to others at times!

The point here is that all of us have paid the consequences for our mistakes, the reader and this writer included. We all ought to thank God for *his* not "rubbing it in," or not one person living, past or present, could or would have a chance for salvation. I for one am glad that God does not judge man the way that much of man judges one another. If God exercised his judging the way some folks do, who would be allowed to sincerely *repent* of their wrongs? Who would have a second chance? Who could redeem oneself? Who could ever be forgiven? Who would be long-suffering? How much sooner would *God's* own long-suffering have ended?

God's never ending love for us, which accompany his desire to save us from our sins, are also what make him *longsuffering*. This was another side of God read about earlier. I refer yet again to II Peter 3:9 where the apostle states as to why God has not carried out his promise to end the world yet: "The Lord is not slack concerning his promise, as some men count slackness; but is long-suffering to us-ward, not willing that any should perish, but that all should come to repentance." The only reason this earth is around even *now* is because Jehovah is giving all of us chance after chance after chance to come to Jesus before it is everlastingly too late. He is "not willing that any should perish." That is why he wants all to "come to repentance." "Repent" means, "To turn around; turn away from." This is why God sent Jesus. Paul tells the young preacher Timothy the following about God: "Who will have all men to be saved, and to come unto the knowledge of the truth" (I Timothy 2:4). God wants you saved from the Devil and Hell more than he wants anything else, no matter who or what you are.

No accountable member of mankind can save *himself*. In Jeremiah 10:23, the writer of that book whom we identified before as the "weeping prophet," is talking to God directly and saying, "O Lord, I know that the way of man is not in himself: it is not in man that walketh to direct his steps." Jesus must be--and can only be--the one to save us. He said to Thomas in John 14:6, "...I am the way, the truth, and the life: no man cometh unto the Father, but by me." If Jesus said, "no man," then he means, "no man!" You and I cannot save our own souls from sin. If such were the case, then Adam and Eve might very well not have disobeyed God in the Garden of Eden, recorded in all of Genesis 3. What is more, if saving oneself from sin were possible, God would have accepted Adam and Eve's own *personal choice* of repentance, or else would have *given* them one or more choices of correcting themselves, after they violated his will. This brings us up to the next point.

In speaking of the Garden of Eden, that is where the sending of Jesus to earth was first promised by God to redeem the soul of sinful man. "Redeem" means, "Buy back." When rebuking and pronouncing the punishments on Adam and Eve for their disobedience by partaking of that forbidden fruit from the tree of knowledge of good and evil, God said specifically to Satan, who appeared in the form of a serpent, "And I will put enmity between thee and the woman, and between thy seed and her seed; it shall bruise they head, and thou shalt bruise his heel" (Gen. 3:15). "Enmity" means, "Positive, active, and typically mutual hatred or ill will." That "enmity" would be between Jesus and the devil, but would not reveal itself *completely* until many centuries later, when Jesus would come down from Heaven, be born, teach and preach, and finally, die on the cross, thus, becoming a sort of *scapegoat* for all of mankind's sins. Paul tells the churches at Galatia, "But when the fullness of the time was come, God sent forth his Son, made of a woman, made under the law, To redeem them that were under the law, that we might receive the adoption of sons" (Galatians 4:4-5). So we just noted where Christ was promised, then his coming was fulfilled, which was at the *time* God saw proper to send him. When Christ was put to death, Satan thought he really had conquered Jesus; but his very *own* defeat was just beginning, for it was Christ's crucifixion which brought about the start of *victory* to the world; victory over sin; victory for all who would obey his words!

Is it not something how Satan tried so excessively hard to defeat God's purpose for sending Jesus to save the soul of man, even by trying to keep Jesus from coming to earth, but lost the battle so miserably! He would never "miss a trick," as the saying goes. (Nor does he "miss a trick" today, you can rest assured!) No matter what this "original sinner" tried, working through the human race in his attempts to thwart the cause of Christ, God's plan of redemption for you and I did not fail! That may very well be called the one *stupid* side of Satan—thinking he could defeat Jehovah God! Sounds like the biggest laugh of all generations, does it not? After all that was said, done, and attempted, God *won out* over the Devil all the way! With our Maker, it was a "landslide victory," to say the very least! With Satan, it was a "no win situation," which is exactly what it will produce for anyone who listens to him, instead of God. Our Maker actually used *all* of Satan's tactics to accomplish his purpose in sending Jesus to this earth. Hence, that "last laugh" is on Satan!

Let us next check on a few verses of scripture in I John. In speaking of Jesus, the apostle says in Chapter 3:16 basically the same thing recorded in John 3:16: "Hereby perceive we the love of God, because he laid down his life for us: and we ought to lay down our lives for the brethren." In I John 4:9-10 John also says, "In this was manifested the love of God toward us, because that God sent his only begotten Son into the world, that we might live through him. Herein is love, not that we loved God, but that he loved us, and sent his Son to be the propitiation for our sins." "Propitiation" means, "The gaining or regaining of the favor or goodwill of." All the repenting and good works that we can do will not, on our own, regain God's favor or goodwill with us. That is how ugly and repulsive sin is, gentle reader. It took Jesus Christ to reestablish our favor with God, for we are otherwise helpless in all our efforts.

Of all beings to send to this earth for the purpose of saving the soul of mankind, why Jesus? This is a sensible question. One answer, if not the only one, is because Jesus lived a *sinless* life, as the Bible plainly records. In I Peter 2:2, the apostle says of Christ, "Who did no sin, neither was guile found in his mouth." The life Jesus lived on this earth was absolutely faultless; perfect; minus any sort of wrongdoing. As already noted, to be guilty of "guile" means to tell a half-truth. What you said was true, but the rest of the facts should have been included. The *entire* story was not told, but was *intentionally* left out. Jesus' very own speech could not ever be stumped or even detected to contain any *guile*! That is how blameless a life he lived. Jesus never sinned. The Hebrew writer says about the life of Jesus, "For we have not a high priest which cannot be touched with the feeling of our infirmities; but was in all points tempted like as we are, yet without sin" (Hebrews 4:15).

Jesus' living a totally *sinless* life while on earth as a man may be another hard thing for a lot of people to accept, but because the good book says it, such must be altogether true. Some try to refute this verse by suggesting things on which God's Word is silent. They will say, "Well, the Bible does not say he was tempted to commit *adultery*!" I have heard this argument, and such will not cut it! The Bible is silent in telling us that Jesus was tempted in any *specific* way. No individual sins are listed in reference to his being tempted such as those of stealing, lying, adultery, murder, and so on. It only states that Jesus was "in *all* points tempted like as we are," but he turned down each and every one of those temptations, for the text goes on to say, "yet *without* sin." So that verse must mean just what it says—that Jesus was "in all points tempted like as we are!"

Every sin came Jesus way in an effort to entice him, but he refused each attempt. I tell the reader again without reservation, it was *every* sin! It took a sinless being, one capable of living a fault-free life in the flesh, (and Jesus did) to be the perfect example for us to try and follow. What a thought! A totally *guiltless* individual took upon his shoulders all the sins of the world, past, present, and future! Jesus committed no sin, and yet, he was the one who took our place at the cross. Referring to God and Christ respectively, Paul told the Christians at Corinth, "For he hath made him to be sin for us, who knew no sin; that we might be made the righteousness of God in him" (II Corinthians 5:21). What supreme love this is that was bestowed by God! What a gift!

However, all the *generics* of Jesus' temptations are recorded in God's Holy Writ. After Jesus was baptized of John the Baptist in the Jordan River revealed near the end of Matthew 3, observe what immediately followed in chapter 4:1-11: "Then was Jesus led up of the Spirit into the wilderness to be tempted of the devil. And when he had fasted forty days and forty nights, he was afterward an hungered. And when the tempter came to him, he said, If thou be the Son of God, command that these stones be made bread. But he answered and said, It is written, Man shall not live by bread alone, but by every word that proceedeth out of the mouth of God. Then the devil taketh him up into the holy city, and setteth him on a pinnacle of the temple, And saith unto him, if thou be the Son of God, cast thyself down: for it is written, He shall give his angels charge concerning thee: and in their hands they shall bear thee up, lest at any time thou dash thy foot against a stone. Jesus said unto him, It is written again, Thou shalt not tempt the Lord thy God. Again, the devil taketh him up into an exceeding high mountain, and showeth him all the kingdoms of the world, and the glory of them; And saith unto him, All these things will I give thee, if thou wilt fall down and worship me. Then saith Jesus unto him, Get thee hence, Satan: for it is written, Thou shalt worship the Lord thy God, and him only shalt thou serve. Then the devil leaveth him, and, behold, angels came and ministered unto him."

In the above reading, we can see that Satan tried every lie and "trick in the book" to lure Jesus into sinning. He baited the Son of God with every sinful work and hook he could produce, but Jesus did not take the bait. Satan perverted scripture. He, too, got Jesus when he was at his absolute weakest—hungry from fasting. The Devil knows not the game of "fair play." Plus, concerning that last temptation for Jesus to obtain all the kingdoms of the world if he would bow down and worship Satan, I have one sensible question to ask: Was this ever so "generous gesture" from the Devil something that Jesus did not already *possess*? No! Satan was not offering Jesus anything he did not already own! Remember: Christ existed before the Creation and executed God's commands of actually bringing the Creation into existence. In view of that, whom did Satan think he was fooling? This episode in the life of Christ shows us that all temptations thrown from the Devil to God's only Son were declined. Not once did Jesus yield. Not once! Remember too again that the Hebrew writer said that although Jesus was tempted in every way like all of us, it was, "yet without sin."

Along with Matthew 4:1-11 stating in detail that Jesus "was in all points tempted like as we are," those verses also reveal that whatever temptations are thrown out to us, each one will always, without exception, come under one of these three categories: (1) Lust of the flesh, (2) Lust of the eye, and (3) Pride of life. I John 2:16 has the apostle telling us just that: "For all that is in the world, the lust of the flesh, and the lust of the eyes, and the pride of life, is not of the Father, but is of the world." In reading carefully Genesis 3:1-6, the reader will find that this was exactly the way Eve was tempted by Satan, posing as a serpent—and in the same numerical order, at that!

So yes, Jesus *was* tempted in *every way* that you and I are, but he refused to succumb. We just read from John that all sin, again, falls under "the lust of the flesh, and the lust of the eyes, and the pride of life." Take the test for yourself. Name every sin you can think of and find, and see which one of these three areas each particular sin fits. There will not be one solitary sin that will not categorize itself in one or more of the above headings.

In the entire chapter of Isaiah 53, the sufferings of Jesus are foretold by that great prophet some seven-hundred years before they actually took place, according to most Bible scholars. I admonish you to read that chapter. Verse 10 is particularly touching to this writer, for it shows all the more, again, as now being discussed, the magnificent *love* God had for man, in spite of the fact that Jesus was his only begotten Son: "Yet it pleased the Lord to bruise him; he hath put him to grief: when thou shalt make his soul an offering for sin, he shall see his seed, he shall prolong his days, and the pleasure of the Lord shall prosper in his hand." In spite of what God *well* knew would happen to his beloved Son, still, "it pleased the Lord to bruise him" and "put him to grief." How gallant and noble of God allowing all those things to afflict his Son, due to his great love for us, irregardless of his great despitefulness for sin! *No* other gift can match it!

Being the father of two sons, along with being a grandparent, I for one would forbid such a thing as what happened to Jesus to be inflicted on any of my offspring. The idea of being physically and verbally abused in every way conceivable does not set well with my parental instincts. If the reader is a parent and/or grandparent, I am quite sure the feeling is no different. However, one does not necessarily have to be a parent or grandparent to feel this way. Yet, God allowed his Son to be scorned, despised, rejected, spit on, mocked, unjustly accused, beaten, and finally *crucified*! Again, all of this was due to his great *love* for us! What happened to Jesus had to occur, due to the terrible and ugly price of sin. It was all part of God's plan of salvation. While God hates *sin*, he (like he wishes us to be) loves the *sinner*! This is more than evident.

There are so many complimentary adjectives one can use to describe this greatest of gifts God sent to you and I. In contrasting himself to false teachers and Satan, such a contrast obviously being as different as day and night, Jesus told a group of people in John 10:10, "The thief cometh not, but for to steal, and to kill, and to destroy: I am come that they might have life, and that they might have it more abundantly." You have not really *lived* until you have completely accepted this most wonderful gift from God into your life--Jesus Christ. You have only *existed*!

Jesus told his apostles in John 14:15, "If ye love me, keep my commandments." Loving Jesus means more than just believing him to be the Son of God, although that is certainly the right and proper place to start. To love him, as before discussed in the previous chapter, means more than feeling something sentimental. In chapter 15:14 he says to those same people, "Ye are my friends, if ye do whatsoever I command you." If we really love Jesus, if we really claim to be his friend, we will obey his *every* word, because we just read where he *said* so. He also told us that *true* friendship with him is based on the condition that we "do whatsoever" he commands us. Jesus said it, so I believe it, and that *settles* it with me. It is like that bumper sticker says about God: "God said it, I believe it, and that settles it!" I truly hope and pray that the reader feels the same way. Jesus Christ died to save you! The word "Christ" means, "the anointed one." He is the anointed one of God, sent to save the world. Jesus is, ..."KING OF KINGS, AND LORD OF LORDS" (Revelation 19:17).

With all the words in mind contained in the above paragraph, I would like to begin drawing this book to a close by offering the following verses of scripture for you as the reader to look up, in hopes that you will accept that beautiful gift of gifts from God--Jesus Christ. I will let the Bible declare for itself, speaking where it speaks and keeping silent where it is silent, so there can be no cause for anyone to think I am just giving my own "interpretation" on what the Bible says. I hope the following texts will be investigated and obeyed. Each are categorized:

CHURCH: Matthew 16:16-18; Colossians 3:17; Acts 4:10-12; Colossians

1:12-18; 1 Timothy 3:15; Acts 2:47; Ephesians 4:4-6; Romans 16:16.

OBEDIENCE: 1 Peter 4:11; Matthew 4:4; 2 John 9; John 12:44-50; John 6:63; Mark 16:16; 1 Peter 3:21; Romans 6:3-4; John 3:23; Colossians 2:12; Galatians 3:27; Acts 22:16; Acts 2:36-41.

All of the above verses are all self-explanatory, as was already said much earlier in this book about so much of the Bible. The passages then, again, should be easily understood, for they obviously say what they mean and mean what they say. I implore all of you in the Spirit of Christ to read them with an open mind, free of any prejudices. Pay attention to every single *word* contained in each verse, and you will not miss anything said to you. Reread and reread, and all will become clear. Study these verses on your own. Paul told the church at Philippi, "Wherefore, my beloved, as ye have always obeyed, not in my presence only, but now much more in my absence, work out your own salvation with fear and trembling" (Philippians 2:12). Study by yourself, so that you will be completely free of someone else's views, and hence, will not be a parrot of anybody's personal beliefs.

Examine that Bible in private! Be totally alone! Paul told Timothy, "Study to show thyself approved unto God, a workman that needeth not to be ashamed, rightly dividing the word of truth" (II Timothy 2:15). The term "rightly dividing the word of truth" means to handle God's Word *correctly*. The only way to do that is to read the Bible *thoroughly*, and not to be selective on what verses are and are not accepted by you as the one reading. When that book known as the Bible is read, that is *God and Jesus* talking to us, not any member of the human race. Jesus, that wonderful gift of God, was given to all of mankind, and is revealed in God's Holy Word for you and I to read, accept, and completely obey. He was prophesied in the Old Testament, and fulfilled in the New Testament. The Apostle James instructs us, "Wherefore lay apart all filthiness and superfluity of naughtiness, and receive with meekness the engrafted word, which is able to save your souls" (James 1:21). Then, after reading, contact me if there be any questions.

God and his many characteristics in which he saw fit to name in his Bible were written there to invite your attention, impress you, and compel you to submit to his will. All were penned and sent to you out of deep concern for your soul. God does not beseech us to surrender to him on account of his being some kind of *killjoy*! He does it out of love, he knows what sin and its consequences are, so the things he proclaims in his book not only instruct us on how *not* to live, but they likewise tell us how *to* live. The Bible is not just a book of "do nots." Its contents are not all negative. There are plenty of "dos" in those pages, as well.

Again, Paul said in Romans 15:4, "For whatsoever things were written aforetime were written for our learning, that we through patience and comfort of the scriptures might have hope." Many characters listed in the Bible are categorized by God in simply one of two ways: acceptable or unacceptable. Learn from *both* types of people, and you will, hence, learn from all of them whose lives God saw fit to record in detail, for their revealed lives will teach you the right ways and the wrong ways to conduct your life on earth, as just cited from Paul. Will you *accept* God's most precious "gift" offered to you? This writer's sincere prayer is that you will. Your *soul* depends on it! To reject Jesus is to lose it all. It is the waste of wastes. When talking to his apostles and a group of people, Jesus said in Mark 8:36-37, "For what shall it profit a man, if he shall gain the whole world, and lose his own soul? Or what shall a man give in exchange for his soul?" This is still yet another question that obviously gives its own answer.

The latter part of John 4 tells of a group of Samaritans who were introduced to Jesus by a Samaritan woman after she spoke with him at Jacob's well. Upon hearing Jesus speak, notice their reaction to him in verses 41-42: "And many more believed because of his own word; And said unto the woman, Now we believe, not because of thy saying: for we have heard him ourselves, and know that this is indeed the Christ, the Saviour of the world." The term, "the Saviour," means Jesus is the "one and only" person who is both capable and qualified to save your priceless, immortal soul. For that matter, this writer is thoroughly sure that you can see the word "save" in the title of "Saviour." Since the jurisdiction of Jesus covers "the world," that means you and I need him too.

As said in the "Foreword" section of this book, so it is declared again, to *God* be the glory in all that is accomplished in his name! What an amazing Creator and Maker we have up there in the heavens! Exalt him immensely. Learn all you can of God in his Word, and let *him* be your guide of guides. He will never lead you wrong, but will always direct you "in the paths of righteousness," (Psalm 23:3). Is it not truly worth it, does it not make the best of sense, and will it not be totally beneficial to allow a completely *sinless* personality guide you? Doing this will guarantee that God and Jesus are right every time without fail. Get to know God, as one thing is for sure, you who read this: He knows you! Love him, for he loves you. Get close to him, for he wishes to be close to you. The first part of James 4:8 has the apostle telling us, "Draw nigh to God, and he will draw nigh to you." Laud your majestic Maker above all people, places, and things every day of your life. Jehovah deserves it. Be assured that he is Lord over all forever and ever. Thank you again ever so much for reading my book. May Heaven be your eternal abode! Amen and Amen!

**Questions**

1. A "gift" is given out of ______________ instead of ____________.
2. "For God so __________ the world, that he __________ his _____ begotten ________, that ________________ believeth in him should not ________________, but have ______________________."
3. "Begotten" comes from the word "beget," and means, "___________ ____________________________________."
4. "Therefore the Lord himself shall give you a _________; Behold, a _______________ shall _______________, and bear a _________, and shall call his name ________________."
5. Since Jesus was sent to earth by his Heavenly Father, he must have already been around ______________ that time.
6. "Before Abraham was, _______________."
7. "And now, O Father, ______________ thou me with ______________ ___________with the _____________ I had with thee ____________ the world was."
8. "In the ________________ was the _________, and the __________ was with ___________, and the ______________ was God. The _____ was in the __________________ with God."
9. "For the ___________ of sin is _____________; but the _________ of God is ________________ life through _________________ our ____________."
10. "That as _________ hath reigned unto __________, even so might _____________ reign through _____________________ unto ______ life."
11. "But God ______________________ his __________ toward us, in that, while we were yet _______________, Christ _________ for us."
12. I for one am glad that _________ does not ___________ man the way that much of man _________________ one another.

13. "For God sent not his __________ into the __________ to __________ the __________; but that the __________ though __________ might be __________."
14. Coming to earth was not the __________ of Jesus, for he __________ no __________ where the subject of __________ is concerned.
15. "Repent" means, "__________."
16. Paul says to Timothy about God, "Who will have ______ men to be __________, and to come unto the __________ of the __________."
17. "__ am the __________, the __________, and the __________: ______ man cometh unto the __________, but by __________."
18. "And I will put __________ between __________ and the __________, and between __________ seed and __________ seed; it shall __________ thy __________, and thou shalt __________ his __________."
19. "Enmity" means, "__________ __________."
20. "But when the __________ of time was come, ______ sent forth his __________, made of a __________, made under the __________, To __________ them that were __________ the __________, that we might __________ the __________ of __________."

www.ingramcontent.com/pod-product-compliance
Lightning Source LLC
Chambersburg PA
CBHW031838090426
42741CB00005B/278

* 9 7 8 1 5 8 4 2 7 2 8 1 6 *